MEMORIES OF ODYSSEUS

For Thomas

MEMORIES OF ODYSSEUS

Frontier tales from ancient Greece

FRANÇOIS HARTOG
Translated by Janet Lloyd

THE UNIVERSITY OF CHICAGO PRESS

FRANÇOIS HARTOG is Directeur d'Études at the École des Hautes Études en Sciences Sociales and Directeur of the Centre Louis Gernet in Paris. Among his previous books is *The Mirror of Herodotus*.

The University of Chicago Press, Chicago 60637

Edinburgh University Press Ltd, Edinburgh EH8 9LF

English translation © Janet Lloyd, 2001

First published in France as *Memoir d'Ulysse*, © Editions Gallimard, 1996

English edition published with the aid of a translation subvention kindly given by the French Ministry of Culture

00 09 08 07 06 05 04 03 02 01   1 2 3 4 5
ISBN: 0-226-31852-4 (cloth)
ISBN: 0-226-31853-2 (paperback)

Library of Congress Cataloging-in-Publication Data

Hartog, François.
[Mémoire d'Ulysse. English]
Memories of Odysseus: frontier tales from ancient Greece/François Hartog;
translated by Janet Lloyd.
p. cm.
Includes bibliographical references (p.).
ISBN 0-226-31852-4 (cloth: alk. paper)—ISBN 0-226-31853-2 (pbk.: alk. paper)
1. Geography, Ancient—Historiography.   2. Voyages and travels—Historiography.
3. Greece—Civilization—To 146 B.C.—Historiography.   4. Classical antiquities.   I. Title.
G84.H3713   2001
938'.007'2—dc21   2001035153

This book is printed on acid-free paper.

Contents

Foreword: Odysseus in Auschwitz
Paul Cartledge

> *On we go, amigos ...*
> *down the ages way across the watery world,*
> *and yearning, yearning for my home,*
> *as you all do, as we do, though we can't go home,*
> *never again ...*
>
> Judith Kazantzis, *The Odysseus Poems*

We are what we remember – and forget. François Hartog, Directeur d'Études at the École des hautes études en sciences sociales and Director of the Centre Louis Gernet de recherches comparées sur les sociétés anciennes, has long been preoccupied with human memory, with special reference to its manipulation in and impact upon the writing of history both ancient and modern.[1] One of his major influences has been the inspiration of the late Sir Moses Finley, a collection of whose essays in French translation he edited in 1981 under the title *Mythe, Mémoire, Histoire*.[2] At one point in the fascinating interview with the editor that is appended to those essays Finley remarks: "yet again the alterity of Antiquity receives confirmation" (p. 257). Alterity too, like memory, has proved to be a major theme of Hartog's own work, most notably in his brilliant and groundbreaking monograph, *The Mirror of Herodotus* (1980–91, 1988), also translated by Janet Lloyd. But a more potent influence still on Hartog, as on most of us born in the shadow of the Second World War, is the crushing experience, even if at second or third hand, of the Shoah (Jewish Holocaust) and its aftermath. That tragedy must, somehow, be remembered, but how is the remembrance best to be achieved and used?[3] The after-shocked suicide of one of the Holocaust's most articulate witnesses, Primo Levi, whom Hartog tellingly recalls towards the end of the present book, cannot fail to excite deep anxieties and doubts.[4] It is hardly surprising that memory and representation have been described as quintessential post-modern concerns.

If memory by itself needs no further justification as a subject of study by a master-historiographer, one can still fairly ask what the point of a memoir or memories of Odysseus/Ulysses might be. There have been many Odysseuses over the ages. What has been called for short "the Ulysses theme"[5] has been traced out from Homer via the Greek tragedians through Hellenistic and Roman antiquity, through the European Middle Ages, and on down to James Joyce and beyond, not least to "the immensely inventive, if flawed, reprise of the Homeric original in Nikos Kazantzakis" (G. Steiner, *TLS*, 15 October 1999). Odysseus has even entered our everyday English language – we speak freely of any unusually lengthy or problematic journey, whether mental or material, as an "odyssey". F. A. Lincoln's *Odyssey of a Jewish Sailor* (1996) is just a serendipitous recent instance. A rather more elevated literary manifest-ation of this tradition, more properly a literary phenomenon, has been the work of West Indian Nobel laureate Derek Walcott, a specifically colonial or postcolonial appropriation of the Ulysses theme, in the form of both a mod-ern verse epic (*Omeros*) and a stage-play.[6] In the world of film one thinks immediately of the Greek filmmaker Theo Angelopoulos's *Ulysses' Gaze* (1995), a meditation on the crisis of identity in post-Communist Balkan Europe.[7] A more popular filmic approach, or perhaps gesture, towards the Odysseus legend or myth, is the Coen brothers' presumably self-referential *O Brother, Where Art Thou?* (2000).

Scholars too have not allowed Odysseus or his reception to escape their attention for long. Recent work deserving special mention includes the col-lection of essays edited by Beth Cohen on the representation of the female in the *Odyssey* (1995), William Thalmann's study of the representation of class in the *Odyssey* (1998) and, closer to the concerns of Hartog, Irad Malkin's *Returns of Odysseus* (1998).[8] Closer – but not all that close. For, as in his book on Herodotus, Hartog unlike Malkin is not much concerned in *Memories of Odysseus* with the reality underlying the representations, but rather with the representations themselves, with what they can tell us about Greek mentality, or Greek culture, at a number of key points between the creation of the monu-mental epic somewhere around 700 BC and the Second Sophistic of the high Roman imperial period, and, in turn, what those representations and recep-tions have meant in key periods and to key cultural figures of the early mod-ern and modern world.

Few perhaps – and certainly not Homer's original Odysseus – would echo C. P. Cavafy's paradoxical urging in "Ithaka" (1911), his famous poem on exile and nostalgia (which means literally the pain caused by the desire to return home), to "pray that the way be long"! Hartog's book is at any rate not at all long, given its immense chronological, geographical and cultural range. For him, the figure of Odysseus in literary representation, from the Odysseus of Homer who always remembers to Philostratus's Odysseus-like Apollonius of Tyana who unifies all the heterogeneous places through which he alone has passed, serves as a guiding thread. It is the figure of Odysseus too who serves as the original inspiration of the invention and practice of historiography in ancient Greece, since the true historian was considered to be he who spared neither time nor effort nor resources to traverse land and sea in order to see with his own eyes.[9]

Two major themes, or perhaps rather variations on a single major theme, identity, recur throughout the space of this new book: ethnicity and alterity. Who the Greeks thought they were, and how they thought themselves as Greeks by a variety of oppositions of themselves to "others" of one sort or another – these are Hartog's principal preoccupations here, as they have been of other recent historians of ancient Greece, in their different ways and from their different perspectives.[10] From the point of view of method Hartog's general approach is distinctively informed by one consistent and recurrent mode of disciplinary crossover, from history towards anthropology. We find ourselves thus in the same general intellectual territory as the American anthropologist James Clifford's punning *Routes: Travel and Translation in the Late Twentieth Century*,[11] even if we are now already in the early twenty-first.

Times move on, as do people and peoples. In such a context the metaphor of travel springs to mind almost unbidden – as we follow the symbolic wanderings of Odysseus through the self-conscious ancient Greek imaginings and constructions of themselves and others, with Dr Hartog's stimulating book in hand as our map and guidebook. And what a journey or rather series of journeys we are treated to here! An opening chapter, "The Return of Odysseus", sets the scene. This is to be a long-run, anthropologically oriented cultural history of ancient Greece, a history of Greek self-representation and self-exploration through the journeyings of Odysseus, through evocations of his name, and through metaphorical interpretations and various other uses of him to formulate and problematize the question of Greek identity. It is to be a history of limits and boundaries, a history of humanity, suffering and escape.

In the second chapter, "Egyptian Voyages", Hartog focuses specifically on Egypt, source of a Baudelairian forest of symbols for Greeks from Homer via Herodotus to Neoplatonist philosophers such as Porphyry. What interests Hartog is the impact of the differing visions of Egypt on the development of Greek cultural identity. The din caused by the clash of intellectual, political, religious and social attitudes over the centuries is very clearly conveyed. "There is no country in the world that the Greeks more enjoy hearing about" – so says an Egyptian priest, in good Greek, in Heliodorus's novel *Aethiopica*. Iamblichus, the neo-Pythagorean philosopher, on the other hand, was moved to comment on the imperfection of all translations: "even when it is possible to translate names, they lose some of their power (*dunamis*)". Perhaps it would not be wise to pursue such reflections too far here. Let us stick rather with Herodotus, who appropriated his Egypt for his Greek addressees through the classic Greek heuristic device of polar inversion: what They do and are, We do not do and are not – and We are who We are precisely because of that negative opposition. Thus, to take just one of his score of supposed illustrations, whereas Egyptian women urinate standing up, Egyptian men urinate sitting down – an unfortunate inversion of Greek norms of masculinity, according to which it was considered manly to be upright, but womanish or (even worse) servile to stoop or squat.

Verbally speaking, this polarization of Greeks and Others was consecrated in the opposition of all Greeks (including women and children, who were otherwise deemed morally and spiritually inferior to adult men) to all non-Greeks, who were collectively lumped together, and often enough denigrated, as "Barbarians". By 500 this new polarity or 'field of Otherness', as Hartog describes it, was fixed and delimited for a very long time to come. Chapter 3, "The Invention of the Barbarian and an Inventory of the World", concentrates mainly on politics and geography. It illustrates the variations that could be played on the general theme of identity through polarized alterity, starting off from the presumption that the norm and centre were constituted by the relatively egalitarian, relatively autonomous Greek *polis* or citizen-state. Every other political formation was deemed more or less abnormal, more or less eccentric, more or less marginal. Another key mode of distinction was by way of the rite of animal blood-sacrifice: you are what, and how, you sacrifice. Finally, a more inclusive, and more bookish mode of boundary-drawing and identity-fixing: Hellenism, following the example of the establishment of the Library at Alexandria, might now also be redefined as a shared literary heritage, regardless of ethnicity in the physical sense of blood or descent.

From Greeks' views of Others to Greeks' views of Themselves: in Chapter 4, "Greek Voyages", we travel with Hartog from Anacharsis the Scythian culture-hopper, defined as an "inside-outsider", to Alexander the Great, founder of a new era and a new space of Hellenism. But in between those two, in Hartog's presentation, come the Greeks Polybius and Pausanias and other later, postclassical travellers in fact and imagination from Virgil to Watteau, all of whom liked to be able to say that in some sense they too had been "in Arcadia". That relatively remote and unthreatening series of images is counterposed to the reception and promotion of Alexander the Great, first by Plutarch and Arrian writing in the second century of our era, his most effective ancient Greek interpreters of those few that survive, and then by J. G. Droysen in the nineteenth, the latter a Hellenic supremacist defending the frontiers of Greek – or rather, a Greek – identity.

Chapter 5, "Roman Voyages", looks at the difficult issue of how the Greeks' fierce conquerors – and cultural legatees – were to be classified according to the traditional bipolar worldview of Greeks v. Barbarians. The historian Polybius, held hostage in and around Rome for many years, reappears here to head the lineage of Greek intellectuals extending down to Aelius Aristides by way of Dionysius of Halicarnassus and Strabo who made the voyage to Rome by adopting a Roman viewpoint. With the imposition of Roman order on the known inhabited world (the *oikoumenê*) came the end of the road for the figure of Odysseus.

In Philostratus's *Life* of the wandering sage Apollonius of Tyana, which Dr Hartog explores by way of a Conclusion, the Homeric poems are still present, if only as a subtext. It is doubtful, however, whether Homer's Odysseus would have recognized himself in Philostratus's "zealot of Hellenism and defender of Greek identity".

To conclude: *Memories of Odysseus* was very well received on its first publication in French in 1996.[12] Translations into Spanish, Italian, Portuguese and Turkish are planned or on their way. It is an honour to have been able to introduce this English translation, which makes available to a new readership some of the ripest and richest fruits of recent French scholarship on ancient Greek – and so, as the author does not fail to observe, our – identity.

Acknowledgements

I should like to express my gratitude to the Getty Center and its director Salvatore Settis for their most generous hospitality. My thanks also go to the students in my seminar, who tolerated my trying out these pages on them; Michel Casevitz, Jacques Revel, and Jean-Pierre Vernant, who were their first readers; and lastly Eric Vigne, for his great patience.

Some books are like voyages: one seldom sticks exactly to the proposed route in either.

Charles Perrault, *Parallels between the Ancients and the Moderns*

MEMORIES OF ODYSSEUS

Introduction: Travellers and Frontier-men

How is the name Ulysses/Odysseus used today? A joint American–European deep space probe has been baptised *Ulysses*. Perhaps because this was to be a voyage into the furthest distance, to see what had never been seen before: the poles of the Sun? But this time "Ulysses" was never to come home! It was presumed to be a voyage from which there would be no return. On a more commonplace level, quite a few travel agencies go under the flag of Odysseus or Ulysses, as do certain cruise programmes, inviting us to follow in his wake and enjoy the charms of the Mediterranean. The name Ulysses/Odysseus thus comes in handy for both the tourist industry and space agencies. It seems that, by reactivating such ancient names, they are seeking to summon up some modern mythology in which they do not really believe; or perhaps they are simply trying to recycle the old mythology so as to forge a link between science and fiction.[1]

In the 1960s, Greece itself became a high spot for worldwide tourism. *Zorba the Greek* (1964) toured the world in the shapes of Anthony Quinn and Irene Papas. Not long after, Jacques Lacarrière, a great walker and lover of Greece, was felicitously evoking other Greek memories, material and physical ones, now threatened, of the country along whose highways and byways he had roamed and on whose boats he had sailed between 1946 and 1966. They were memories that went back to the days before the floods of visitors and before the dictatorship of the colonels, and that for centuries had lived on in the Greek language, where they had taken refuge and were concentrated: immaterial, fragile memories but still alive to those who could listen. A poem by Seferis is all you need to embark or re-embark upon the Greek voyage and rediscover "the deeply breathing historical body of Greece".[2]

3

The pages that follow are about the anthropology and history of ancient Greece, about a long-term cultural history that sets its sights upon the figures of a number of "travellers", adopting them as guides. The first and most famous of all of them is Ulysses, or Odysseus, as he is generally called in English, the hero who "was driven to wander far and wide … [seeing] the cities of many people and [learning] their ways".[3] Others, inspired by him, were to follow, travellers both real and fictional, who take us to Egypt, into the Greek heartland, to Rome, and round the world. Odysseus was the man who had *seen* and who knew because he had *seen*. This, right from the start, alerts us to a relation to the world that is central to the Greek civilization: here, the seeing eye was the means of knowledge valued above all others. Seeing, seeing for oneself, and knowing "came to the same thing".[4] Aristotle declares: "We prefer sight, generally speaking, to all the other senses. The reason for this is that of all the senses sight best helps us to know things, and reveals many distinctions".[5]

Whether they be far-distant voyages, to the edges of the very edge, as in the case of Odysseus, or voyages in Greece itself or in Rome, or – inevitably – literary voyages such as those of Apollonius of Tyana, within the space of a particular language and a particular culture, what we shall be studying are travellers' tales.[6] The objective will not be to draw a map of this ancient culture, unfolding before the eyes of the reader a heavy, synoptic machine in which changes are conveyed by the gradual or, on the contrary, sudden narrowing of the spaces between the contour lines. Rather, we shall simply pick out a few travellers and follow them for a while. So it will be a matter not of topography or geography, but rather of keeping on the move and looking: topology and keeping going. These travellers' journeys through the space of the world can also be read as so many itineraries that leave trails more or less deep and lasting across their own culture.

Odysseus, in his travels, through the very movement of a return journey that is constantly blocked or deferred, sketches in the outlines of a Greek identity, encompasses it. He marks out frontiers (between the human and the divine, for instance) or rather, he, the One who Endures, tests them out, at the risk of losing himself altogether. Ever on the move, tossed here and there by the waves, constantly obliged to set out yet again, he himself is a frontier-man, a memory-man. He goes as far as is possible, to the point beyond which there may be no return, to the extreme limits of the Underworld, where Hades rules, as close as possible to the shores of the island of the Sirens, the enchantresses of Death, shores heaped with "the bones of decomposing

4

bodies with rotting flesh". Among the Lotus-Eaters, even with Circe the magician, he still longs for the day of his homecoming, and on Calypso's island, "sitting on the rocks or sands", he looks out "with streaming eyes across the watery wilderness".

Pioneer travellers such as these make for frontiers, are themselves frontier-markers, but mobile ones. As they travel onward they are, so to speak, on both sides of frontiers both great and small: at once inside and outside, in between, boundary-crossers, translators. Alongside those extreme travellers we find the "globetrotter", tracking across the world, humping his bundle; he is known as *poluplanês*. One such is Pythagoras, traditionally recognized as a great traveller: impatient to leave Samos, the isle of his birth, he visited Egypt, stopped off in Crete, and visited the Chaldeans and the magi, before eventually settling in Magna Graecia. According to other biographies, however, he was of Etruscan or possibly even Syrian origin. He was also a time-traveller, and he remembered all his earlier lives. Another was Hecataeus of Miletus, also dubbed *poluplanês*, the author of a *Journey around the World*, who had visited Egypt before Herodotus.[7] And then there was Solon, who, while visiting Croesus, the king of Lydia, combined his "travelling" (*planê*) with "learning" (*sophia*), his quest for knowledge with travels round the world.[8] All of them (except Anacharsis the Scythian) were "insiders" who came to know the "outside" so well that they sometimes even acquired the "look" of outsiders, at least to the eyes of the "inside". Their proper names, which all stand for "traveller", are linked with stories from elsewhere, brought back by them, but then rendered intelligible, acceptable to the "insiders", translated and appropriated despite their otherness.

As frontier-men, they sketch in the outlines of a Greek identity, understood as a "bounded entity to which no experience corresponds in reality".[9] Furthermore, beyond the *Odyssey* itself, seen as the story of a founding voyage and a pioneering itinerary, subsequent voyages made in the name of Ulysses/Odysseus, evocations of that name, metaphorical interpretations of it, and the various other uses to which it is put in the long term all illuminate the changes and reformulations of that question of Greek identity made within the context of ancient Greek culture and even beyond it.[10] So after the voyages made by Odysseus and in his name, we shall be following the travels of the Scythian Anacharsis, who appeared out of the cold wastelands of Scythia and travelled in the longer term through Greek culture, from the fifth century BC down to the second century AD at least, taking in works ranging from the *Histories* of Herodotus to the writings of Lucian of Samosata,

5

a native Syrian who became one of the masters of Greek prose. The echo of Anacharsis' name was still to be heard in 1788, thanks to the famous *Voyage of the Young Anacharsis*, written by the scholarly Abbé Jean-Jacques Barthélemy. Then, for a while, we shall be accompanying Apollonius of Tyana, sage and magician, a tireless pilgrim obsessed by the memory of Pythagoras, about whom Gustave Flaubert was still "rhapsodizing" many centuries later.[11]

We shall be visiting Egypt too, the land of ancient knowledge by which the Greeks had always been fascinated, or at least had been ever since the visit that Menelaus involuntarily paid it on his return from Troy, right down to the lucubrations of the Neoplatonists, and from the time of Book II of Herodotus' *Histories* down to that of the recent *Black Athena*, written by Martin Bernal, who seeks to remind us of the Egyptian and African origins of Greek civilization.[12] In Greece itself we shall find, reflected in Pausanias' gaze, a very ancient and primordial Arcadia, not exactly the one that Goethe was thinking of when, on his way to Rome, he wrote at the beginning of his *Voyage in Italy*, "*Auch ich in Arkadien*", "I too have been to Arcadia". Next, we shall visit the lumpen Boeotians, and then move on to consider the people of Abdera. Were the inhabitants of the city of Abdera stupid or mad, or perhaps more mad than stupid? Theirs is a famous case on which much wisdom of the moderns has been expended, and Abderitism, as a category, is still present in Kant's *The Conflict of the Faculties*. Then Alexander, in the guise of the latest civilizer, a new Achilles, passes rapidly by, linking Greece and Rome. Finally Rome, the conquering city, imposes its presence and, as an inevitable corollary, a series of voyages are made to Rome. That is a detour that we have to undertake if we are to have any chance of understanding a completely different world and finding answers to the questions: "Who are the Romans? Are they Barbarians or are they Greeks?". And also to questions such as: "And *we Greeks*, who were we?" and "What place can we expect today, and on what basis?".

This whole voyage – an itinerary, it should be repeated, not a map – produces a succession of names, places and perceptions that interconnect, intersect and overlay one another, marking out points of reference and moments when things become confused or take a new turn. It suggests the flow of the history, itself in flux, of Greek otherness.

For the Greeks, who were the "others"? How did they circumscribe and define otherness? There were "others" who were non-human: either super-human, such as the gods and demi-gods; or subhuman, such as monsters and animals; and there were "ordinary" others: foreigners (*xenoi*), in practice anyone outside the restricted community constituted by the city.[13] We know that, in the classical period, Sparta was said to be closed to foreigners. Thucydides contrasts the Spartan *xenelasia* (the expulsion of foreigners) to the openness of Athens,[14] which indeed created the status of *metic* (resident foreigner) for foreigners who wished to settle there. And there were also "internal" foreigners, excluded people such as slaves, whether helots or chattel-slaves.[15] Herodotus notes that the Spartans applied the category of *xenos* to *all* foreigners, both Greeks and non-Greeks, in other words Greeks and Barbarians alike.[16] The famous pair Greeks/Barbarians, which we shall be returning to consider, does not seem to have meant anything to them. It was as if their view of otherness had been arrested in a time prior to the diffusion and general recognition of that pair, which – as an antonymous structure, at least – was destined to a long future. For the Spartans, any individual who was not a member of the Spartan community, whether Greek or non-Greek, was a *xenos*.

Further afield, when a traveller approached frontier areas, the limits of the *oikoumenê*, he would without fail describe the foreigners or Barbarians, strange peoples composed of both admirable sages and daunting savages, situated on the border between the human and the non-human; and yet further away, other strange beings, or frankly monsters. The above, briefly listed, represent no more than the principal categories of the Greek concept of "otherness". Nor were they fixed categories, but rather so many major points of reference (with interconnections), intellectual operators thanks to which the Greeks, when they spoke of others, could define themselves: question themselves, reaffirm themselves, assign themselves the leading role and the first place, or even entertain doubts about themselves, but always with themselves still in control of the situation.

The question was: how do we define *ourselves*, and, even more, what is our *sophia*? No Greek could ever identify with the questioning of the Book of Job: "Whence then cometh wisdom? and where is the place of understanding? Seeing it is hid from the eyes of all living, and kept close from the fowls of the air. ... God understandeth the way thereof, and he knoweth the place thereof".[17] For the Greeks it was a question of: where does *our sophia* come from? It is something that, since long ago, has belonged particularly to us, and yet we have produced thousands of stories that say that it came from elsewhere. Egypt, in particular. How can something that is *ours* come from elsewhere? It is this movement, this pulse, almost this breath which links the same with the other in Greek culture that we shall be exploring through the image of a voyage.[18]

So it is not the voyage itself, in its material aspect,[19] that is important here, but rather the voyage as a discursive operator and a narrative device: the voyage as a perception and resolution of a problem or as the answer to a question. A voyage *to* Egypt, *to* Arcadia or *to* Rome, but also and even more a voyage *in* Egypt, *in* Arcadia, *in* Rome, with all that that entails in the way of imaginary representations. It is the (almost) always astonished perception of Herodotus or the (almost) never surprised perception of Apollonius. It is the perception of the Greek tourist, who never ceases to evaluate what is other according to the yardstick of what is the same, and who always knows, deep down, where he is coming from; or it is, on the contrary, the "distant perception" of someone who, by taking a detour by way of somewhere else, sets what is the same at a distance, or even calls it into question, a perception which, by dint of his moving elsewhere and evaluating what is other, transfers his doubt concerning what is the same to what it is that he is himself; or it may be a perception that, by constantly reconsidering the past and reappropriating it, finds reassurance through "rediscovering" signs and traces of an ancient Greek identity that can be recomposed and reactivated. This last is the perception of Apollonius, the Pythagorean, and also, in its antiquarian way, that of Pausanias, the second-century AD author of the *Description of Greece*.

Two observations, borrowed from two contemporary philosophers, may serve to circumscribe the field of enquiry, or rather the two poles of the investigation. The one, on Odysseus, is lifted, in passing, from Emmanuel Levinas, who sees in Odysseus' voyage the very image of Western philosophy. His "world adventure was simply a return to his native island – complacency about what was the same, rejection of what was other".[20] Complacency, a lack of understanding, a rejection of everything "other": that is all Odysseus' adventure amounted to (and is all that Western philosophy amounts to too). And what about Otherness? The Greeks, it is true, never were expecting anyone; no Revelation ever casts its light upon Olympus, and Lycurgus, for all he was a "divine" legislator according to the Pythia, never recorded any divine Word. Nevertheless, before changing the constitution of Sparta, he did travel, visiting Crete and possibly Egypt.[21] In Greece, according to Thales, "everything was full of gods", but the point is that those gods were *there*, part of the world – in a sense part of the same world as men, whom they could sometimes visit, in order either to help them or to lead them astray. The only difference was that they possessed in full what human beings could only ever obtain in a partial and precarious fashion.[22]

Odysseus, an unwilling traveller, dogged by Poseidon's hatred, was in the last analysis in quest of no Absolute; he was not even particularly curious about the world. Nothing could have been more alien to him than the idea of the seafaring of Baudelaire, who sought to "Plunge into the depths of the Abyss, be it Hell or Heaven, into the depths of the Unknown, to find something new". All Odysseus, for his part, could dream of was getting back to what was familiar to him.

If that is truly the case, what are we to make of the many declarations, written in Greek and by Greeks, about the Barbarian origins of *sophia* and, in particular, of philosophy, declarations sometimes fully affirmative, sometimes expressive of at least an element of doubt? Christian apologists were, by and large, to echo those declarations, taking them over for themselves. Hence the whole theme of the "Greek theft". For instance, Clement of Alexandria, in the mid-second century AD, who was at once culturally Greek and "Barbarian by vocation", praised the superiority of "Barbarian culture", first and foremost the pre-eminence of the wisdom of the Hebrews.[23] He also pointed out that Zoroaster was "emulated by Pythagoras", that philosophy only reached Greece at a late date, and that Anacharsis, even though a Scythian, was considered superior to many Greek philosophers.[24]

The situation was such that Diogenes Laertius, at the start of the third century AD, was to begin his *Lives of Famous Philosophers* on a note of uncertainty that his entire work, in its very conception, then proceeds to dismiss: "There are some who say that the study of philosophy had its beginning among the Barbarians". This is followed by a list of the possible initiators and high places of Wisdom: the magi of Persia, the Chaldeans of Babylon, the gymnosophists of India, the Druids of Gaul ... .[25] Then comes a swift riposte in the form of a refutation pure and simple: "These authors forget that the achievements which they attribute to the Barbarians belong to the Greeks, with whom not merely philosophy, but the human race itself began". So it is certainly "from the Greeks that philosophy took its rise: its very name refuses to be translated into foreign speech".[26] It is impossible to translate. In the last analysis, Greek alone, or later (failing Greek) German, is the language of philosophy! This is also recognized by Clement, in his own theologian's language, when he declares that philosophy was given to the Greeks "as their peculiar covenant", just as the Law had been given to the Jews (up until the *parousia*, that is to say the coming of the Messiah).[27]

In his *Alien Wisdom*,[28] Arnaldo Momigliano drew attention to the doubt harboured by Greek intellectuals on the score of their own *sophia*. Questions

9

and doubts were expressed as early as the fourth century BC and continued to constitute a kind of counter-tradition, cited, repeated, enriched or attacked over the centuries. Zoroaster was to be remembered with respect, as were the magi, the brahmins and Hermes Trismegistus (another name for Egyptian wisdom). The *sophia* of others is greater than our own, more divine, above all more ancient. Plato makes the Egyptian priest of Saïs exclaim, during his famous dialogue with Solon: "O Solon, you Greeks are always children; there is no such thing as an old Greek".[29] Was this a belated recognition of the greater antiquity of the East on the part of Greeks who had finally become less infatuated with themselves?

The name of Plato is indeed often associated with this "opening up" of Greek wisdom towards the East. But what kind of opening up was it, and towards what kind of East? As always with Plato, things soon become complicated.

Did he really ever travel in Egypt? *To* Egypt, certainly, but *in* Egypt is less sure. But in any case he is one of the major travellers, in the sense in which the word is understood here, of and in Greek *sophia*; albeit probably the most devious, the one who most clouded the issues. In the first century AD, Flavius Josephus, on the basis of the ideas developed in the *Timaeus*, was to set out to prove that the Greeks were relative newcomers compared to the Egyptians, the Chaldeans and the Phoenicians, not to mention the Jews themselves, of course:

> All those peoples live in countries that are not at all exposed to the ravages of the atmosphere, and their major preoccupation has been not to forget any of the events that happened in their countries, but always to consecrate them with official annals produced by the wisest among them. The land of Greece, in contrast, has suffered a thousand catastrophes that have wiped away the memory of past events.[30]

Less than a century later, under the Antonines, the philosopher Numenius, a native of Apamea, was definitively to place Plato within an Eastern configuration of wisdom, when he remarked: "What is Plato, really, if not Moses in Athenian garb?".[31]

But the main point is that the Greek intellectuals assumed they would remain in command, Plato in particular. Or else, in more modest fashion, when a whole string of authors paraded Anacharsis of Scythia in Greece, they used him to look at themselves through the eyes of a foreigner, but it was always they who dictated what he should see. When Diogenes of Sinope, the Cynic philosopher, sang the praises of the uncivilized life, he was out to subvert the centre of the city or of Greekness in general through its outlying areas, by showing that the truly civilized were not those who believed themselves to be such. This certainly constituted a moment of doubt and crisis in society; yet his concern was still with the centre, and his only real interlocutors remained the Greeks themselves.[32]

The *Lives* of Diogenes Laertius would, on the contrary, appear to reflect a moment when such doubts were repudiated, and to express a desire for reassurance. Equally, *The Life of Apollonius of Tyana*, in its novelish way, supports a similar view. This "holy" man, with a confidence based on his extremely close relations with Pythagoras, proclaims the antiquity and pre-eminence of Greek "wisdom". This "biography", published around 220–30 AD, was written by the sophist Philostratus, who claimed that he did so at the behest of Julia Domna, the wife of Septimius Severus. She was of Syrian origin and the daughter of a priest of the cult of the Sun at Emesa. This appears to have been a moment of doubts and reassertions of assumptions of Greek pre-eminence. The work declares that the elite Greeks may, indeed should, place their trust in their culture, through and thanks to which they can claim their place and legitimate their rights in the Graeco-Roman empire that emerged from the Battle of Actium.[33] That was also the message conveyed by the literary and political movement, or cultural strategy, known as the Second Sophistic. The *Life of Apollonius* played its part in the enterprise of reconquering and actively reappropriating the Greek past, in other words to recreate it – a process in which every living society bent on fabricating or inventing its own traditions tends to engage.[34]

But in all these cases, whether it was a matter of calling Greek pre-eminence into question or of rejecting all attempts to do so, the defined intellectual field and the rules of the game were always Greek. That is not to say that the Greeks, solely cultivating solipsism, never learnt anything from non-Greek wisdom. But as a general rule they never really took an interest in it for itself – only for themselves, within their own context and, above all, in the language that was their own means of expression. "The Greeks were great tourists, but were not given to participant observation".[35] They were, and remained (with a few exceptions) even in the Hellenistic period, "proudly mono-lingual", as Momigliano pointed out. "Conversing with natives in the language of the natives was not for them". Nor did they translate foreign books into Greek. The existence of the Septuagint, the Bible in Greek, represents not so much an exception as a confirmation of that, given that, according to Momigliano, it should be regarded almost certainly as a private initiative undertaken by the Jews of Alexandria and then placed under the patronage of the king, Ptolemy Philadelphus. So if there was indeed, despite everything, a dialogue between the Greeks, the Romans, and the Jews, it was initiated by the Romans and the Jews, not by the Greeks.[36]

Momigliano, as a historian, takes in the whole of the Hellenistic period, whereas Levinas, as a philosopher, is interested only in Odysseus' return journey. However, their points of view, each in its own register, are strikingly similar.

In total contrast, Cornelius Castoriadis, reflecting on "the Greek *polis* and the creation of democracy", lays strong emphasis on the unprecedented "opening up" introduced by the Greeks:

> Until the Greeks, and outside the Graeco-Western tradition, societies were established according to a principle of strict closure: our vision of the world is the only one that makes sense and is true; "others" are bizarre, inferior, perverse, evil, treacherous … True interest in others was born with the Greeks, and that interest was never anything besides another aspect of the critical and appraising look that they turned upon their own institutions. In other words, it was part of the democratic and philosophical movement created by the Greeks.[37]

Greece set on foot the transition from "heteronomy" (law that came from elsewhere) to "autonomy" (in which a society explicitly regarded itself as the source of law). Here, for the very first time, a society instituted itself. And the result was that, because it could take a long view of itself, it could afford to call itself into question.

Hence, according to Castoriadis, the beady eye that it fixed upon itself, but also upon others. The gaze that it turned upon others originated in the gaze that it turned upon itself, of which it was simply "the other side". This way of thinking attempts to accede to what is essential without bothering too much with historical considerations (for example, what are we to make of the Greeks–Barbarians dichotomy? And what about Greece after the fifth century?). It links the question of the Greeks and "others" to the particular moment and the particular development represented by the constitution of the *polis*. The whole problem is placed in the context of beginnings and in the perspective of a Greece that stands for inauguration.

Where Castoriadis sees openness and recognition, Levinas (like Momigliano) sees closure and a lack of understanding. Clearly the two theses are incompatible: the latter sees the Greeks "from outside", while the former sees them "from inside": two, quite literally, completely different points of view. Rather than reject them both, or use one to reject the other, or seek to reconcile them, I should like to begin by establishing them as polar opposites, in order to determine and thereby create the space for my own questioning. What I should like to do is orient those *Greek itineraries* and give meaning to those journeys, meanwhile, in the background, posing a question of my own: whether they were ambassadors representing certainties or bearers of doubts, and whether they sought to bring reassurance or were bent on destabilization, did not these frontier-men embody a real anxiety, to which they gave a face and expression and at the same time a means of resolution? Do not the accounts of their travels constitute a way of making room for "others", of assigning them a place, even if they do so by speaking (in Greek) for them? All of which boils down to saying that frontiers constitute both closures and openings, spaces between two different things in which travellers-translators can do either their best or their worst.[38]

CHAPTER 1

The Return of Odysseus

Odysseus returned full of space and time.
Osip Mandelstam

In Greece, it all began with epic, and for centuries everything was to remain under the sign of Homer. It is in epic that we must first expect to find the principal categories of Greek anthropology established and used. The *Odyssey* is not a geography of the Mediterranean, nor an ethnological enquiry, nor a collection of nautical instructions (Phoenician and others) expressed in verse and set to music. It is an account of a voyage intended from the outset to be a return and bent upon achieving its completion. It tells of the return journey of a man who "for years wandered, ... suffering much anguish in his soul, upon the sea", a man who, in response to a question put to him by King Alcinous, declares that he is "but a mortal", and possibly the most unfortunate of all mortals. The sea is there throughout, omnipresent and detested: a sea of sudden storms and nocturnal wrecks, which sweeps seafarers to a pitiful end. Odysseus is certainly a navigator and a better one than most, but he is an unwilling one, with no hankerings for dawns at sea or for islands "greener than dreams".

A VOYAGE AND A RETURN JOURNEY

Unlike Dante's Odysseus, spurred on by his desire to know the world, Homer's is basically a traveller against his will. It would not enter his head to murmur to himself the words whispered to him by Constantine Cavafy: "When you set off for Ithaca, pray that the route be long, rich in adventures and discoveries ... and that there will be many summer mornings when you

15

sail into ... unknown ports".[1] Only very seldom does he express a desire to see or to learn. Exceptionally, when on the Cyclops' island, he wants to stay, against his companions' advice, in order to "see" him; and when passing the island of the Sirens, he is seized by a "desire to listen".[2] His determination to go home to Ithaca, never to lose sight of the day of his return, is part and parcel of his resolute choice to retain the condition of a mortal. Only once, as the days pass on Circe's island, do his companions need to urge him to remember his native land.[3]

The fact that Odysseus remembers means neither that he worships the past nor even that he has a particular taste for recollection.[4] He is determined always to remember what he is, above all his name. In the end he does reintegrate his identity, starting with his name ("No-Man" once again becomes Odysseus). Likewise, he once again becomes the legitimate king of Ithaca, the husband of Penelope and the father of Telemachus, but he also knows, beyond all doubt, that at the end of the road death awaits him: "his own death", just as the infallible seer Tiresias warned him when he went all the way to Hades to seek him out.[5] Before that, though, he must suffer the experience of not recognizing his native land, even when he is at last returned to it, and of failing to win recognition from his own household.[6]

From the point of view of the Greek perception of others, it is probably by no means irrelevant that this first canonical and inaugural voyage is no one-way journey, but most emphatically a return. What should simply have been a return crossing turns into a ten-year voyage. Before the *Odyssey*, Odysseus was simply an Achaean chieftain with a particularly glib tongue and greatly skilled at deception. It is his Return that turns him into the hero of Endurance, the *Polutlas*, and that confers upon him, right down the centuries, a position that is altogether exceptional, one analogous to that which the *Iliad* conferred upon Achilles.

Is it possible, generally speaking, to draw a distinction between a voyage and a return? Would a voyage from which there was no return, not by accident but by definition, really still be a voyage? Would a quest for the Absolute, for instance, a losing of oneself, a final voyage, a disappearance leaving no trace? In truth, even a "voyage" such as that leaves behind it a story, a song, tears, the hollow space of an absence. And, on a more worldly and more Greek level, were not the colonization expeditions that the Greeks undertook from the eighth century BC on, within the Mediterranean area, conceived as one-way voyages for those who, as volunteers or conscripts selected by lot, set out under the leadership of an *oikistês* (founder), never to return? In a sense, they were. They set sail in order to found a completely new city. Hence all the precautionary foundation rituals, designed both to mark a new beginning and to ward off the perils attending it. Hence the consultation of Apollo in Delphi and the "investiture" of the founder, the recourse to diviners before setting out, during the voyage, and at the moment of settlement, and the transfer of a spark of fire from the communal Hearth of the mother-city. But, except on voyages of that kind, one usually set out without any baggage: without any ancestors or any of the dead (unlike Aeneas when he departed, with his father slung over his shoulders, to found a new Troy).[7] "Ordinary" voyages, for their part, certainly presuppose a return: the story to be told (upon one's return) is one of their "organizing" principles, as was pointed out by Pascal, who went on to condemn it as mere curiosity, on the grounds that "curiosity is nothing but vanity. More often than not one only wants to know so as to be able to talk about it; were it not for that, one would never undertake sea voyages at all, never to speak of them and for the sole pleasure of seeing things, with no hope of ever communicating them to others". Nobody travels solely for the pleasure of seeing. A voyage encompasses more than the present moment; it looks forward to a future that will make it possible for the traveller to contemplate himself seeing, to remember what there was to see, and to relish that pleasure of seeing.

But as for a voyage that is purely an account of a return, in which all the adventures and all the lands visited are no more than detours and diversions, does that not tell us something different? Odysseus wants to think of nothing but the day of his return. The many successive stages in his journey seem simply occasions that carry the danger of making him forget it. So the management of such a voyage is quite different. The most successful return journey is that of Nestor, who, having left the shores of Troy, returns to Pylos as quickly as possible, without "seeing anything". For that very reason there is nothing to say about it, except that his meticulous and unfailing piety carries him safely home without delay. Menelaus and Odysseus, on the other hand, "bungle" their returns: so they get to see many lands before eventually savouring "a return as sweet as honey".[8] A delayed return is caused by some "error" being committed (where the gods are concerned). It is within the space opened up by that delay (which the bard exploits) that "otherness" is experienced and that, as the tale develops, the great divides of Greek anthropology are revealed. Otherness is invariably a threat, and extreme otherness means extreme danger. In order to maintain or to recover his identity, to regain his own name, Odysseus the Endurer must also be Odysseus the Vigilant.

His return to himself comes about despite the "others", whether the other one is Polyphemus, who is ready to devour him, or Calypso, who wishes to give him immortality if only he will stay with her. The latter episode is the first ever to formulate "a heroic rejection of immortality".[9]

But in the last analysis, the *Odyssey* also tells us that simply to return does not guarantee that everything will again be as it was in the past. The *Odyssey*, a poem about a return journey through space, clashes with time. Ithaca is still there but is no longer Ithaca, or rather no longer the same Ithaca. Time has forced its way in and has changed everything. The old dog Argos dies when he recognizes his master. As soon as the poem begins, we move into the time of memory. Forgetfulness, now feared, now longed for, lurks. The memory of the dead haunts the living: when Menelaus at last returns to his palace in Sparta, he mourns the warriors "who died long ago on the broad plains of Troy, so far from Argos where the horses graze", but there is one in particular whose memory haunts him, spoiling his sleep and his appetite: Odysseus.[10] Odysseus, too, weeps when, among the Phaeacians, he hears Demodocus sing of him, Odysseus, in the third person, as though he were dead. The experience of not being himself is a painful one. Otherness is temporal as well as spatial.[11] Achilles, cheated of any return, has escaped time: he can be celebrated forever as "the best of the Achaeans", the epic hero *par excellence*.[12] But to win such *kleos*, he had first to die. The contrast between Achilles and Odysseus is partly a matter of each of them relating to a different time: the one shines forever in epic time, while the other makes the painful discovery of historicity and "the time of men".

If the *Odyssey* is no more than a return journey, what are the spatial schemata that organize the accounts of other, founding, voyages? In a sense, the *Aeneid* takes up where the *Odyssey* leaves off. The ships of Aeneas plough through a sea that has already been traversed, taking a route already recognized in the Homeric epic. But is not the general movement quite the reverse? Odysseus' aim is simply to return to Ithaca, once Troy is finally destroyed. Aeneas, in contrast, leaves Troy in flames, never to return. The *Aeneid* is the very model of a voyage with no return, even if the whole story is focused on the foundation of a new Troy. Where and how is what the whole story is about. It is the account of an enforced colonization: a matter of dying or fleeing, fleeing so that Troy will never die. *Feror exul in altam* ("An exile, I fare forth upon the deep"), declares Aeneas.[13] As Creusa's ghost tells her husband Aeneas, he and his companions are to be "wanderers", destined to a long exile: "Long exile is your lot, a vast stretch of sea you must plough".[14]

It will be a long time before they find the place to land in order to found (*condere*) a new Troy or to resuscitate (*resurgere*) the old one.

But whatever the reality of that quest, its current moves at surface level; the source of the propulsion that drives them lies deeper. By means of prophecies, oracles and dreams, Virgil strives to turn those wanderings into a return, albeit one that he represents as unwitting – a return to the unknown land of the wanderers' origins. The reader of the poem very soon discovers what it takes the travellers much longer to realize. Already in Delos, Apollo tells the descendants of Dardanus, "The land of your ancestors, whence you are sprung, shall receive you on your return (*reduces*) to her generous bosom. Seek out your ancient mother". The Trojans all wonder where the walled city to which Apollo is urging them to return (*reverti*) lies.[15] Anchises fancies he remembers that it must be in Crete. So they immediately make for that island and even found a town there, giving it the fine name of Pergamum. However, no sooner are its walls in place than a disease strikes the trees, the harvests and the colonists, so they are forced to set sail again, with all speed.

In which direction are they to steer? Now the Phrygian Penates appear to Aeneas as he sleeps and disclose to him that the Hesperia of which Apollo spoke was really Ausonia, or Latium.[16] The tribulations of exile are far from over, but at least they now know. To found the City (*condere Urbem*) or the Roman race (*Romanam gentem*) will in effect be to resurrect the kingdom of Troy (*resurgere regna Troiae*), but this return to the past can only take place, can only find *its place,* in the motherland of origins.[17] The foundation is to be a refoundation, a repetition, but at the same time totally new. Troy "returns" to somewhere it has never been, yet where it has always been and will forever be.[18] But this is not the end of the story, for Aeneas has to fight before founding, not Rome immediately, but Lavinium. And then there will remain the delicate matter of transferring from the one to the other. But even after the foundation of Rome, Lavinium would still, even in the historical period, remain the seat of the divine Penates of Rome and also of the Common Hearth.[19]

The exile is transformed into a return. It is as if the *archê*, the original foundation or absolute beginning, was impossible to confront head-on and was bound to prompt discursive operations and narrative side-stepping strategies, which, even as they made it possible to speak of that beginning, averted any excessive violence. The ploy of an account of a voyage is clearly just such a strategy.

"Remember this day, in which ye came out from Egypt, out of the house of bondage; for by strength of hand the Lord brought you out from this place".[20] Those are the words – founding words if ever there were – with which Moses addressed the liberated children of Israel. The Lord heard the prayers of his people and brought it out from Egypt to guide it to a "fine, wide land, flowing with milk and honey". Egypt, the land of misery and oppression, left forever, stands in contrast to the future felicity of the land of Canaan, to which the children of Israel "go up". The basic meaning of "exodus" (*exodos* in Greek) is certainly "exit".[21] The spatial pattern seems simple enough: they exit, then enter a new land. There can clearly be no return from the exodus march (for a return would be catastrophic); it must advance towards the future, confronting all hazards. This is no simple return journey.

Forty years of tribulations were to pass before the people, led by Joshua, would finally be allowed to cross the River Jordan. Moses, on the point of death, would be vouchsafed a glimpse of the land of Canaan in the distance, but would not be permitted to enter it. The march through the desert represents the beginning and development of a history. But the "land flowing with milk and honey" that the Lord has promised to give, to be fully possessed by his people, is not uninhabited: it first has to be conquered. War awaits at the end of the journey, just as it does for Aeneas, confronted by Turnus, and even for Odysseus, who must first eject the suitors from his house. Finally, and most importantly, this land is the one which the Lord first promised to Abraham, then to Isaac, and then again to Moses: "I am the Lord: And I appeared unto Abraham, unto Isaac, and unto Jacob ... And I have also established my covenant with them, to give them the land of Canaan, the land of their pilgrimage, wherein they were strangers".[22] To Abraham the Lord had announced: "I will give unto thee, and to thy seed after thee, the land wherein thou art a stranger, all the land of Canaan, for an everlasting possession; and I will be their God".[23] So in that sense, for the children of Israel Exodus too is the story of a return to the land of their fathers, but it is a return, long delayed, to a land that they did not possess and never had possessed. This visited land or land of "pilgrimage" is described in the Septuagint as a "land visited by temporary residents" (*gê paroikêseôs*).[24] Abraham's status, after all, was that of a domiciled foreigner. The same expression is used when Abraham is told of the Jewish people's future "sojourn" in Egypt, where they will, *par excellence*, be "stranger[s] in a land that is not theirs".[25] Upon their "return", in contrast, the people of the covenant is to become the proprietor of the places trodden by its ancestors in the past.[26] And will remain so, provided it becomes and continues to be a people of priests and a nation that is holy.

In his wanderings over the sterile sea, Odysseus is in danger of losing everything, his possessions, his reputation, even his name, and in the end returns home all alone, obliged to pass himself off as someone else, after losing all his ever-forgetful companions. In contrast, Israel, in its wanderings in the desert and under the guidance of its inspired lawgiver, learns how to become an instituted people, altogether different from the band of slaves that fled from Egypt.[27] Moulded by its god, who dictates its Law, Israel is firmly warned never to forget about Egypt, for if it does, the time of oppression may recommence and Egypt may "return". Remembering is the antidote. In the course of its long march, this people does not clash with "others" – other, strange peoples or monstrous beings – yet otherness is present within itself. It alienates itself, of its own accord, when it is overcome by the temptation of paganism, as is shown by the episode of the golden calf. Aaron is told, "Up, make us gods, which shall go before us; for as for this Moses, the man that brought us up out of the land of Egypt, we wot not what is become of him".[28]

In *Exodus*, we are confronted by a spatial economy that uses "voyage" and "return" in a fashion far more complex than the *Odyssey* or the *Aeneid*; above all, we find ourselves in an altogether different world, where the courage to begin stems from a willingness to obey.

ANTHROPOLOGY

The sea is both one and diverse. It encompasses several heterogeneous spaces, which it separates rather than unites, yet all of which Odysseus – and only he, carried along by the swell of the deep – eventually visits. But his endless journey is more than simply a visit to those near or far-flung places, some with human, some with non-human inhabitants. It is a journey that creates and communicates a Homeric or Greek (to the extent that Homer really was the "master" of Greece) anthropology: it tells of the place and the lot of mortals on the earth, and the condition of those whom the poem calls, precisely, "eaters of bread".

In the *Theogony* and the *Works and Days*, Hesiod recounts how Prometheus, in conflict with Zeus, institutes the first blood-sacrifice. This aetiological (almost theological) *muthos* elaborates an extremely forceful model to explain and justify the respective fundamental and definitive shares allotted to human beings, the beasts and the gods.[29] Homer, on a quite different level, in his account of Odysseus' wanderings, sets to work or rather sets in motion those same major anthropological categories. Where Hesiod is static and normative, Homer is dynamic and narrative. The conditions allotted to each group are animated and illustrated by the adventures of Odysseus and his companions as they journey through successive spaces, themselves shaped by the interplay between those categories: the space of the "mortal eaters of bread", the space beyond, and, eventually, a non-human space that is inhabited by monsters, but also by divine creatures. In short, this first anthropology, which structures the space of the "stories told at the court of Alcinous", is at work in the very logic of the narrative.

"Neither god nor beast" might be the watchword of this anthropology. Hesiod's poems strive to conceptualize the dividing lines; the *Odyssey* makes a story out of them.[30] Defined as mortal, and feeding on bread and the flesh of sacrificed animals, human beings mark out their territory, always ephemeral, ever needing to be reconquered, in between the gods and the beasts. Odysseus strives always to maintain not only the distance separating humans from animals but also that which must separate humans from the gods. When Calypso offers him immortality, he replies: "My lady goddess, do not be angry at what I am about to say. I too know well enough that my wife Penelope's looks and stature are insignificant compared with yours. For she is mortal, while you have immortality and unfading youth. Nevertheless I long to reach my home and *see* the day of my return. It is my never-failing wish".[31] Unlike him, his companions fail to remember. Ruled by their stomachs, they gorge on the "honey-sweet" lotus, cannot resist the meal that Circe sets before them, and end up sacrificing the cattle of the Sun.[32]

Mortals' need of domesticated animals is twofold: they need them to cultivate the earth, since, as eaters of bread, they are by vocation cultivators; and they need them in order to honour the gods, who are unfailingly punctilious in claiming the share of a sacrifice that is their due. To sacrifice is an essentially human activity. Within this first division another is at work: the division between animals that are domesticated and those that are wild, between spaces that are cultivated and those that are uncultivated. The Greek language has two words to designate wildness, each with a different register: *thêrios*, based on *thêr*, the wild beast, and *agrios*, which gives *agros*, uncultivated land, outlying land, fallow land.[33] Thales was said to count himself lucky to have been born a man rather than a wild beast, and furthermore a male rather than a female, and a Greek rather than a Barbarian.[34]

The world of mortal eaters of bread from which Odysseus hails and to which he indefatigably longs to return is the world of Ithaca, Pylos, Sparta, Argos and many other territories. There lie expanses of "wheat-giving earth" and land on which plump flocks pasture; there, a traveller's eye immediately seizes upon the "works of men": these are fields where men must labour hard in order to grow the cereals which, once milled and cooked, form what Homer calls the "marrow of men". With this bread, they eat the meat of sacrificed animals, divided into equal portions, and they drink wine: no banquet would be complete without these truly human foods.

This space that is cultivated is also socialized. Here humans, as a rule, are neither alone nor isolated. Each one belongs to a lineage, is a member of an *oikos*, which is at once a dwelling-place, a family system, and a power-structure: each one belongs to a community (*dêmos*, *polis*, *astu*).[35] For preference, humans live in "towns". A number of practices involving exchange are current there: warfare is one frequent and codified form; the exchange of women another; hospitality regulated, among nobles, by the giving of gifts and counter-gifts; and banquets, again among nobles or at the king's table.[36]

Such wholly human space is also tightly circumscribed. It consists of no more than modest settlements, separated by vast, wild expanses that are both linked and divided by the sea. This "sterile" sea, Poseidon's domain, is a familiar but dangerous space into which one never ventures with pleasure. Above the "wheat-growing earth" is the sky, sometimes described as "bronze", where the Immortals dwell; below it, the house of Hades and the land of the dead.[37] Overall, the earth appears as a flat disk, surrounded by the River Ocean, which is the source of all its seas and waters. It has not yet been divided into continents.

But even within the world of the mortal "eaters of bread", it is possible to make out a series of increasingly distant zones. The most familiar of these is encompassed by Telemachus' voyage from Ithaca to Sparta and by Nestor's return route from Troy to Pylos. Beyond it lies a second circle, through which Menelaus travelled, as did Odysseus, as far as Crete. It encompasses Crete, set in "the middle of the wine-dark sea", and extends as far as the shores of Phoenicia, swarming with sly, rapacious seafarers, of Libya "where the lambs are born with horns", and of Egypt, "a region so remote that one might well give up all hope of return once the winds have blown one astray into that wide expanse of sea, which is so vast and perilous that even the birds cannot cross it in a year".[38] Even more distant lies the boundary zone, the home of the "last" human beings (*eschatoi*): the Ethiopians, visited by

Poseidon, but also by Menelaus; the Cimmerians, shrouded by the Ocean mists; and the Phaeacians, with their magic ships, whom only Odysseus encounters. These people of the outer limits are certainly mortals, but they enjoy a rather special status, for they are still close to the gods and have preserved certain features of the life of the Golden Age.

This space contains a veritable airlock. It is situated between the Cape of Malea, a steep promontory in the south of the Peloponnese, and the island of Cythera, which lies beyond it. Everything may be decided within this strait. Nestor, the embodiment of piety, passes through without even noticing it. As a result, he returns directly from Troy to Pylos. But if the channel is closed, seafarers are forced to wander away, carried by the "great sea-swell". Such is the fate of Menelaus, whose pilotless fleet is scattered afar among people with "foreign tongues" (*allothrooi*), distant strangers with whom relations are virtually impossible.[39] Such too, above all, is the fate that assails Odysseus, who, repulsed from Cape Malea and blown off course for nine days by stormy winds, eventually lands among the Lotus-Eaters, in alien space, not the space of mortal eaters of bread. In this non-human space of the "stories told at the court of Alcinous", Odysseus now encounters a radical otherness, where the whole matter of boundaries is brought into question, and the categories separating human beings, beasts and the gods are all confused.

The space, the reverse of the humanized space from which Odysseus has come, seems to be devoid of cultivation or sociability, isolated and without detectable boundaries. To pass through it is to encounter diverse ways of life and dietary regimes that even encompass the most extreme forms of cannibalism. But every place where the travellers pause presents them with the same disconcerting discovery: nowhere is the land cultivated (even if it happens to produce of its own accord, as in the Golden Age), and even where herd-raising is practised – as among the Cyclopes and the Laestrygonians – it is never accompanied by agriculture. Shepherds they may be, but cultivators they are not (yet). There is no wheat, no bread, so it is difficult not only to eat food befitting human beings, but also to honour the gods as they should be honoured, with sacrifices of a kind to please them.[40]

Some of the beings who inhabit this space eat the food of the gods, which is forbidden to men: Circe and Calypso are thus served with ambrosia and nectar. Others, such as the amiable but forgetful Lotus-Eaters, eat flowers. Yet others happily consume human beings, when they happen to catch them or fish them from the sea: the giant Laestrygonians harpoon Odysseus' companions like so many tuna fish, and Polyphemus is a man-eater and a drinker of neat wine (a double anomaly in relation to the norms), even if his usual diet consists of milk and cheese.[41] Not until he reaches Phaeacia (by which time he is on his own), will Odysseus find cultivated fields and the bread of human beings (despite the fact that King Alcinous' orchard is still very close to the Golden Age).[42]

In this space, there is no communication between one being and another. Calypso lives alone in her cave, apart from the other gods; even Hermes, their messenger, has never visited her. Circe, the enchantress, also lives alone, and changes into animals those imprudent enough to entrust themselves to her hospitality. Aeolus, the king of the Winds, is not alone, but lives trapped on his island of bronze, surrounded by his sons and daughters, who dispassionately practise incest. The Laestrygonians do constitute a society, with a king, a palace and an agora, but these giants do not practise agriculture and are, moreover, cannibals. As for the Cyclopes, after Homer they came to represent a type of primitive life in which each individual, living on his own in his cave, unconcerned by others, was a law unto himself.[43] Polyphemus, a shepherd, is a consumer of milk products who is, nevertheless, partial to fresh meat and pure wine.

Whenever he is about to land on new shores, Odysseus wonders whether he will encounter people who are "violent savages without justice, or hospitable beings who fear the gods" (*Odyssey*, VI, 121–2). The answer, invariably, is that in the non-human world, hospitality, as a general rule, has no place. Strangers are not welcomed.[44] Circe pretends to be hospitable, the better to achieve her ends. Polyphemus, for his part, squarely makes a mockery of hospitality, telling Odysseus that he has no truck with Zeus Xenios (the Hospitable One), but nevertheless, by way of a hospitable gesture, he will devour *No-Man* last of all, after he has consumed all his companions.[45] It is again only in the land of the Phaeacians, those infallible boundary-crossers stationed where one world meets another, on the frontiers between categories, that hospitality recovers its rights: only the Phaeacians are capable of reintegrating Odysseus into the space of the eaters of bread, of so to speak getting him to pass beyond Cape Malea in the "right" direction, returning him from extreme otherness to the heart of what is familiar.

The *Odyssey*, with its poetic anthropology, provides the basis for the Greeks' vision of themselves and of others. Not in abstract form, but through an adventure story, it produces a long-lasting paradigm – albeit one that was later to be reshaped, reworked, completed, reassessed and criticized – that made it possible to see and explain the world so as to explore it and represent it, "inhabit" it and make it a world that was "human", that is to say Greek. It was thus with total justification that, as late as the first century, Strabo called Homer the *archêgetês* (founder) of geography.[46] As the creator of a Greek understanding of space and the organizer of a Greek space of understanding, Homer was certainly a founder, in the strongest sense of the term. Like those who landed on unknown shores and there founded new cities and who, when they died, were buried in the agoras of their towns, where they became the objects of a cult, Homer lies at the centre of Greek memory.

THE RETURN TO ITHACA

At the shore's edge, where the waves break, the unavoidable, perilous sea begins. It belongs primarily to Poseidon. It is he who, barring the way on Odysseus' return journey, makes him the sea's "prisoner". He is "Poseidon, the great god, mover of the earth and the sterile sea", to whom the gods have allotted "a twofold office, ... to be tamer of horses and a saviour of ships";[47] though it is also he who destroys the latter. Armed with his trident, he unleashes squalls and churns up the sea or, alternatively, calms it and creates a gentle breeze. He demands homage in the form of the appropriate sacrifices before a vessel sets to sea and also when it comes in to land. As the father of Polyphemus, the lord (*anax*) of the Pylians and the Phaeacians, and a willing guest at the banquets of the Ethiopians, he is constantly present in the *Odyssey*. Although he is the king of the sea, he is not a sailor: the techniques of ship-building and navigation neither interest nor concern him.

Those skills belong to Athena, who, through them, intervenes in the domain of the sea. It is she who knows how to build and guide the swift ships that are the "horses of the sea". She guides the hand of the carpenter, so that he "saws straight", just as she guides that of the pilot, so that he "steers straight". The key word for "to steer" is *ithunein*, to go straight. A good pilot knows how to steer straight even when the wind drops or veers; he knows how to steer straight even when reference points themselves are constantly shifting; he can keep the ship on course even when a sudden squall sweeps down from all sides, seizing hold of the ship. If "wet paths" do exist across the sea, they are never visible in advance and vanish as soon as the wake of the vessel disappears. For every crossing, the paths must be reinvented, and they are easy to lose from one moment to the next. A good pilot must possess the kind of supple, cunning intelligence, as swift as the sea itself and quick to adapt to circumstances and seize opportunities, that will enable him to cut out a route and find a way through (*poros*): "By skill ... the helmsman keeps his quick ship running straight over the sparkling sea, though the winds are buffeting".[48] More than any other hero, Odysseus possesses that kind of intelligence, for he is "the inventive one", the man with multiple *mêtis*. Yet, as a captive of the sea, he, more than any other, suffers "as he seeks for ways through".

On the "misty sea" where he has to navigate, a helmsman uses the sun, the stars and the prevailing winds to help him to find his way. The course of the sun is the major axis. For a traveller, the sign of being lost is an inability to distinguish the East (*eôs*) from the West (*zophos*). But *eôs* and *zophos* are far more than two cardinal points: they mark out the limits of different zones, levels and spaces. *Eôs* is the point where, each morning, the sun, rising up from Ocean, appears on the horizon, but it is also the entire zone of (visible) sunrises; and it is daylight, that is to say the whole portion of space that extends between the East and the West, passing by way of the South; it is the region lit by the sun, the world above, that of the living, the world of Zeus. *Zophos*, in contrast, is the point where the sun sets, but also the entire space that extends between the East and the West, taking in the North; the sunless world below, the world of the dead, where Hades dwells. And the sea can get you lost in those spaces, as it were beyond it, where nothing is visible.[49]

Even without moving outside the world of mortal eaters of bread, more and more distant zones appear, zones whose boundaries are drawn by voyages and the tales told of them. In the first place, there is the zone marked out by Telemachus' journey from Ithaca to Pylos and the stories that Nestor tells of his return from Troy to Pylos. But that zone shows no trace of Odysseus' passing.

That is why Nestor sends Telemachus on, on to Sparta. For, even if Sparta belongs totally to the space of human beings, Menelaus, for his part, has returned from the land of Egypt, "a region so remote that one might well give up all hope of return once the winds have blown one astray".[50] And even in that distant world Odysseus is not to be found. It is only through the mediation of the Old Man of the Sea, Proteus, that Menelaus learns that Odysseus is alive, but is detained at sea. This distant space is that of the voyages of Menelaus and of the "Cretan tales" (the lying tales that a disguised Odysseus is subsequently to tell, upon his return to Ithaca). Crete, which is still close enough, yet already distant, occupies an important place in that space: in the presence of Eumaeus, Odysseus is able to pass himself off credibly as a Cretan and relate that, after Odysseus set sail for Troy, while rounding Cape Malea he was washed ashore on Crete; and similarly, part of Menelaus' fleet, which is taken by surprise beneath the Cape, is wrecked on the Cretan coast.

Odysseus (the Cretan) has been to Troy, to Egypt, to Phoenicia, and eventually landed among the Thesprotians, who were supposed to carry him onward to Ithaca.[51] Menelaus too knew Phoenicia, Egypt, and its river, and Libya. Beyond lay the zone of the outer boundaries, those of the "last" men (*eschatoi*), the Ethiopians, the Cimmerians and the Phaeacians. These are human beings, for they are mortal, but their situation, their way of life and their relations with the gods make them rather more than humans.

As soon as Odysseus sets foot on the island of Circe, he climbs to the top of a hill in the hope of seeing cultivated fields, but all he can make out is a wisp of smoke rising far away, in the middle of a thick wood.[52] However, smoke is not a reliable sign of the presence of human beings, as Odysseus and his companions have already learned to their cost among the Cyclopes and the Laestrygonians, and as they are about to learn again from their encounter with Circe herself. So, in this space where it is not possible to eat the food of human beings, once the ship's provisions are exhausted and they are suffering from hunger, the only option is hunting (or fishing). But to hunt in order to eat is not a glorious business and may even be dangerous if one treats as game animals that are not strictly wild or, worse still, if one transgresses a prohibition and strikes down beasts that belong to a god, such as the cattle of the Sun, which appear to be truly human food but are in truth absolutely prohibited.[53]

This world, devoid of any true sociability, is immobile. It has no past, no memories. It is a world where nothing is remembered, where no itinerant bard lives, and where all those cast ashore will be wiped out: the lotus is a flower of oblivion, and Circe's drug is a *pharmakon* that effaces all memories of one's homeland. Circe and Calypso sing as they weave, but nobody hears their songs; Aeolus and his companions feast all day long, but their endless banquet lacks what should be its joy and ornament, namely the song of the bard: which is why Odysseus himself is obliged to recount the capture of Troy, episode by episode. Furthermore, the "vision" of bards such as Phemius or Demodocus cannot penetrate this space. When inspired by the Muse, the blind Demodocus sings of the trials of the Achaeans camped outside Troy, just as if he had been "present in person", but he can "weave" no song about the tribulations of Odysseus, far away on the misty sea and living among savages. The bard, who sings of the high deeds of heroes, is the master of *kleos*, which means both glory and renown; so the non-human space is fundamentally *akleês*, devoid of glory. For any hero unfortunate enough to be dragged there, there is nothing to be gained and everything to be lost – even his name. Ultimately, the only bard of this space of distress and oblivion is Odysseus himself, the man who always remembers. Alcinous indeed compares his *muthos*, the account of his adventures, to the true song of a bard.[54]

However, Odysseus is not a bard. He is not inspired by the Muse: simply, he himself has physically endured and witnessed with his own eyes all that he recounts.[55] He speaks in the first person, offering himself as the sole guarantor of his words (a fact that raises the possibility that he may be lying), whereas a bard always relates his tales in the third person, placing himself under the authority of the Muses, who, for their part, were present when it all happened. The Muses, the daughters of Zeus and Memory, are "absent" from this space of "stories", or rather, the only Muses encountered there are the Sirens, who are the Muses of death and oblivion: anti-Muses.[56]

In this unknown space devoid of points of reference, the knowledge of a helmsman is of scant avail, for there can be no real navigation here. What is needed is a guide who is more than human. When Odysseus disembarks on Circe's island, he says that it is thanks to the guidance of some god; and the same goes for his landing on the island of the Cyclopes, which, furthermore, is engulfed in the darkness of the night: "This is where we came to land. Some god must have guided us through the murky night, for it was impossible to see ahead. The ships were in a thick fog ... Not a man among us caught sight of the island".[57] Odysseus is cast by a god and during the night upon Calypso's shores. And in order for him eventually to set foot in Scheria, not only is the intervention of Athena required, to intercede with the winds (she, exceptionally, steps out of her own particular domain of competence here), but also the talisman veil given to him by Ino. All these narrative details emphasize the inaccessible nature of these places, where one can set foot without knowing where one is, during the night, whereas normally a sailor, upon finding he was approaching an unknown land, would anchor at a distance and wait for dawn, or would land there only involuntarily (following a shipwreck).

There is no proper route between these inaccessible places, no route that links them or that would make it possible simply to move from one to the next: no chain of islands dotted here and there, separated by vast stretches of water. Just one place after another, without any transition, or rather through the transition of a linking formula between two episodes, a formula that is frequently used: "So we left that country and sailed with heavy hearts. And we came to the land of ...".[58] Sometimes that transition does involve a period of time, but it is never anything but a formulaic period: after nine days of sailing or drifting, they arrive, on the tenth day, among the Lotus-Eaters or on Calypso's island, or on the twentieth day they reach Phaeacia. In contrast, a single day, from sunrise to sunset, suffices to pass from the island of Circe to the edge of the boundary-limit of the world constituted by Ocean.

This world, whence there is no return for whoever, despite himself, has ventured there, is a heterogeneous and limitless space for stories: neither the gods nor the dead are far away. Of course, the gods Above dwell on Olympus, that place of eternal light, beyond the movements of the air, the earth, and the waters, a fixed and immobile (*asphalês*) point in the universe. And they have no liking for this space shaken by the winds and battered by the waves, where Hermes is loath to go when he is sent to tell Calypso of Zeus' decision. However, the point is that Calypso and Circe are goddesses: exiled and isolated they may be, but they are still goddesses, and they eat the food of the gods. Unlike most of the gods when in the world of ordinary humans, they do allow simple mortals to see them, although Circe, when she wants to, is able to avoid being seen. Calypso the goddess perforce obeys the male gods, who cannot tolerate a goddess living with a mortal man. More generally, within this non-cultivated space, no sacrifices are made, for here no one is bound by the practice that regulates relations between the gods and human beings and through which, by repeating the division of a ritually sacrificed animal, those human beings acknowledge themselves to be mortal eaters of bread. The absence of sacrifice is the sign of a different kind of space, one that is close to the world of the Golden Age, in which savagery and proximity to the gods coexisted perfectly well, as Polyphemus baldly declares: "We Cyclopes care nothing for Zeus with his aegis, nor for the rest of the blessed gods, since we are much stronger than they are".[59]

Odysseus sets sail in the morning, with no need of a pilot, departing from Circe and the land of dawns and sunrises and, swept along by a brisk Boreas, that very evening comes to the extreme edge of River Ocean, itself a frontier of the world, and reaches the land of darkness. There, having beached his craft, he has to press on further, in the direction of the house of Hades, at the confluence of the rivers of the underworld. It is now impossible to descend any lower, short of passing through the "gates of Hades", so it is time to resort to ritual: the customary libations, the slaughtering of a lamb and a black ewe, as these animals turn their heads toward Erebus, and a holocaust for Hades and Persephone. Immediately, the shades of those who have disappeared emerge, attracted by the blood. "Green with fear", and grasping his sword, Odysseus has to ward them off until such time as Tiresias, the diviner, the only one in this place to have retained his "wits", has quaffed the blood.[60] The blood momentarily brings "life" to the dead, these heads without strength, making recognition and conversation possible, but then they are obliged to redescend into Erebus, mere shades among other shades.

But even while invigorated by the blood, a shade is only an illusion, and all physical contact with it is impossible. Three times Odysseus vainly tries to embrace his mother, without success, for she is no more than a dreamlike illusion. Again "green with fear" at the idea that Persephone might send up "the gorgon head of some ghastly monster", Odysseus hurries away. As a living man at the extreme edge of the land of the dead, he must not lay eyes on the frightful Gorgon, the very sight of whom would turn him to stone. She marks the ultimate limit of the world of darkness, where everything is confusion and chaotic noise.[61]

It is not yet time for Odysseus to cross the threshold of Hades, nor is he to remain a captive of the misty sea. For at last he must leave the space of no return, albeit by now totally alone after the last shipwreck, and only saved thanks to the Phaeacians, the infallible ferrymen. The Phaeacians dwell at the interface between two spaces, the non-human space and that of the eaters of bread. They practise hospitality and recognize Zeus the Hospitable One.[62] Nausicaa is not yet wed, but there is no question of having her marry one of her brothers, as in the case of Aeolus, and Odysseus would make a fine son-in-law for Alcinous. For the first time since the start of Odysseus' wanderings, Athena is directly present (initially taking the form of a young girl carrying a pitcher),[63] whereas the space of stories had up until now been closed to her. The Phaeacians are mortals, but intermediate ones.

They are also the "last" of men. They have no dealings with others and have regarded strangers with suspicion ever since Nausithous settled here, apart from others, and far away from the troublesome Cyclopes, who used to be their neighbours. In contrast to Ithaca, a society whose development is blocked and where all forms of sociability are disintegrating, Scheria is a community at ease with itself, where life passes amid joy and good humour. Alcinous is not so much a king "ruling by might", but rather a master of banquets who organizes the dancing and games that follow the songs of the bard. This is a society unacquainted with violence and warfare, where there are neither heroes nor *kleos* and where, according to Alcinous, the deaths of so many warriors beneath the walls of Troy were engineered merely in order to provide future men with songs to listen to. The land is tilled here, but the king's orchard is still very close to the Golden Age and his palace is a place of wonder. Sacrifices are performed in Phaeacia, but the immortals frequently honour the banquets with their presence, for the Phaeacians are "close to the gods". Alcinous and Arete are man and wife, but also brother and sister, so their union is incestuous.

The Phaeacians excel not only at singing and dancing, but also as oarsmen. Among these shipowners, everything – even their name – is geared towards the sea. Like the Phoenicians, who roam all the seas, they are professional sailors, but unlike the Phoenicians they exchange nothing, trade nothing, but are content to fulfil their function as scrupulous ferrymen. In short, they live for, not from, the sea.

Their magic ships know instinctively where to go: "Hidden in mist and cloud they make their swift passage over the sea's immensities with no fear of damage and no thought of wreck".[64] The Phaeacians, who are the seamen of Poseidon, not Athena, have no need of a pilot's skills or of a rudder in order to "go straight". Setting sail at sunset, they carry away Odysseus, sunk in a sleep "the very counterfeit of death", speeding faster than a falcon and "leaping forward to make short work of the course"; and the journey is completed, not at the break of day, but while it is still dark, before dawn, in the cave of Phorcys, a sheltered harbour where the Naiads live. This too is a double space and so is a possible point of contact between the space of stories and that of men who are eaters of bread. Then the nocturnal ferrymen depart in their ships that have no need of winds and waves, returning to their own destiny. Whatever that may be, whether or not Poseidon carries out his threat, and whether or not the Phaeacians are immobilized and disappear, there will never again be any ferrymen between the two spaces: Odysseus is the last to make that voyage, and the Odyssey can never be repeated.

Life, like a homecoming, is "as sweet as honey", and death is always hateful. But there are ways and ways of dying. A hero accepts death in battle, and is willing to cross the threshold of the gates of Hades and oblivion provided that, in exchange, he obtains *kleos* and lives on through the songs of the bards and in the social memory of the group. Achilles, choosing to die before the walls of Troy, forwent a return (*nostos*) to his loved ones, but was convinced that he would win "imperishable glory". In contrast to a heroic death such as this, at the head of one's warriors, death at sea is totally horrifying, for the dying man loses everything, in return for nothing at all: his life, his homecoming, and also his renown and even his name. Worse still, although he loses his life, he is not truly dead. For until such time as he is given the last rites his shade is left "wandering in vain along the broad-gated house of Hades",[65] unable to cross the threshold. Such a soul, with no place to go for the time being, is furthermore likely to present a threat to the living. When Odysseus arrives at the gates of Hades, his companion Elpenor, left unburied on Circe's island, begs him to be sure to complete the last rites for him: "Do not sail away and forsake me utterly nor leave me there unburied and unwept, in case I bring down the gods' curse on you … Burn me there … and raise a mound for me on the shore of the grey sea, in memory of an unlucky man, so that men yet unborn may learn my story".[66]

That is why, drowning in the stormy sea, Odysseus regrets not having died before Troy, near the corpse of Achilles, for there he would have received the funerary honours due to him, and the Achaeans would have "carried home" his *kleos*. Telemachus would also have felt that his death at Troy was less cruel, for his father would have had a tomb and "would have bequeathed his great glory to his son". As it is, instead of being ritually consumed on the funeral pyre, his maltreated corpse has probably been eaten by the dogs, the birds and the fish, and instead of his white bones being gathered up for burial, they are probably "rotting in the rain upon some distant land or rolling in the salt sea waves".[67] As Telemachus sees it, Odysseus, neither dead nor alive, but vanished, has been carried off "without glory" (*akleiôs*) by the Harpies, those winds of storms and death, and has departed invisible (*aïstos*) and undiscovered (*apustos*).

Telemachus' voyage thus has a double purpose: to seek out the *kleos* of his father, all that men are saying about him; and also, if ever he comes across someone who "saw" him die, to return forthwith to Ithaca and there build him a tomb (*sêma*) and pay him due funerary honours. For even if that memorial is no more than a cenotaph,[68] it will "signal" that Odysseus is dead and, standing as a memorial stone, for future men it will remain a visible and undeniable sign of his *kleos*. Similarly, Menelaus, detained in faraway Egypt, builds a tomb to commemorate his brother Agamemnon, "so that his glory shall never fade". Furthermore, once the death of Odysseus is attested and marked on the landscape, it will be possible to resolve the situation in Ithaca. The competition for Penelope and the throne will really begin; and Telemachus will claim his rights and defend his chances on the strength of the "glory" of his father.

Throughout his life, and even at the expense of it, a hero struggled to elude the crowd of those who were "nameless". But a death at sea reduced all his efforts to nothing. Outside the space of human beings, in the world of the sea where no fame endures, death meant an anonymous disappearance. When

Penelope learns that Telemachus has set sail, she asks whether he wishes "his very name to be forgotten in the world".[69] In the watery space of stories, the *kleos* of Odysseus and his very name are, so to speak, worth nothing (except from time to time, thanks to ancient predictions). As he tells Polyphemus, here his name "of fame" (*kluton*) is No-Man. Even at the risk of himself and his crew being smashed to bits by the rocks hurled at them by the blinded Cyclops, he cannot, in the end, resist claiming the exploit of having escaped in his own true name: *noblesse oblige*. But it is not until he reaches Phaeacia and hears Demodocus sing of the Trojan horse and the cunning of Odysseus that he can really reassume his name as a man and, in response to Alcinous' remark that nobody "is altogether without a name", can spell out his own identity: "I am Odysseus, Laertes' son. The whole world talks of my stratagems, and my fame has reached the heavens".[70]

Odysseus wandering over the seas is nobody, or no longer anybody; and Telemachus, for his part, is not at all sure who *he* is: "My mother certainly says I am Odysseus' son, but for myself I cannot tell".[71] Not even the assurances of Penelope or his physical resemblance to his father, so striking in the eyes of Mentes, Nestor and Menelaus, suffice to assure him of his affiliation: is he the son of Odysseus or of nobody?

Yet within non-human space there is one place where the name of Odysseus does mean something: the meadow of the Sirens.[72] The Sirens know of Odysseus, know of his sufferings before Troy, for they know "what happens on the fruitful earth", that is to say in the world of human beings. With their clear voices raised in song, they enchant (and deceive) whoever draws near, and that puts paid to any homecoming for him: trapped by his desire to listen to them, there he remains until he rots on the shore, unburied and forgotten. For, in contrast to the true Muses, who, through the songs of the bards, confer "imperishable life" upon dead heroes, these Muses of death offer nothing but the oblivion of an ignominious death, without burial, without memorial. By listening to them (as if he were listening to a bard singing of him after his death), the hero loses everything: both his *kleos* and his *nostos*, both fame and homecoming. He is already dead.

However, in the end Odysseus wins everything, both his homecoming and his fame: the pillager of Troy returns to Ithaca, where, "with his strength", he slaughters the suitors. For, even though hated by Poseidon, he was never destined to find a pitiful death in the storm-swept night. Yet, having returned home and having once again become Odysseus of Ithaca, he was to be forced to set out as a traveller once more, according to the extraordinary and mysterious prediction of Tiresias. As he tells Penelope when they are reunited, "Dear wife, we have not yet come to the end of our trials ... Tiresias told me to ... wander on from city to city":[73] not so as to see the towns of men once again but, on the contrary, until such time as he becomes an object of general curiosity. Shouldering an oar, he is to make his way towards lands where people know nothing of the sea, until a passerby is curious enough to ask why he is walking along in this way carrying "a winnowing fan". At this point, knowing that he has reached his destination, he will stick his upright oar into the ground and offer up a sacrifice to Poseidon. It is as if, through this expiatory sacrifice, made on the very spot where Poseidon's authority ends, on the frontier of his sphere of influence, he will be offering Poseidon the final homage. For that last time, he must go to the very limit and mark the frontier. After that, Tiresias has told him, when he has returned to Ithaca and grown old there, a gentle death will come for him "*ex halos*":[74] does that mean a death "from the far away sea" or "a death far away from the sea"?

Both interpretations are possible, and both have been upheld or entertained. For instance, Apollonius of Tyana, like a latter-day Tiresias, told the future Emperor Titus that for him, as for Odysseus, death would come from the sea.[75] The Neoplatonic philosophers fastened upon this prediction in their efforts to turn Odysseus' travels into a mystical voyage. For Numenius of Apamea, writing in the second half of the second century AD, the meaning was certainly "not in the sea" or "away from the sea". Having at last escaped from the trials of terrestrial life, Odysseus, far from the seething waves, would recover the calm of his heavenly homeland: "To die is to escape from the rough waves of this earthly life spent amid matter".[76] The figure of Odysseus stands for the soul exiled in the perceptible world. Plutarch, meditating on the situation of that exiled soul, related it to the general condition that makes all humans transient beings in exile.[77]

What is, in the future, to make Odysseus an emblematic figure is not so much his wide experience of the world, but rather his ability to escape from it: not the voyage itself, but the endurance of it and all its perils, and the final deliverance from it. This was the exegesis of Odysseus that was elaborated by a number of philosophical schools, all of which regarded him as the embodiment of their ideal of humanity: a cynical Odysseus, a beggar in his own palace, stoical in his ability to endure, scorning pleasure, and a butt of hostile Fortune; an Odysseus able to resist the attraction of the Siren temptresses; an allegory now of pleasure, now of poetry and knowledge.[78] In this series of interpretations of the figure of Odysseus, the journey through the world is also transformed: it becomes simply a metaphor for another "voyage", a far finer one, reserved for the philosopher, a motionless traveller embarked on an altogether internal journey.

Maximus of Tyre called Odysseus a "sage". Yet what exactly was it that he had seen? "Savage Thracians and Cicones, Cimmerians bereft of sunlight, Cyclopes who killed their guests, a female poisoner, the sights of Hades, Scylla, Charybdis, the garden of Alcinous, and the hovel of Eumaeus: all of them perishable, ephemeral things, the stuff of fable". And what of the spectacle that the philosopher is invited to contemplate? It is like a dream which, embracing the entire world, is all clarity and totally true.[79]

The pedestrian, terrestrial voyage through all the "otherness" of the world becomes no more than a pale approximation, or worse still, an obstacle, a diversion that distracts the philosopher from his scrutiny of what is Above and from his contemplation of life. Odysseus has finally become a monk.

THE VOYAGES OF A NAME

With a death "far from the sea", Odysseus/Ulysses can represent a man who, like Joachim du Bellay, *exiled* in Rome, dreams only of returning "to live out the rest of his time among his kin". Or, with "a death from the sea", he may, on the contrary, as in the *Odyssey* of Nikos Kazantzakis (1938), be an old sea-captain departing at dawn from Ithaca on his last voyage of no return, proclaiming that "abroad is his native land".[80]

That ambiguity has made it possible for the name of Odysseus/Ulysses to embark on other voyages in space and time, far beyond the spaces of Homer's *Odyssey*. But before that, Odysseus, a reluctant voyager who saw and visited the cities of so many peoples, though propelled by no desire to see or to know, soon became an expert on the vast world, a patron of voyagers, ethnographers and historians, even the ideal for statesmen and sovereigns. It is as if the very first lines of Homer's poem have been detached from the rest of it and the fact that, immediately following them, he is presented as the only hero, the last of all, still deprived of his homecoming and his wife, has been forgotten.[81] That anomaly is precisely why the bards sing of him. In the epic cycle of *Return Journeys*, he represents the exception: the only one who has not (yet) returned. Why? How? The element of suspense is already there; all the skill of the bard will now consist in deferring for as long as possible a return that everyone knows must eventually happen. Given that Odysseus did not die beneath the walls of Troy, nor did he disappear at sea, he is bound to return. Bound to, even if, as the words of Tiresias warn, that return will not quite bring his tribulations to an end.

The prologue to Herodotus' *Histories* directly echoes the opening lines of the *Odyssey*. Herodotus the historian sees himself, too, as a voyager, and identifies with the experiences of Odysseus. He likewise sets out to visit the cities of men, both great and small, and to understand them. But he has an advantage over Odysseus, for he knows that "those that were once great have for the most part become small; and those that are great in his own day were once small": he understands that time is vicissitude.[82] For that reason, he must make equal mention of both the great and the small, moving on from that which is there to see to that which is no longer visible, and paying attention to all remaining traces. According to Herodotus, a historian is indeed like the Odysseus described by the poet Mandelstam, a man who returns "full of space and time". To tell his story.

Polybius was to subscribe to that picture, stressing that a historian must have seen with his own eyes and endured with his own body, thereby combining the qualities of a historian with those of a statesman.[83] Then, in the first century, Diodorus Siculus was to begin his *Universal History* by invoking Odysseus. But the point of view had changed: it was no longer a matter of the experience of the historian, rather that of the reader. History had something to teach but the historian was not obliged to have experienced all its misfortunes in person.[84] A more comfortable position to be in, it must be said.

The Romans extended a hearty welcome to this Odysseus, the man of experience and also an *exemplum virtutis*, as is testified by their paintings and sculptures, based on Hellenistic models. Bernard Andreae, who has traced that image in Rome, skilfully reveals the complementarity and opposition between the image of Odysseus and that of Laocoön: Odysseus represents inventive, autonomous man, capable of forcing destiny; Laocoön represents the just man, crushed by fate.[85]

Skipping over a number of centuries, in particular the Renaissance, itself a great time for discoveries and voyages, and for validating autopsies and re-evaluating story-tellers and "liars" such as Herodotus,[86] in the eighteenth century we come upon Father Jean François Lafitau, claiming to have inherited the authority of Homer and Odysseus so far as knowledge of mores and customs is concerned. That knowledge is so useful and interesting, he writes, that Homer "saw fit to make it the subject of an entire poem. Its aim is to publicize the wisdom of Odysseus, its hero, who ... profited from all his navigational mistakes and learned about the customs of many nations".[87] And what was the point of all that instruction of his, if not to instruct us? Odysseus' belated return results from navigational mistakes which the hero, like a modern explorer, puts to good use in order to fill in the blank spaces of maps and to cram his notebooks with observations. Contrary to what Pascal said about voyages, they are not a matter of "vain curiosity", for the knowledge that is their goal is by no means "sterile".

But the long itinerary of voyages in the name of Odysseus[88] had already been glorified many years earlier, by Dante. The poet meets Odysseus in the eighth circle of Hell. Virgil, his guide and alter ego, questions the damned soul, asking him where he eventually died. Dante was clearly following up the riddle of Odysseus' death; and he opted without hesitation for a death "from the sea". The Greek hero's reply consists of an extraordinary account in which an Odysseus of modern times comes to the fore, possessed by a thirst for knowledge and punished as it were twice over, both as a pagan Ancient and as an (excessively curious) Modern. Petrarch was soon to comment that Odysseus was a man who wished to see "too much" of the world.

Strangely enough, the attitude of Dante's Odysseus/Ulysses is similar to that of the narrator of the *True History*, by Lucian of Samosata (second century AD). In this parody of travellers' tales, the model for which was, precisely, the tales told in the palace of Alcinous, where Odysseus got "the poor, simple Phaeacians" to swallow a pack of lies, Lucian – or rather the narrator, who calls himself "I" – begins with a preliminary declaration of duplicity that subverts the initial contract of a writer. He says not "I have seen", "I have heard", but "I declare that I have seen nothing, heard nothing; nothing has befallen me. So you should not believe me". Quite simply, "I have decided to lie, but with more honesty than most people as there is one point on which I shall tell the truth, and that is that I am recounting lies". Once into the story, however, we find all the usual marks of authentication: details of the voyage, observations, claims of "I saw", and even an inscription composed by Homer himself in honour of Lucian: "Lucian, beloved of the blessed gods, saw all of this country and then departed to his dear homeland"![89] By cutting himself down to size as a writer of parody, Lucian, with his story, casts doubt upon all those other stories that opened with a preliminary declaration of veracity: "I have seen with my own eyes and heard for myself...". Lucian–Homer and Lucian–Odysseus then continue: the reason for this journey to the Ocean was "my intellectual activity and desire for adventure, and my wish to find out where the end of the Ocean was, and who the people were that lived on the other side".[90] This fictitious story thus explicitly declares that its hero is spurred on by curiosity, a desire to see. But this fictional traveller who is so curious about the antipodes is poles apart from Odysseus! He has the makings of a true discoverer, but his primary purpose is to make fun of all explorers and historians who falsely claim to be producing autoptic accounts: they are out to make us believe that they know because they have seen, and in most cases that is simply not true. Meanwhile I, who have seen nothing, am proclaiming my desire to see!

Dante's Ulysses, like Lucian's explorer, opted, in preference to a return to Ithaca and the duties of a loving husband, for the lure of the "open sea" and for his ardent ambition to become "an expert on the world". He wants to see the uninhabited world and discover its limits, so he too sails beyond the pillars of Hercules and strikes out across the Ocean:

> Night then saw all the stars of the other pole and ours so low that it did not rise from the ocean floor ... when there appeared to us a mountain, dim by distance, and it seemed to me of such height as I had never seen before. We were filled with gladness, and soon it turned to lamentation, for from the new land a storm arose and struck the forepart of the ship. Three times it whirled her round with all the waters, the fourth time lifted the poop aloft and plunged the prow below, as One willed, until the sea closed again over us.[91]

That high mountain, a fatal bourn, where the ship foundered, was the Mount of Purgatory, situated exactly at the opposite pole to Jerusalem. Just as Odysseus and his companions were rejoicing at the thought of at last reaching land again, they were brutally driven away. The land of salvation was, could only be, inaccessible to them. The poet George Seferis has brilliantly and justly written that that shipwreck in which, "as One willed", all bodies and souls were lost left him "as it were deeply and ineffaceably scarred by the definitive disappearance of the ancient world".[92] For Odysseus, no return was any longer possible.

CHAPTER 2

Egyptian Voyages

Egypt, situated between Africa and Asia, with easy communication routes with Europe, occupies the centre of the ancient continent. This is a land with nothing but great memories, the homeland of the arts, many monuments of which are preserved here. Its principal temples and the palaces where its kings dwelt still stand, although even the least ancient of those buildings were constructed before the Trojan War. Homer, Lycurgus, Solon, Pythagoras, and Plato all travelled to Egypt to study its sciences, religion, and laws.[1]

Those lines, the very first in *La description de l'Égypte*, were written by Jean-Baptiste Fourier, who, in a long historical preface, reflects upon the importance and significance of the Egyptian Expedition which, under the command of General Bonaparte, on 2 July 1798 landed an expeditionary force, accompanied by a 150-man commission for the sciences and the arts. Fourier, who had been recruited by Monge, was a mathematician. While in Egypt, he worked chiefly as the permanent secretary of the Institute of Egypt, which had immediately been set up on the model of the Institute in Paris. Upon his return to France, Bonaparte made him a prefect. As prefect of the Isère department, Fourier was joined by a collaborator, Champollion-Figeac, who introduced him to his younger brother, Jean-François Champollion, who was already passionately interested in Egypt. At the Restoration Fourier returned to his studies and became the permanent secretary of the Académie des sciences.

Bonaparte had also taken the artist Vivant Denon along with him to Egypt. Two years later Denon had become the Director General of Museums. His *Voyage dans la basse et la haute Égypte*, published in 1802, was a great success. Much curiosity was aroused and many people wanted to see Egypt for

41

themselves. Denon claimed that, his whole life long, he had "wanted to travel in Egypt", and he described himself as a "soldier-scout" who had "drawn and described everything from nature", carrying his portfolio strapped across his chest as he rode with Desaix's soldiers, and making his sketches on his knees, at times even under fire from the Mameluks. Alongside the ruins of the Egypt of the pharaohs, with its fine architecture uncontaminated by any borrowed influences, the exotic "Barbarian" Egypt of the nineteenth century was presented for all to see in his sketchbooks: these showed faces, silhouettes, scenes of daily life, even maps and battle-plans. When he returned to Cairo, Denon showed his collection of drawings to the general-in-chief, who, having examined "them all attentively", declared that the "mission" was now completed.

SEEING EGYPT

Observation was one of the key concepts of the above texts: observation in order to describe. The particular purpose of the Academy of Cairo was, in fact, "painstakingly to observe the country that was about to be given a new administration". What was wanted was "a full and faithful description of the richest museum in the universe". To this end it was necessary to "examine", "measure", "distinguish", "conceive", "reflect", "make maps", "trace plans", "draw pictures", in short document Egypt, quantify it, depict it so that it became "known". Fourier wrote as follows:

> No land has been the subject of such extensive and varied research, and none has more deserved to be. Knowledge of Egypt is of interest to all civilized nations, either because it is the cradle of the arts and civil institutions, or because it has become the centre of the political relations and trade between empires.

In the name of both what it had been and what it might become, Egypt was thus much prized, at once a conservatory and a laboratory, a place to be submitted to a new rational and triumphant examination that would miss nothing yet not be gullible.

Yet even as it set out to submit everything to a meticulous examination that would then produce full and exact descriptions, Fourier's report depended upon ancient observations and accounts, as was already suggested by the opening words of his preface to the *Description of Egypt*, which reiterated the traditional idea that Egypt was the motherland of the arts and the place where Greece had been schooled. More generally, the whole vision of ancient Egypt as a land ever ruled by good laws and administration came directly and virtually unmodified from Bossuet. And much of Bossuet's own description was derived from the first book of the *History* by Diodorus Siculus (first century BC) who, for his part, had used the work of an author of the late fourth century, Hecataeus of Abdera. Furthermore, Hecataeus, who had visited Egypt at the time when the Ptolemaic dynasty was establishing itself, had himself inevitably been influenced by earlier descriptions, in particular the most famous of them all, that of Herodotus . . . . Through a whole succession of writers ranging from Herodotus (but also Hecataeus of Miletus and the Ionian "natural philosophers") down to Fourier, descriptions of Egypt had thus followed one upon another, not mechanically or in a direct line of course, but rather amid clashes, fragmentation and entanglement, and in accordance with a variety of preoccupations and shifting intellectual and other (political, religious and social) attitudes.

In Bossuet's view, the Egyptians deserved all the more consideration given that God had ordained that Moses "be instructed" in all aspects of their wisdom. Their ancient past went back so far that it approximated to eternity: "They delighted in losing themselves in an infinite abyss of time that seemed to bring them close to eternity". Their country was "the most beautiful" in the universe and the first in which "the rules of government were recognized". It was a place where kings, more than anyone, were obliged "to live according to the laws". No people had ever "preserved its customs and laws for longer" (one century later this was to be the principal quality attributed to the Spartans). The Egyptians had invented astronomy, geometry and medicine, and their architecture was noble and simple. Furthermore, they practised "esteem and love for their country".

Bossuet did not dwell upon their religion. However, the eighteenth century certainly did. Abbé Rollin, in his *Histoire ancienne*, raised the question of the coexistence of wisdom and idolatry: what was to be made of the sacred crocodiles? Was the cult really addressed to animals, or were the latter simply symbols? Had the Egyptians, thanks to the great ambiguity of their culture, preserved scraps of some primitive revelation, or was their religion fundamentally just a cult of nature?[3] Alternatively, was Egypt, the indubitable cradle of the sciences and the arts, also the cradle of "pagan superstition", as Diderot suggested in his article "Égyptien" in the *Encyclopédie*?[4] Had the priests exploited the credulity of the people and passed on to them no more than "the vain and pompous display of their cult" in order to ensure and extend their own privileges? Seeing Egypt through the question of superstition opened up a wide breach in the myth of its excellence and wholesomeness.

Another notion recalled by Bossuet, again following Diodorus, was that the Egyptians had settled in various parts of Greece at precisely the time when Moses was being raised by Pharaoh's daughter.[5] This vision of Egypt playing a civilizing role in Greece was also to be purveyed, in somewhat dramatic vein, by Abbé Barthélemy in the opening pages of his *Voyage of the Young Anacharsis*:

> According to ancient traditions, the dwellings of the first inhabitants of Greece were simply deep caves, from which they emerged only to compete with animals for crude and sometimes harmful types of food. Later, when marshalled together under uncouth leaders, they increased their knowledge, their needs, and their misfortunes... Wars broke out; great passions were kindled; the consequences were terrible...
>
> But, either because men eventually tired of all this ferocity or because the climate of Greece sooner or later softens the character of those who live there, several hordes of savages sought out legislators, who set about civilizing them. These legislators were Egyptians who had recently landed on the shores of Argolis. They came seeking asylum; and they founded an empire. How splendid it must have been to see those cruel, rustic peoples approaching the foreign colony in fear and trembling, admiring its peaceful pursuits, felling forests as ancient as the world itself, to discover beneath their very feet an unknown land which they rendered fertile, spreading out over the plains with their flocks, and eventually passing peaceful and serene days in an innocence that caused those bygone centuries to be called the Golden Age.
>
> That revolution began (in 1970 BC) under Inachus, who had led the first Egyptian colony to Greece; and it continued under Phoroneus, his son. In a short space of time, Argolis, Arcadia, and the neighbouring regions altogether changed in appearance.
>
> About three centuries later, Cecrops (in 1657), Cadmus (in 1594), and Danaus (in 1586) appeared.... They brought with them new colonies of Egyptians and Phoenicians. Industries and arts crossed the borders of the Peloponnese; and their progress so to speak added new peoples to the human race.

Barthélemy was by no means a nonentity. He was an orientalist, numismatist, epigraphist and decipherer of Palmyrian, who knew all the sources and who set out to write an encyclopaedia of the Greek world which, for all it was amusing, was nevertheless certainly encyclopaedic.[6] His account of the beginnings of this world is accompanied by numerous notes that refer the reader, in particular and indifferently, to the Plato of the myth of Protagoras, the first book of Diodorus, of course, Pausanias, Cicero and Eusebius, and Nicolas Fréret for the dating. All these texts seem to be set on a par. The important thing was to show the reader that every assertion had a reference, a citation or a note to back it up. Barthélemy's account starts off with the original, impossibly dispersed life of the first human beings, as presented by Protagoras; but it was not from Hermes' equal distribution of *politikê technê* (as the basic social link) amongst all those human beings that the emergence from savagery resulted.[7] In Barthélemy's version of history, the "civilizers" of these hordes were, precisely, colonists from Egypt. "Myth" was at this point left behind for "history". The model was already that of the legislator, and the motivation was a desire to imitate. The idyll of the Golden Age found its place and meaning here. The Egyptians were introduced as a functional equivalent of Protagoras' *politikê technê*, or a historicized version of it. The well-known antiquity of their roots sufficed to guarantee the verisimilitude of Barthélemy's account.

Barthélemy, as the representative of scholarly eighteenth-century opinion, did not consider that this version of the Egyptian origin of Greek civilization presented any particular problems. But the same cannot be said of the following century, which rejected, or rather abandoned, the Egyptian or "Ancient Model", as Martin Bernal calls it, in favour of what he calls the "Aryan Model".[8] Civilization came not from the South, but from the North. Greek civilization was the product of a combination of Northern (and Indo-European) invaders and the pre-Hellenic peoples whom they conquered. The first, historiographical, volume of *Black Athena* is entirely devoted to the "fabrication" of this ancient Greece. According to Bernal, the shift occurred between 1790 and 1830, in Protestant Northern Germany, at the time of the establishment of the pioneering discipline of philology and the development of the vision of an ideal Greece to be imitated, a Greece with which the Germans had particular affinities. The voyage to Greece no longer passed by way of Egypt.

To be more specific, it was the work of Karl Otfried Müller that clearly indicated the rejection of the "Ancient Model". In his *Geschichte hellenischer Stämme und Städte*, he rejected the legends of colonization on the grounds of their late development (Cecrops was an autochthonous figure, not an Egyptian colonist) and attributed the earliest role to the Dorians.[9] It is not surprising, but not a matter of indifference either, that the first volume, devoted to Orchomenus and the Minyans, opens with a quotation in which Pausanias attacks the Greeks for being so prone to admire the wonders of Egypt and to ignore those of their own homeland: "Many distinguished historians have described the pyramids of Egypt in great detail, without even mentioning the treasury of Minyas or the ramparts of Tiryns, despite the fact that these are no less wonderful".[10] Pausanias, a defender of the Greek past and a promoter of the Greek heritage, was in this respect an ally for Müller. Then George Grote, whose *History of Greece* was one of the principal landmarks of the nineteenth century, strongly emphasized the break between mythical time and historical time, suggesting that, strictly speaking, Greek history began in 776 BC. He thereby "reinforced the impression that classical Greece resembled an island in both space and time", an island that, one fine day, had emerged "out of nothing".[11] The "Greek miracle", with certain national variants, was now ready to take off. As Bernal sees it, the ancient model was not abandoned for "internal" reasons produced by new developments in the discipline, but as a result of "external" motivations: quite simply, it no longer suited the racism, or Eurocentrism, of the day.

But Bernal does not stop there, nor did he ever intend to. After taking apart the "fabrication" of this ancient Greece in the German universities, he sets out to prove the fundamental validity of the ancient model. As he sees it, the demonstration is all of a piece, but it is really its second part that underpins his entire enterprise and definitively validates it. The ancient model admittedly has to undergo a number of "revisions" in terms of chronology, and to take into account the fact that Greek is undeniably an Indo-European language; but it is substantially correct. The Greeks were right; they were even more right than they realized. Beneath their myths one can unearth the history of Sesostris' expeditions to the Aegean, to Anatolia, and even as far afield as Scythia. There really were Egyptian and Pheonician settlements in Greece, and their influence there was "massive". Archaeology and etymology prove it. Bernal at this point transforms himself into an archaeologist and specialist in the Bronze Age, in order to study the available documentation. But I shall not be following him there.

Why not? Partly because I am not an archaeologist; partly because, until more evidence is found, I am by no means convinced by this second part of his enquiry; and finally, because what interests me is not Bernal *per se*, but rather, thanks to the current reactivation of the Egyptian question manifested by his work, the possibility of studying how the Greeks themselves saw Egypt. In short, overturning previous schemata – "the colonies, invasions and conquests are no longer Indo-European but Afro-Asiatic"[12] – Bernal is led to substantialize a pre-existent "Greek" entity. To be sure, the inversion is a handy ploy and one to which the Greeks themselves, beginning with Herodotus in his attempt to understand the Egyptians, often resorted. But all in all, it reproduces that very same configuration of knowledge that it sets out to contest. "Move over, so that I can take your place" is what it says. But what we find is the self-same world of invasions and, even more, colonizations.

GREEK VIEWS

Egypt had been known to the Greeks ever since the Mycenaean period, and over the centuries they maintained continuous military and commercial relations with it. Even before they established themselves there as masters with Alexander and the Ptolemies, Egypt had never been a matter of indifference to them. On the contrary, it occupied a prime place in their imaginary representations and their thought, sometimes exerting a positive fascination, which was eventually passed on to the modern age. There was no single view of Egypt, no single, unified model, but if there was one long-lasting (albeit post-Homeric) feature associated with Egypt, it was clearly its antiquity. For a Greek intellectual, to travel in Egypt was to go back in time and catch a glimpse of how it all began; to collect stories about the beginnings of civilized life in general and this or that cultural practice in particular, and to hold forth with verisimilitude on these matters. The Egyptians were "the first to ...", according to the schema of the "first inventor", much used by Greek cultural historians.[13] In short, to make the voyage to Egypt was, for a Greek, to acquire "more memories than if he was a thousand years old" – to find memories that he did not possess or to recover memories that he had lost. Pythagoras, the memory-man, was inevitably fated to visit the land of Egypt.

The purpose of the following pages is to trace the development of the Greek visions of Egypt which continued to be constructed and developed from Homer down to the Neoplatonic philosophers, that is to say from the eighth century BC down to the third century AD. It aims to mark out just a few of the moments when Greek views of this strange land were formed or transformed, not so much from the point of view of their degree of reality or veracity as from that of the arguments which, from within the Greek culture itself, organized and informed them. It also aims to suggest how a particular theme, when transmitted and re-expressed, may exert a different impact on

Greek culture, which was itself undergoing profound transformations.[14] One such theme was the importance of religion, which was heavily underlined from Herodotus, the fifth-century BC traveller from Eastern Greece, all the way down to Porphyry, the third-century AD philosopher from Tyre, who was a disciple of Plotinus.

Going to Egypt involved "a long and weary trip over the misty seas";[15] for it was the faraway land to which, as has been mentioned above, Menelaus was blown off course and from which he returned only with the greatest difficulty. Odysseus, for his part, did not land there, but only claimed to have done so, while masquerading as Odysseus the Cretan, when he judged it altogether plausible to tell Eumaeus: "I had spent only a month in the delights of home life with my children, my wife, and my possessions, when the spirit moved me to fit out some ships and sail for Egypt".[16] For the riches of Egypt certainly beckoned: it was a good destination to aim for on a voyage, or rather a raiding expedition. No sooner had they landed, he says, than his men went on the rampage among the fine Egyptian farms, plundering and killing. Menelaus, while there, eventually amassed many treasures, most of them gold, which he took home to Sparta. The rich, faraway Egypt of the Homeric epic also seems to have been a rather magical land of herbal remedies and doctors. From it, Helen brought back the famous *nêpenthes*, which produced "forgetfulness" of all pains and worries. Herodotus was later to note that the country was full of doctors, each with his own speciality.[17]

Plunder and mercenary warfare also went hand in hand in one of the stories recounted by Herodotus. When King Psammetichus was ousted from power, he went into hiding in the marshes of the delta. A number of Ionians and Carians landed near by and set about seeking plunder. When an Egyptian who spotted them took Psammetichus the news that "men of bronze" had landed, the king had them brought to him and, with their aid, recovered power, for an oracle had predicted that he would do so when he saw men of bronze coming from the sea.[18] Psammetichus I (636–610 BC) was the first pharaoh to employ the services of Greek mercenaries. This "originary myth" of the use of mercenary forces has been confirmed by the discovery of a dedication engraved on a cuboid statue found in the neighbourhood of Priene, an offering made by an Ionian Greek by the name of Pedon. The inscription reads as follows: "Pedon, the son of Amphinous, who brought me back from Egypt, consecrated me, and Psammetichus, the king of Egypt, rewarded him with a gold bracelet and a town, for his valuable [assistance]".[19] This mercenary had himself depicted as an Egyptian, bare-chested and wearing a loin-cloth, but he dedicated the statuette, with its inscription in Greek, in his own native city.

Further written evidence of the presence of mercenaries is to be found on the left leg of the colossus of Rameses II, placed at the entrance to the temple of Abu-Simbel, in Nubia. It is slightly later (591) and was the work of Greek mercenaries recruited by Psammetichus II: "King Psammetichus having come to Elephantine, here is the inscription of those who sailed with Psammetichus, son of Theocles, who travelled to just above Kerkis, as far as the river allowed; the people of a different language had Potasimto as their leader, the Egyptians Amasis. We have been written by Archon, son of Amoibichus, and Pelecus, son of Oudamus". This text is followed by a number of signatures. Interestingly enough, these men, who wrote their graffito in Greek, refer to themselves as *alloglossoi* (people of a different language). Homer used *allothrooi* to designate foreigners "with other languages", for they were too distant for it to be possible to establish links of sociability founded on regulated exchanges. In Egypt, however, it was they, the Greeks, who were the people with a different language. They provide advance confirmation and illumination of what Herodotus was later to write about the Egyptians, who called all those who did not speak their language Barbarians.[20] Just like the Greeks! At any rate, this handful of men, isolated in their distant garrison in upper Egypt, by resorting precisely to this Greek word to convey the Egyptians' perception of them, seem to be speaking of themselves in the third person. Their own image of themselves is by now that assigned to them by the Egyptians. "We", that is to say "they", the *alloglossoi*, regard ourselves as our employers do: as Barbarians, "men of bronze". And we are inscribing this (in Greek) on the leg of one of their kings.

Soon, in the course of the sixth century BC, Egypt became a subject of research, attracting the scientific reflections and speculations of the thinkers of Ionia. Fourier's words, "Egypt, situated in between Africa and Asia…, occupies the centre of an ancient continent", contain a distant echo of the first Ionian ponderings on this strange land. Once it had been decided to divide the earth into three continents, which (for reasons that were not apparent, according to Herodotus) had been given the three feminine names Asia, Europe and Libya, where was Egypt to be placed?[21] Between Asia and Libya, with the Nile forming the frontier? Or did Egypt, on its own, constitute a fourth continent? Or should the name Egypt be applied only to the delta, as some Ionians believed? For what was Egypt, after all, if not a creation, a "gift" of the Nile? It presented the observer with the paradox of a land that was at once very ancient and yet still in the process of formation. The Nile, which for Homer was simply the river of Egypt, now became the focus of attention. For many years any investigator worthy of scientific credibility felt himself in duty bound to propose an original theory on this unique river with its "inviolably healthy waters".[22] In his *Histories*, Herodotus mockingly recapitulated those theories and then, of course, produced one of his own, thereby demonstrating that he was well able to hold his own in the controversies of the day.[23] But, to avoid the dead ends into which the Ionians had stumbled, he began by defining Egypt as the country occupied by the Egyptians.[24]

He devoted an entire book to Egypt, which is certainly an indication of its importance.[25] Since it is the country that presents the most "marvels" to the eyes of travellers, it is also the country that occasions the longest commentary. However, as soon as the "otherness" of the country's places and people is recognized, and even if Herodotus continues to repeat that its marvels (*thôma*) always exceed the report of them, the narrator adopts a number of ploys to apprehend and "domesticate" it. The first ploy is inversion, a very convenient rhetorical figure that converts the reality of "others" into a simple inversion of all that is not other and is ours, i.e. is Greek. It is an effective way of establishing the frontier between them and us, clearly indicating the differences and pinpointing the reasons for them. However, such a frontier is a brutal break that is both a mutilation and a simplification. So, after introducing it, Herodotus wastes no time in "forgetting" it, when enumerating all the things that the Greeks have borrowed from Egypt, particularly in the religious domain. His next ploy is a constant preoccupation with surveying, measuring, numbering, quantifying, which is, of course, a way of translating, transcribing and reducing, – in short, a way of making the *thôma* manifest.

However singular Egypt maybe, it nevertheless finds its place in Herodotus' representation of the world: symmetry, inversion and analogy make this possible.[26] Egypt is a strange space, at once natural and artificial (created by a river, then modelled by human beings), the depth of whose alluvial levels makes it possible to recognize (and measure) its great age. And its relation to time is even more remarkable: this is an exceedingly ancient country, and the Egyptians have existed for as long as human beings generally. Above all, it is a land that has been unchanging, without a break, without modification (*ouden eteroiôthênai*), where the "time of men" – purely human time, as opposed to the time of the gods – is far more ancient than is thought by the

Greeks, who are much mistaken when it comes to divine and human chronologies. Take Hecataeus of Miletus, for example, who, although a knowledgeable man, proudly spelled out his genealogy to the priests of Thebes,
imagining that he would encounter a god sixteen generations back.[27]

Their great antiquity makes the Egyptians men with long memories and,
hence, great knowledge. For their scribes have always written everything
down: they keep records and register the passing of the years; and they note
down all omens and preserve them in an archive.[28] That antiquity also
explains how it is that, in the religious domain, they were inventors: the very
first to regulate relations between men and the gods, to lay down the rules of
piety, and to organize religious cults. Which is why Herodotus has no doubt
at all that, essentially, the religion of the Greeks has an Egyptian origin. He is
a diffusionist, who reconstructs itineraries and points out where the links
occur. Not only do Dionysus, the Orphic cults, the belief in metemsomatosis,
prophecy and even the Thesmophoria come from Egypt, but even the very
"names" (*ounomata*) of the gods.

Previously, there had certainly been gods (*theoi*), but they remained undif-
ferentiated. The Pelasgians honoured them as the "orderers of the universe"
(*kosmôi thentes*). Herodotus resorts to etymology to explain their primitive
religion in which the deity, a faceless power, was simply apprehended as a
principle of order (*theos* is connected with *tithêmi*, "I set up").[29] But once
they had heard (*akouein*) the "names" handed on by the Barbarians and had
obtained the agreement of the oracle of Dodona (the most ancient of the
Greek oracles) for their use, another time began first for the Pelasgians
(although they too were regarded as Barbarians), and then for the Greeks,
who received those names from them. It was now possible to pronounce the
names well enough and to divide up the substance of divinity as seemed
appropriate.[30] Polytheism was born. Later, with Homer and Hesiod, there
would come the next stage: the organization of a proper pantheon by dint of
fixing the gods' genealogies, areas of power and honours. But that happened
only yesterday, or not much earlier: barely four hundred years ago.[31] The visitor to Egypt discovered that the time of the Greeks and that of the Egyptians
(who were nevertheless also men) were not commensurable. The time scale
was dauntingly different.

Such was the image of Egypt, with its long swathes of time which, thanks
to a variety of interpretations (mainly on the part of Greek travellers),
became the land from which the Greeks had borrowed much. But for
Herodotus, those borrowings did not imply simply imitation of or dependence

upon the Egyptians; let alone the latter's superiority. On the contrary, Herodotus established a clear cultural divide between the two countries, a distance revealed in a number of ways, particularly through his treatment of his sources. At a stroke, Herodotus manages on the one hand to demonstrate the Egyptian origin of Greek religion and, on the other, to indicate, frequently by implicit comparison, how very different certain Egyptian practices are from those of the Greek world. For example, the division between human beings and animals in Egypt is different from that fixed by Hesiod in the myth of Prometheus and reactivated in a Greek city every time it performs a ritual sacrifice,[32] as is clearly shown by the different features of Egyptian sacrificial ritual and the existence of sacred animals in Egypt – most extraordinary sacred animals, such as crocodiles. However, the very framework of reference precluded Herodotus, unlike later writers, from detecting and condemning zoolatry (the worship of theriomorphic idols) in the Egyptians' relations with certain animals. Furthermore, the panoply of the Greek sacrificer (knife, spit, cauldron) served to define the Greek identity and so, by extension, also the Egyptian identity, since Egyptians totally rejected such instruments, which they considered to be impure once they had been in the possession of a Greek.[33] However, the distance between the two cultures was not yet as great as it was later to be, when it became a matter of blood-sacrifice on the one hand and "pure" sacrifice on the other.

Although sacrificial practices did reveal a distance that touched the heart of the religious identities of Greece and Egypt respectively, they also allowed Herodotus to reject a story which, for its part, seemed to express an excessive difference: this was the story of Busiris.[34] As a result of a lengthy drought that had afflicted his country, Busiris had, it was said, decided to make an annual sacrifice of a foreigner who happened to be passing through. Heracles arrived. At first welcomed as a guest, he was about to be treated as an "animal" and led to the slaughter. But Heracles made his presence felt: he burst his bonds and killed many people, including the king and his son. Herodotus dismisses this story (which has more to do with the adventures and personality of Heracles than with Egypt) as a *muthos*, for it is not credible. A single man could not slaughter whole battalions (Heracles, at this point, is just a man); besides, it contradicts the very strictly regulated sacrifices of the Egyptians, who, at precisely ordained points in time, only sacrifice a few carefully chosen animals. Never human beings. Such excesses have no place in their practices.

The distance between the two cultures is also manifested in Herodotus' description of the funerary rituals of the Egyptians. Greek cities, in order to contain the ever possible excesses of mourning, had laid down strict rules concerning everything to do with how the dead were treated.[35] From this point of view, Egypt (along with the funerary rites of Scythian kings and those of the kings of Sparta, who were quite exceptional Greeks) was judged to be on the side of excess. The practice of embalming, the minute description of which constitutes a particularly choice *thôma* and a bravura episode in Herodotus' *History*, is for all that (if not all the more) a practice that is very alien to the Greek culture. Normally a corpse is buried.[36]

Similarly with Dionysus: many Greeks are mistaken about his origins. Dionysus, that is Osiris, is Egyptian. He was introduced into Greece by Melampus, a Greek "well-versed in the Egyptian religion". In the opinion of Herodotus, two points corroborate that. He appeared in Greece fairly late and his cult "was not in harmony with the ways of the Greeks" (*homotropos*). If he was Greek, his cult should have been *homotropos* with the customs of the Greeks. But it was not, so he must have come from somewhere else. Maybe from Egypt, but Herodotus thinks that he knows that, in between Egypt and Melampus, Cadmus the Tyrian had intervened, as had those who came with him to settle in what then became Boeotia. Even with the passing of time, this borrowing never shed its foreign look.[37]

The Egyptians were great writers. They kept archives and they consulted their books. But in Herodotus' view, their undeniable great knowledge implied neither great value for writing as such, nor any devaluation of the principle of orality. It is true that he himself was a writer (and produced a work even longer than the *Iliad* or the *Odyssey*). But in the world of fifth-century Greece the oral modes of knowledge remained active and important.[38] In his account of his relations with Egyptian priests, Herodotus never mentions "lessons to be learned from writing". He was neither a savage nor even a semi-savage compared with these learned people. Because, after all, they themselves were Barbarians.

From the narrator's point of view, it made sense, in his strategy of persuasion, to reveal the borrowings of the Greeks. It testified to his own skill as an enquirer and at the same time upset, or at least brought into question, a number of convictions that were current in Greek culture. By not properly recognizing elements that had been borrowed from Egypt, or sometimes even presenting them as discoveries of their own, certain Greek religious reformers had acquired considerable renown. Writing on the subject of the immortality of the soul and metemsomatosis, Herodotus declared: "The whole period of transmigration occupies three thousand years. This theory has been adopted by certain Greek writers... who have put it forward as their own. Their names are known to me, but I refrain from mentioning them".[39] All the same, everyone knew that he meant Pythagoras and Orpheus. Such remarks were intended not so much to magnify the Egyptians as to give credit where credit was due, and not to allow the wool to be pulled over one's eyes. "I, who have travelled, I know how things really were".

When the Egyptian *logos* is considered, not for itself, but in relation to the fundamental cleavage that runs right through the *Histories*, namely the division between Greeks and Barbarians, the Egyptians, despite their antiquity, their piety and their long memory, are inevitably on the side of the Barbarians.[40] However, Barbarian does not mean barbaric (he rejects the accusation that they use foreigners as sacrificial victims). What Barbarian refers to, even more than the fact of not speaking Greek, is the fact of being ignorant of city life and, instead, living in subjection to a king. "Barbarian" is above all a political term. And ever since the earliest times, Egyptians were incapable of living without kings. Their whole history is a succession of kings.[41]

Egypt, the land of religion, the space of a thousand marvels, which became a subject of enquiry for the thinkers of Ionia, is a reservoir of knowledge and a land from which to borrow (not always with due acknowledgement), where Greeks of the past found much to appropriate. They were doing so already in the above-mentioned earliest days, before shares were apportioned and iden-tities stabilized, when the Pelasgians were not yet Greeks but were already visiting Dodona, and travellers, cultural go-betweens called Danaus, Cadmus and Melampus, were already on the move; and likewise, more recently, Pythagoras, for example, to whom Herodotus deliberately refers but without actually naming him. A voyage to Egypt thus enabled an enquirer or *theôros* – one who wished neither to trade in Naucratis nor to be engaged as a mer-cenary fighter, but only to "see"[42] – to retrace the (human) history of Greek cultural practices, sometimes as far back as their first inventors: those who had introduced, brought back, transmitted particular examples of such prac-tices. And even if certain Greeks did go to Egypt for instruction, for Herodotus that did not mean to say that Egypt, as such, taught the Greeks how to found cities.

By the end of the fifth century a veritable Egyptian corpus had been estab-lished, presenting a collection of features that could be reused, criticized, var-ied, but that unmistakably designated Egypt. For instance, the Danaids, through their physical appearance and their clothing, were identified as non-Greeks as soon as they stepped ashore.[43] Book II of Herodotus' *Histories* clearly constituted an essential and very well-known record of this Greek knowledge, for in *The Birds*, performed in 414 BC, Aristophanes could parody some of his descriptions without even naming him, and the *Thesmophoriazusae*, for its part, parodied Euripides' *Helen*, which was set in Egypt. In about 385, Isocrates' *Busiris*, which turned a pharaoh with a bad reputation into a civilizing and legislating hero, swept the Egyptian "mirage" to the peak of its popularity.

Plato too, on several occasions, produces "Egyptian discourse". He was clearly well acquainted with the records of Egyptian material, for he reused, imitated and even parodied the *Aiguptika*. But to what end, and why Egypt in particular? "How clever you are at composing Egyptian stories!", the admiring Phaedrus exclaims. To which Socrates' crisp rejoinder is that what matters is the truth of what is said, not who is speaking and where he comes from.

More generally, these Egyptian stories constitute an important element in the ever-open file on Plato and the East. Did he really travel to Egypt, as an entire later tradition asserts? Did he "see" Egypt?[44] Or did he simply imagine it? Did he actually travel to Egypt or was his a mental Egyptian voyage? And however that may be, how important is the strong presence of Egypt and what is the function of Plato's references to it?[45] Perhaps the first point to be noticed is the link between Egypt and Atlantis. As the beginning of the *Timaeus* recounts, it was in Egypt that Solon learnt, from the priests of Sais, the story of that ancient hubristic power that was vanquished by ancient Athens. Just as Atlantis, despite mountains of books and generations of researchers, remains a fictional creation of Platonic discourse, it may well seem that Egypt too is used largely as a fictional land, conveniently to hand and plausible, which Platonic discourse can take over, setting up its own stage, on which to present its own play. Just as Atlantis is a *logos* that is mostly about Athens,[46] similarly the account of Egypt, which is also about Athens, articulates authentically Platonic discourse. Plato is speaking Greek here, that is to say Plato's own language for Greeks who know how to understand it.

Let us consider two instances of these stories: the inventions of Theuth and the beginning of the *Timaeus*.[47] Pondering upon writing, Socrates makes a detour by way of Egypt and tells Phaedrus of an ancient tradition of which he learnt through *akoê* (oral transmission). The Egyptian scene is set in a few words "in the region of Naucratis". Theuth, the inventor, is probably a version of the Egyptian Thoth, although the characteristics of the latter are more complicated than the features of the civilizing hero that Plato mentions. As soon as Theuth, with his new *technai*, comes to see King Thamous (another name for Ammon), there can be no doubt that we are in the Greek world, with Plato. The opposition of the king to the inventor, and that of judgement (*krinein*) to conception (*tekein*), are Greek: the user or consumer wins out over the inventor or producer:

> Most ingenious Theuth, one man has the ability to beget arts, but the ability to judge of their usefulness or harmfulness to their users belongs to another; and now you, who are the father of letters, have been led by your affection to ascribe to them a power the opposite of that which they really possess. For this invention will produce forgetfulness in the minds of those who use it, because they will not practise their memory. Their trust in writing, produced by external characters which are no part of themselves, will discourage the use of their own memory within them. You have invented an elixir not of memory but of reminding.[48]

The undervaluation of Theuth's invention is truly Platonic, since it stems from Plato's theory of knowledge and education. For Theuth, writing is a *pharmakon* (remedy) which will assist human memory and increase knowledge. For the king, on the contrary, it seems clear that, as it makes souls forgetful, it will promote forgetfulness. He sets "anamnesis", the remembrance of what is essential, which is positive, in opposition to "hypomnesis", the mere recollection of what is written down. Hypomnesis, which is external, thwarts anamnesis, which is internal. Theuth's remedy/poison will thus turn out to be more of a poison than a remedy.[49] Finally, Theuth's "letters", as described in the *Philebus*, totally resemble the characters of the Greek alphabet: this writing is not "hieroglyphic" at all, but "phonographic", and notes down sounds.[50] But at any rate, the story of Theuth, which plays upon the association between Egypt, long memory and writing, does help to transmit the idea (accompanied by a scholarly warning) that writing was definitely invented on the banks of the Nile, in this land of first beginnings.

At the beginning of the *Timaeus*, Egypt is again mentioned, and in an Egyptian setting. Nothing is lacking, neither names, nor a Herodotus-like parodic note to the effect that the name of the goddess Neith is the equivalent of Athena, nor an incalculably ancient account passed down through a succession of oral intermediaries.[51] The scene is set in Sais, a town on the delta founded by Neith (i.e. Athena), where Solon paid a visit to those who were "in a way" the parents of the Athenians. What unfolds there is also told in a somewhat Herodotean manner:

> On one occasion, when [Solon] wished to draw them on to discourse on ancient history, he attempted to tell them the most ancient of our traditions, concerning Phoroneus, who was said to be the first man, and Niobe; and he went on to tell the legend about Deucalion and Pyrrha after the Flood, and how they survived it, and to give the genealogy of their descendants; and by recounting the number of years occupied by the events mentioned he tried to calculate the periods of time.

These lines seem reminiscent of those in which Hecataeus, faced with the priests of Thebes, is proud to recite his "long" genealogy. In both cases, the same comic ploy is used: the difference in the chronological scale. In the case of Hecataeus, the priests' response is to point silently to the three hundred and forty-five statues of Egyptian high priests, men and only men, who have succeeded one another so far. To Solon, struggling with his calculations, the very old Egyptian priest exclaims, "O Solon, Solon, you Greeks are always children. There is no such thing as an old Greek".

Out of this situation and in the name of the theory of periodic cataclysms, Plato then develops a picture which, repeating elements already present in the *Aiguptika*, sets Greece in opposition to Egypt. Thanks to "the Nile, Egypt's saviour", Egypt is saved from such catastrophes. As opposed to a Greece which, for its part, constantly changes and never lasts, Egypt is a land of continuity and immutability, just as it was for Herodotus. In Greece, every time things become more or less organized, and writing begins to link memories together, a cataclysm occurs, and as the fire or the floods spread, so does oblivion:

> Your people and the others are but newly equipped, every time, with letters and all such arts as civilized States require, and when, after the usual interval of years, like a plague, the flood from heaven comes sweeping down afresh upon your people, it leaves none of you but the unlettered and uncultured, so that you become young as ever, with no knowledge of all that happened in the old times in this land or in your own.

Egypt, in contrast, from the height of its ever-continuous archives, looks down upon those youngsters who are perpetually making new starts. So those "ancient" accounts that the venerable Solon was struggling to date in reality differ very little from the tales of children. Greece, in truth, is a country of, not history – as it would like to believe – but mythology, while Egypt is the place of *archaeology* or, better still, *archaeography*.[52] In this perspective, which is not that of anamnesis but rather of the memory of the past and how it is recorded, writing wins out over speech, and *grammata* over *logoi* that are forgetful and that fade away. The Egyptian priest is again speaking in the language of Plato.

However, at this point in a well-crafted and virtually orthodox Egyptian story, Plato organizes a dramatic reversal: the Athenians have forgotten that they are descended from a more ancient race. "This has escaped your notice because, for many generations, the survivors died with no power to express themselves in writing. For verily, at one time, Solon, before the greatest destruction by water, what is now the Athenian State was the bravest in war and supremely well organized also in all other respects". Athens was in reality founded a thousand years before Sais, and was a city of "great achievements (*erga megala*)",[53] above all in the struggle against Atlantis. Chronology is thus abruptly reversed. Now the first inventors are not the Egyptians, but the Athenians, and Sais, with its long memory, is no more than a degraded image and imperfect copy of Athens. Origins and originality lie in Greece.

But for it to be more than a mere manipulation of Greek stories about Egypt, this reversal needs to make sense within the Platonic discourse itself. The Egyptian archaeography is substituted for Greece's own memories, but "through a stroke of genius and a mirroring effect, that extremely ancient memory coincides exactly with the memory of the (Platonic) Forms: the prehistoric Athens of the *Timaeus* and the *Kallipolis* of the *Republic* are one and the same city".[54] The philosopher's construction of the present is embodied in a city of the past. Both in the philosophical city, that forgotten and vanished Athens, and in Egypt we find the same tripartite division of society (into priests, warriors and producers). So Egypt is introduced neither for its own sake nor in a cultural dialogue between Greece and Egypt, but is there to testify, through its archives (which Solon's interlocutor knows by heart) and through the "effective" tripartite division of its society,[55] that the city of the *Republic* did once exist and so might, one day, exist again. With one considerable difference though: instead of priests, it is philosophers who will occupy the prime position. The city of the *Republic* is a fiction, designed to testify within a current of thought that is Greek through and through.

Egypt is ancient, but Athens is even more ancient. Theuth invented writing, but writing does not give direct access to intelligibility. Writing supports and extends ordinary memory, but what really matters is memory "from within", anamnesis, through which the soul attains to true knowledge. Philosophy is certainly Athenian, if it is true that Athena, the *philopolemos* and *philosophos* goddess, decreed that "this spot ... was likely to bring forth men most like unto herself".[56] An echo of that expression of Plato's is to be found in the opening sentence of Winckelmann's *Reflections* on the fact that the land of Minerva would be the one to produce the most intelligent of men.[57] The Platonic Egypt is thus not a univocal signifier: it is not always and inevitably superior to Greece. Following Aristophanes, the *Laws* also recognized the "trickery" of the Egyptians, whether the explanation for it is bad legislation, their preoccupation with amassing great riches, or even the noxious effects of the climate.[58] The Egyptians were thus sometimes depicted as "Orientals" even by Plato.

Plato, the "traveller" in Egypt, thus seems to have stirred up a great deal of trouble: both in his own texts and well beyond them. Both in Greece and outside Greece, what was later remembered was his depiction of Greeks as having no memories compared to Egypt, while what was "forgotten" was his inseparably linked affirmation of Athens's greater antiquity. Eventually he, like Pythagoras, came to be seen as a man who went to Egypt to study the hieroglyphics and to decipher the "sacred stelae" of Hermes.[59]

An examination of this series of views on Egypt reveals not only how they overlap but also the fact that one and the same eye could perfectly well, depending on the moment and the context, see things quite differently or, on the contrary, present apparently contradictory features as being all of a piece. Hecataeus of Miletus noted that the Peloponnese had at first been occupied by Barbarians as had, in truth, the whole of Greece (although it may have been Strabo who first applied that remark to Greece generally).[60] Herodotus provided a rapid description of those days before Greece, or rather before the Greeks, when there were apparently no solidly fixed frontiers in any domain: peoples migrated, their names changed,[61] they borrowed from one another. And Barbarian seafarers might put into port or settle and multiply, playing the role of cultural go-betweens or "first inventors" (but of course in those days the Athenians or, to be more precise, the future Athenians were themselves Barbarians). Danaus, for example (like Lynceus), came originally from Chemnis in Egypt, and from there set sail (*ekplôsai*) for Greece.[62] Very well. But why does Herodotus draw attention to that origin? In order to explain how it is that, even in his day, the inhabitants of Chemnis are still the only

Egyptians to hold games in honour of Perseus, in the Greek manner. And Perseus was a descendant of Danaus. So it is only to account for an Egyptian peculiarity that he recalls Danaus' voyage to Greece.

Knowledge of such migrations makes it possible to provide more and better explanations, but the major "event" is the arrival upon the scene of Greeks and of such Barbarians (the Athenians, for example) as became Greeks in a qualitatively different period of time. This was when history really started: once these changes (*metabolai*) had taken place there began, so to speak, on the one hand the time of the Barbarians and, on the other, the time of the Greeks: the former was static, the latter active and productive.[63]

Thucydides, in his account of beginnings, also recalled the initial instability that reigned in the space later known as Greece. People did not settle permanently; they were constantly prepared to move on in search of refuge and sustenance elsewhere, if or when danger threatened.[64] They came and went; and strangers arrived, such as Pelops (who came from Asia and who acquired his power thanks to his great wealth). Only Attica, protected by the very poverty of its soil, was unaffected: as no newcomers coveted it, it continued to be inhabited by the same, original people. And that inferiority was eventually commuted into a strength, for the influx of refugees from all over Greece little by little increased the power of Athens.

The exceptional nature of Athens (the Arcadians, too, were autochthonous, but they reaped no benefit from it) is here presented as a historicization of its stories of autochthony. If they had been there forever, the Athenians had either no history or the finest history of all! This was an unanswerable riposte to all those who reckoned that when it came to genealogies of nobility, Athens had very little to offer, but was a city of latecomers and upstarts. Thucydides goes on to explain that even after the combined expedition against Troy, which marks the true beginning of Greek history, peoples continued to migrate. It was thus only after a long time and many difficulties that the population of Greece finally stabilized (*hēsuchasa bebaiôs*). Only then did Greeks start to colonize beyond their shores: the Athenians in Ionia, the Peloponnesians in Italy and Sicily. This new phase is clearly seen as a kind of reversal of the earlier migrations. Isocrates was to present it as a movement of veritable revenge.

As the fourth century dawned, the cities, first and foremost Athens, found themselves swept by insecurity and each of them turned or even clung to its past. They invoked the past, claimed it as their own, sought it out even as they became increasingly aware that it had gone forever.[65] The Athenians celebrated the high deeds of their ancestors and indefatigably continued to proclaim their autochthony. The funeral speeches delivered in honour of the year's war-dead afforded them plenty of scope. The "Athenian history of the Athenians",[66] by which law this genre was governed, was disinclined to welcome foreigners. Plato was full of praise for Egypt, but in his *Menexenus* he also had Socrates declare that only the Athenians nurtured an inexorable hatred for Barbarians, as only they had always been pure from any intermingling with them. Unlike other Greeks, they had entered into no promiscuity with figures such as Pelops, Cadmus, Aegyptus, Danaus and others who were Greek in name only and Barbarian by nature.[67] Such discourse seems as radical as it is uncompromising. Egypt is totally Barbarian and the Athenians, who, only yesterday, were "somehow" related to the inhabitants of Sais, are enclosed within the endogamy of their own excellence. Miscegenation and Barbarians are the enemy! But exactly what kind of discourse is the *Menexenus*? A funeral oration supposed to have been delivered by Socrates but which simply repeats by heart a speech composed by Aspasia. A funeral oration, that is to say an official speech in which the city honours its yearly dead, yet entrusted to a woman! This is a real mix-up. In these circumstances, what of all the fine words about Athenian purity and uniqueness? Does their excessive nature in itself suggest that they should not be believed? The very fact that everyone knows perfectly well that "cohabitation" with Pelops and the rest did, in truth, take place makes it all the more necessary to proclaim that it never did.

Isocrates too testifies interestingly to all these uncertainties and shifts between Barbarians and Egyptians. No writer was more committed, both intellectually and politically, to the opposition between Greeks and Barbarians, Europe and Asia. In his *Helen* (written in about 370 BC), he presents the Trojan War as a kind of turning point. For him, unlike for Thucydides, it marked the first combined operation of Greeks against Barbarians, and thus constituted the first victory over Asia:

> In consequence, we experienced a change (*metabolê*) so great that, although in former times any barbarians who were in misfortune presumed to be rulers over the Greek cities (for example, Danaus, an exile from Egypt, occupied Argos, Cadmus of Sidon became king of Thebes, the Carians colonized the islands, and Pelops, son of Tantalus, became master of all the Peloponnese), yet after that war our race expanded so greatly that it took from the barbarians great cities and much territory.[68]

Yet his *Busiris*, composed in about 390, sets this pharaoh on stage as a civilizing and lawgiving hero and describes Egypt as "the most beautiful place" in the universe! It has been claimed that this was simply a rhetorical, youthful work in which Isocrates was in competition with another sophist who had also written an encomium to Busiris, one that Isocrates considered to be inept. Perhaps. But nevertheless, what is interesting is that Isocrates credits Busiris, previously generally considered to be an unedifying figure, with positive characteristics which enhance the image of Egypt. Why did he produce a political fiction that was so much at odds with his pronouncements on Barbarians? Was it a sign that the Egyptians were no longer classed as Barbarians, on account of their great age and recent re-evaluations of royalty, Barbarians now being considered to be Asiatics, and because the Egyptians had fallen under the domination of the Persians? Without question, all these factors combined to make it possible now to associate Egypt and politics and to regard it as the land where not only religion but also a just version of monarchy originated. The frontier drawn by Herodotus between them and us, the Greeks, quite simply no longer existed.

Busiris, the son of Poseidon and Libya (herself a granddaughter of Zeus), is presented as the first king of Egypt. However, his function and role are defined and assessed in the light of Greek categories: the lawgiver (*nomothetês*), the inventor (*heuretês*), the king (*basileus*). The excellence of his constitution was such that it became a key reference point for philosophers reflecting on such matters; and the Spartans imitated some of his "laws" (in particular the division of society into three classes), for all the world as if the revered and admirable constitution of Lycurgus was in need of an even more ancient and admirable model. Not only is the excellence of his country and his regime praised, but likewise his piety. The priests, exempted from all responsibilities and duties, were able to devote themselves to the care of the body (medicine) and the soul (philosophy): "They unveiled the practice of philosophy, a pursuit which has the power not only to establish laws but also to investigate the nature of the universe". When Pythagoras visited Egypt, he studied under them and was the first to introduce philosophy into Greece.[69]

Unlike Plato, Isocrates thus opted for a priestly and Egyptian origin for philosophy which, he claimed, was then brought to Greece by Pythagoras and his disciples. The model for a philosopher was a priest. His regulated, almost monastic life, not yet quite outside the world, but certainly somewhat apart from it, which made it easier to understand that world and to guide it, made him the prototype of the man of "theory" (*anêr theôrêtikos*) and a

62

guide for the "contemplative life". Now one no longer went to Egypt simply "to see" (*theôria*), as Herodotus and the Ionian thinkers did, that is to say to undertake an enquiry that involved both travelling and *sophia*; instead, one went there to learn how to see what is not visible and to be initiated into the asceticism of the contemplative life. To that end, it was better to close one's eyes and practise "reminiscence" than to move about with wide-open eyes, surveying and interpreting the world and human beings.

For Aristotle, Egypt was the "cradle of mathematics, because it allowed the priestly class much leisure". Thanks to its strict division into separate classes, it provided the first example of a social organization concerned to promote a life of theorizing.[70] In the *Protrepticus*, one of Aristotle's youthful works, contemplation is said to provide the remedy for the deceptive appearance of human life, which suggests that the soul is linked to the body as to a corpse. Why did nature engender us? Pythagoras' reply had been "with a view to our contemplating heaven", and he had declared that he himself was a contemplator of nature and it was for that purpose that he had entered life. Similarly, it was said, Anaxagoras, when asked why we should prefer to be born and to live, replied "In order to contemplate heaven, the stars in it, and the moon and the sun", adding that all the rest did not deserve to be studied.[71]

Egypt – this Pythagorean or Pythagoreanized Egypt – now became a place of apprenticeship and pilgrimage, where religion and philosophy were brought together under the guidance of the priests, and which all great Greek minds were in duty bound to visit. Pythagoras may have been the pivotal figure here but, according to Diodorus Siculus, the list of those who went to Egypt to study "theory" also included Orpheus, Democritus and Oinopides of Chios.[72] Pythagoras, "attracted by the life of the Egyptian priests and wishing to share it, asked the tyrant Polycrates to write to Amasis, the king of Egypt, his friend and guest, requesting that he be associated with the training of these priests". Having arrived in Egypt, equipped with recommendations from Amasis, he visited first Heliopolis, then Memphis, then Diospolis (Thebes). At each place the priests tried to get rid of him. Those at Diospolis imposed particularly severe rules upon him, rules that were "altogether alien to Greek life. He obeyed them steadfastly and earned such admiration that he was allowed to sacrifice to the gods and join their cult, something that no other foreigner had ever been allowed to do".[73] This "Greek" Pythagoras, though still a part of the political world of the fourth century, had his heart set upon making the journey to Egypt and passing his initiatory test.

EGYPT, THE FIRST CIVILIZING POWER?

When, after Alexander's death, Ptolemy, son of Lagus, was established in power, he at first made an effort to reconcile the Egyptians, in particular the priestly class, which had regarded Alexander's conquest of Egypt as a liberation from Persian oppression. Appreciation of the Egyptian civilization was a theme upon which all parties could agree to their own advantage: the Egyptians themselves, obviously; the new sovereign, who thereby killed two birds with one stone, in that he wished to become part of the Egyptian tradition and to root himself in its continuing history; and also the Greek intellectuals. The latter had been trying to express the doubts and uncertainties of a Greece traumatized by the Peloponnesian War; they had made an appeal to the authority of the past; and they had already long since granted Egypt a place in their reflections and aspirations and had themselves embarked on the *voyage to Egypt*. Was Egypt an origin (*archê*) for Greece, and could it serve as a model?

The work of Hecataeus of Abdera appeared at the intersection of all these various interests and all the different meanings that were attached to the signifier *Egypt*. His book on Egypt testifies to the interrelation of all those ideas at a precise historical moment, and suggests a way of articulating them. He had studied under the sceptic philosopher Pyrrhon and had also written *On the poetry of Homer and Hesiod* and *On the Hyperboreans*, a mythical people of the far North. His work on Egypt is better known, thanks to Diodorus Siculus, who made considerable use of it. Before ever Alexandria became the capital, before the Ptolemaic dynasty became well established, Hecataeus had not only made the voyage to Egypt but had settled and worked there from 320 to 305 BC.[74] He was a Hellenistic intellectual of the very first generation! His intellectual interests were extremely wide-ranging: philology, ethnography, history and perhaps above all philosophy, which provided him with a general framework for interpretation and investigation. There is no reason to believe that his approach to the Hyperboreans was structurally different from that adopted to describe the Egyptians. Agatharchides of Cnidus, slightly later, followed in the same current of philosophical ethnography when he set out to describe the peoples who lived in the far South.[75]

Hecataeus claims to base his findings on the temple archives, but he was no more capable of deciphering them than his Greek predecessors had been. Like Isocrates, he ascribes great importance to the king, but emphasizes the controls to which he is subject: he must obey the law and present his accounts. That was something that Bossuet was to remember! So is Hecataeus mainly reflecting the point of view of the priests, and doing so rather more than the Ptolemies might have wished or were to wish? Or is he thinking of some royal ideal written into the margins of the constitution, an ideal similar to that which Isocrates had attributed to Busiris? Even before Euhemerus, he establishes order between the world of the gods and the world of human beings, suggesting that some of the gods were originally kings who had been deified after their deaths. Above all, he stresses that the Egyptian civilization is more ancient than not just the Greek one, but all other civilizations. The Egyptians, who were the first to use an articulated language, were also the first to name the two primordial deities, Isis and Osiris. Osiris travelled the whole world, establishing communal life and agriculture and putting an end to cannibalism.[76]

This first humanization of the world was later followed by the establishment of colonies (*apoikiai*): in Babylon, for instance, where priests, called Chaldeans, organized themselves on the Egyptian model. The Jews too emerged from Egyptian colonies. In Greece, Danaus founded Argos, the most ancient of the Greek towns; and the Athenians were colonists from Sais.[77] Furthermore, some of the Athenians' leaders were of Egyptian birth, Cecrops and Erechtheus for example. Erechtheus was adopted as king in gratitude for his having saved the Athenians, for at the time of a great general drought, he had brought them wheat from Egypt. Once he was king, he instituted the mysteries of Eleusis, modelled on Egyptian rituals.[78]

His treatment of Cecrops is even more interesting. Herodotus simply mentioned him as one of the kings of Athens. Hecataeus, for his part, reckoned that Cecrops' Egyptian origin explained his double nature better than the Athenians ever managed to. He was reputed to be half-man, half-animal (snake), and this form clearly reflected his double allegiance or "nationality", which was both Greek and Barbarian.[79] Such a suggestion had scant chance of being accepted by the Athenian historians of the day, the Atthidographers. The stories that they wrote about Athens from its origins down to the present day were a combination of erudition and patriotism, sharing in the fascination with the past that was so characteristic of the period. Certainly Philochorus, in his *Atthis*, categorically asserts or reasserts the Athenian roots of Cecrops. When the land was being laid waste by the Carians and the Boeotians, Cecrops set about a preliminary gathering (*sunoikisai*) of the population into twelve cities. Later, Theseus united those twelve, making them a single unit.[80] No hint of anything Egyptian here – nobody but Greeks involved. Cecrops was no foreigner.

Diodorus was certainly not convinced by colonizing pan-Egyptianism such as that of Hecataeus, in connection either with Athens or with the rest of the world. He did not believe the Egyptians had any "proofs" to back up their claims,[81] and reckoned they were only so insistent about Athens because of its reputation. In his preface, he is careful to point out that just because he starts off his account with the Egyptians, this in no way implies that he shares Ephorus' opinion regarding the greater antiquity of the Egyptians. These opening chapters of his are cast in the form of "The Egyptians say that ...", but "I, Diodorus, reckon that ...". But Hecataeus really needs to be slotted in there, between Ephorus and Diodorus. So it should, rather, be "[Hecataeus says that] the Egyptians say that...",[82] as Hecataeus maintains that his sources are the Egyptian archives. Clearly, however, both the general framework of the explanation and the type of argumentation adopted are always Greek, whether it is a matter of finding the key to Cecrops' double nature, accounting for the Mysteries of Eleusis, or explaining history by colonization.

Martin Bernal, without realizing it, thus turns out to be a disciple of Hecataeus, rather than of Herodotus! This pan-Egyptianism, which served the cause of the Ptolemies, gave rise to polemics and considerable controversy, thereby confirming the impact made by Hecataeus' book.[83] Megasthenes, an Ionian Greek and Seleucus I's ambassador to King Chandragupta, spoke up for India; Berosus, a priest of Baal, wrote the *History of Babylonia*, in Greek, in three volumes (stretching from the time of origins down to the death of Alexander), which he dedicated to Antiochus I. There is no reason to believe that the Seleucids were any less concerned than the Ptolemies to defend their ancient Greek roots. Nor were the Jews to be left out: standing Hecataeus' schema on its head, the historian Artapan suggested that Moses was the initiator of Egyptian civilization.[84] Diogenes Laertius, referred to above, carried on the polemic where the above arguments left off, but also concluded categorically (at least where philosophy was concerned) that in truth it had all begun in Greece, and in Greek.

Of course this overview of Greek attitudes to Egypt does not include the Greeks *in* Egypt. Alexandria and its culture constitute a vast subject in itself, which deserves to be studied separately.[85] When you actually live in a country (even if Alexandria was always said to be "close to Egypt", not *in* Egypt), your attitude changes, you engage in a whole process of accommodation, and sometimes the result is that you no longer want to see clearly or, more often, that you no longer know what it is that you see.

In the Hellenistic period and then the Roman, when the Ptolemaic kingdom eventually became simply a property belonging to the Roman emperor, interest in Egypt never flagged. Even more or less run-of-the-mill travellers now made the trip to Egypt: tourists such as Aelius Aristides, soldiers, official travellers, pilgrims ... .[86] Keen to "monumentalize their lives", to borrow Vivant Denon's expression, many left marks to commemorate their passing, in the form of Greek or Latin inscriptions. The colossus of Memnon, which became the object of a veritable cult, was particularly sought out. The visitors proclaimed their admiration, their veneration, and recorded the prayers that they offered up for their loved ones and themselves.[87] A religious, devotional, even miraculous dimension was thus continuously present or just below the surface, ready to emerge.

In his novel, *The Aethiopica*, Heliodorus (third century AD) recapitulated this curiosity of the Greeks, in all its dimensions. When his Egyptian priest, Calasauris, sporting the statutory white locks and beard, pays a visit to Delphi, the religious heart of Greece, he replies to the questions put to him by Greek philosophers:

> They asked a variety of questions about the Egyptian gods and cults and the various animals worshipped by my compatriots, and they were amazed at the diversity, and eager for explanations of each of the cults and of the construction of our pyramids and labyrinthian tombs. In short, they overlooked none of the curiosities of Egypt, for there is no country in the world that the Greeks more enjoy hearing about.[88]

Two centuries earlier Strabo, who was accompanying the prefect Aelius Gallus on a tour of inspection, had described the Egypt that was by then a Roman province: he assessed the revenues that it provided, noted the pacific disposition of the Egyptians, and described Alexandria and the country's other major curiosities. The Nile was no longer rated as one of these, since *witnesses* had by now revealed that the summer floods were provoked by heavy rainfall in Ethiopia.[89] In Heliopolis, they had even been shown where Plato and Eudoxus had lived, studying for thirteen years among the priests, whose main concern was to keep their secrets hidden.[90]

But in between Strabo and Heliodorus two discordant voices made themselves heard, expressing a desire or quest for reassurance. One was the irritated voice of Pausanias (echoed much later by K. O. Müller), complaining that the Greeks were always too ready to admire in others things that they themselves possessed; the other, which was forthrightly critical, was that of

Apollonius of Tyana. He had been told by the king of the Indians that the Egyptians held the *genos* of the Greeks in low esteem, maintaining that they were nothing but ruffians, "inventors of legends and prodigies", whereas they themselves were true sages and the authentic "legislators" of the Greek religion. Needless to say, Apollonius soon set straight this poor fool who had been deluded by those conceited Egyptian priests.[91] But Apollonius' most fundamental riposte came when, while visiting Egypt, he put those Egyptian sages in their place, declaring that, in truth they were merely distant descendants of the gymnosophists of India, descendants who had forgotten their origins. A sure sign of the degradation of their sagacity lay in "the strange and ridiculous forms" that they had given their gods.[92]

The Egyptians thus discovered others more ancient and wiser than themselves, and the seat of sagacity shifted further east. Apollonius' conversations with his Indian hosts had already re-established that Pythagoras' wisdom was not so far removed from theirs: even if they had a slight edge over him in terms of antiquity, the quality of wisdom was the same. But how was it that Apollonius, the spiritual son of Pythagoras, launched such a sharp attack on Egyptian *sophia* when Pythagoras, ever since Herodotus at any rate, had always been closely associated with Egypt in every domain, wherever ritual, dietary prescriptions, rules for living, and the origin of philosophy were concerned? When he made Pythagoras independent of the Egyptians and introduced the Indians instead as the primary term of comparison, Philostratus was continuing the cultural battle against Hecataeus. To *de-Egyptianize* Pythagoras and *Indianize* him a bit was to extend his field of influence and make him into a sage of worldwide stature, just as his successor Apollonius was to be (at least in the dreams of Philostratus, who, like him, was committed to defending and lauding the Greek cultural identity).

Yet, despite the protestations of Apollonius, the vocation of Egypt as the land of religion to which both Pythagoras and Plato had turned in their quest for wisdom continued to be affirmed. Apollonius himself won sufficient fame for an oracle of Apollo to recognize that he had been granted the rare privilege, shared only by Hermes and Moses, of a direct vision of a god, during his lifetime.[93] The very mention of the word "Egypt" was enough to conjure up an abstract space humming with the revelations of Hermes, the Thrice Greatest One, also known as *the Egyptian*.

Sacrificial practices provided a different way of approach. For the philosopher Theophrastus, Aristotle's successor, Egypt was where purely vegetable sacrifices originated. The Egyptians, the most knowledgeable of people, living in the most sacred of lands, "are so far from killing a single animal that they turn their likenesses into images of the gods, so sincerely do they consider them to be appropriate and related (*suggenê*) to the gods and to human beings".[94] So now the Egyptians' zoolatry is no longer "ridiculous", but on the contrary a sign of the purity of their way of life. We may here detect an echo of the on-going debate that continued more or less throughout the history of the Greek city. What should one sacrifice, and how? And the corollary to that debate was that the Greeks' type of sacrifice constituted the most powerful definition of their identity, for their manner of sacrifice defined their dietary regime, their lifestyle founded upon agricultural labour, the development of various forms of sociability (such as the communal meal), and a particular conception of the relations between the gods, animals and human beings.[95] To indicate Egypt as the initiator of "pure" sacrifices was thus to join a marginal movement that brought into question the very centre and heart of the city by rediscovering Pythagoras and embracing his struggle.[96] The fact was that murder was ensconced at the very heart of the city.

Plutarch adopts an original position, for he is both an admirer of Egyptian religion and a defender of Greece. He sides with Plato and Pausanias. When he attacks Herodotus, deploring his lies, his malice, his systematic *philobarbarianism*, he is defending the memorial heritage of Greece (that of the glorious Persian Wars), and also the inviolability of the Greek identity. Herodotus' treatment of Io is unacceptable (she certainly was not a girl of little worth raped on a beach by a band of Phoenician traders). It is altogether shocking to exonerate Busiris of the charges laid against him so as to show Menelaus, a Greek, behaving in Egypt as a faithless and lawless individual. To present Perseus as an Assyrian, to suggest that Thales, one of the Seven Sages, was of Persian origin, that Heracles was Egyptian, and that Dionysus and the Mysteries of Eleusis are totally Egyptian is simply not seemly.[97] Plutarch's depiction of Herodotus as the advocate of a cultural *panbarbarianism* is itself not unmalicious, but it does show that the subject was a sufficiently sensitive one for some people indeed to interpret the *Histories* in that fashion. Plutarch was, as it were, relegating Herodotus to an equivalent of the Roman Catholic Index, warning readers that this was a beguiling but dangerous author, to be approached with caution.

However, in his treatise *Isis and Osiris*, possibly the last that he composed, the same Plutarch praises the purity of the lifestyle of the Egyptian priests and proposes an allegorical conception of religion. Osiris is not the Nile, but the principle of the wet, just as Typhon is all that is opposed to that principle.[98] Clearly, the story of Isis and Osiris should not be taken literally. Egypt explains Pythagoras just as Pythagoras, "the greatest admirer of the priests and the most greatly admired by them", explains Egypt: the same applies to the Pythagorean precepts as applies to *hieroglyphics*.[99] The enigmatic maxims of Pythagoras are analogous to hieroglyphics: the former are spoken, the latter deciphered, but the hermeneutic process is the same in both cases. Once again, Pythagoras, as if positioned at the interface of Greece and Egypt, operates as a go-between.

All the same, when he comes to the question of the "names" of the gods, Plutarch recovers his Hellenocentric or anti-Herodotean reflexes. In his view, the etymologies of Isis, Typhon and Osiris are Greek:[100]

> There is no occasion to be surprised at the revamping of these words into Greek. The fact is that countless other words went forth in company with those who migrated from Greece and persist even to this day as strangers in strange lands; and when the poetic art would recall some of these into its use, those who speak of such words as strange or unusual falsely accuse it of using barbarisms.[101]

As for Isis and the deities who accompany her, they should not be confined to Egypt, or be said to have emerged "from its marshes and lotuses", for since the beginning of time people have been capable of distinguishing and revering their respective powers, even if it is only recently that they have learnt the name by which they are designated in Egypt.[102] In short, the gods are greater than their names and are not bound by the linguistic limits of the names that designate them, even if it was Greek (disseminated by migrant Greeks) that made it possible to arrive at how many, in principle, there are of them.

The philosopher Porphyry, a highly cultivated man,[103] was also interested in Egypt and the question of the names of the gods. In his treatise *On abstinence*, he argues in favour of vegetarianism, showing that, everywhere, vegetable sacrifices preceded blood-sacrifices. For Greece, he cites Dicaearchus and his theory of the successive stages through which the first human beings passed.[104] Theophrastus then serves him as a reference for Egypt. It was there that the very first sacrifices in honour of the gods were introduced: grass and roots cast upon a fire, as those were the first products of the earth, even earlier than the trees and the animals.[105] We are back with the familiar image of Egypt, the place of origins. Furthermore, it was *the Egyptian*, that is to say Hermes, who intimated that the souls of those who died violent deaths presented a danger to the living, particularly anyone who sought to draw near to the gods.[106] Here we move to a different level – the level of forms, the degrees of divinity and how to communicate with it – where Egypt again occupies a central position.

Porphyry, naturally enough, pondered upon such matters. He wrote a book, in the form of a letter addressed to an Egyptian priest, on "the gods and the good demons, and the philosophical doctrines relating to them". He is interested in divination and the various vulgar forms that it takes, but would really like to find rather more satisfactory explanations. Whether real or fictitious, this letter proves that Egypt, with its priests, was still considered the greatest authority on such matters by those inclined to question and criticize. Porphyry's letter is addressed to a man whom he calls Anebon, but the name Chaeremon, an authentic Egyptian *hierogrammateus* (sacred scribe) and a Stoic philosopher of the first century AD, also appears in the text.

On the ancient and vexed problem of the naming of deities, Porphyry writes as follows:

> What do all those unintelligible words mean, and why affect to resort to barbarous foreign names? If the Being who is listening is only interested in the meaning of the prayer, it is thought only that counts, not the choice of words! For the god who is invoked is not, I presume, an Egyptian by birth, is he? And even if he were, he would be no more likely to speak Egyptian than any other human language.[107]

Gods cannot be assigned to a particular place or a particular language: so it is mistaken to believe that having recourse to foreign, Barbarian names brings one closer to the "language" of the gods.

The answer (in Greek) was to be provided later, not by Anebon but by Master Abammon, alias Iamblichus, himself a pupil of Porphyry and his successor as head of the Neoplatonic school. The ten books of *The Mysteries of Egypt*, placed under the patronage of Hermes, do offer some solutions to the difficulties raised by Porphyry: both on the subject of the names and also on prophecy and theurgy generally. Let us concentrate for the moment on the names: Iamblichus defends the superiority of the Barbarian names. Names are not simply a matter of convention; they depend upon the nature of beings. And those that are the closest to that nature are also the most agreeable to the gods. It is therefore right to prefer the language of *sacred* peoples to the languages of others. Consequently, translations are never satisfactory: each people has specificities that another language cannot signify; even when it is possible to translate those names, they lose some of their power (*dunamis*). "The Barbarian names possess great solemnity and great concision; they are less ambiguous and less varied, and the words that express them are less numerous [than in Greek]; for all these reasons they are suitable for superior beings". So the real question is not: is the god who is invoked Egyptian and does he speak that language? Rather, one should say to oneself: "Since the Egyptians received as their privilege communication with the gods, the gods like to be invoked according to the rules of this people".[108] With nothing added and nothing overlooked.

In contrast to the Greeks, always keen on changes and new words, the Barbarians, for their part, are constant in both their customs and their ways of speaking. And their discourse is pleasing to the gods. So it is altogether pointless to declare that the names are unpronounceable and Barbarian; they are simply "ritual" (*hieroprepeis*). Herodotus appeared to assume that at some juncture the time of the Barbarians became differentiated from the time of the Greeks, the former being stagnant and repetitive: *cold*; the latter active and progressive: *hot*. Iamblichus' remark confirms that there has been a reversal in the perception of those temporalities. Now the advantage has definitely swung to the side of antiquity and whatever is unchanging and sacred. The other side has been devalued, not so much on account of its youth as because of its inconstancy.

The land of Egypt, saturated in divinity, appears increasingly as a temple or a forest of symbols, where priest-philosophers devote themselves to the contemplative life. One such is Chaeremon. He, like Manetho, is Egyptian and is at once a priest and a Stoic philosopher. He *speaks* both Greek and Egyptian, or rather both Egyptian and Greek. Set apart from the profane, except during festivals, silently the philosopher leads a pure and austere life, stamped through and through with self-control. He never laughs, sometimes smiles, controls his gaze and walks solemnly, his hands tucked into his sleeves. He washes in cold water three times a day and eats sparingly, training himself to endure hunger and thirst. Mathematics, astronomy, hymns sung in honour of the deities at various moments during the day provide the rhythm for a life placed entirely under the sign of research and oriented towards contemplation. Chaeremon also makes it clear that philosophers consider travel to be an impiety and are wary of foreign customs.[109] The closed temple and the temple rules now provide the conditions and the instrument of *theôria*: one must first close one's eyes to the world in order to know it as it really is, and separate oneself and renounce it the better to master it. Within this space, the philosopher, engaged in turning himself into a "divine man" and a "friend of god", can rise towards god "and, one to one and of his own volition, approach the supreme principle".[110]

Lucian focuses upon this same phenomenon, but in a satirical mode, intent upon denouncing it along with all the ambitious charlatans that it attracts, such as Alexander, Peregrinus and – to single out one in particular – Pancrates. The latter was the sacred scribe of Memphis and a learned scholar of the sciences of Egypt. He had lived a life of retreat for twenty-three years (one year longer than Pythagoras, according to Porphyry) in an underground temple where Isis, in person, had taught him the art of the magi. All the prodigious feats that he accomplished, in particular his skill at riding on the backs of crocodiles, certainly won him renown as a "divine man".[111]

FROM THRICE GREATEST HERMES TO CHAMPOLLION

Egypt was gradually transformed into an abstract space in which the writing of the revelations of Hermes Trismegistus, known as "the Egyptian" *par excellence*, "he who knows all that is hidden behind the vault of heaven and beneath the earth", was an on-going process.[112] To mention Egypt was to conjure up this god, who was a combination of Hermes and Thoth, and the whole series of books that were attributed to him. There was thus a shift from Egypt, the reservoir of marvels and curiosities that prompted so many questions on the part of Greek enquirers, to the composite space of the *Corpus Hermeticum*, which confirmed the centrality of an Egypt regarded as "the temple of the universe", which concealed behind a veil divine mysteries that the profane could never reach.[113] The *Corpus Hermeticum* is a vast collection of magical, philosophical and religious texts, written in Greek between the late first and late third centuries AD, on which a number of eminent scholars such as Festugière and Nock have worked extensively. But I shall concentrate on no more than a few points from it, which relate directly to the question of how Egypt was seen by the Greeks at that period and later.[114]

Greece *or* Egypt? That was the question for the moderns. Were they dealing with an ancient and authentic Egyptian wisdom translated into Greek? Or were they moving in a world of Greek speculations that claimed to be sanctioned by the authority of the One who was able to decipher the secrets of heaven? Clearly, as cultural history has taught us, the answer to such a question is bound not to be simply univocal, so it is probably better to think in terms of interactions:[115] interactions between Egypt and Greece, of course, but also taking into account what was concurrently being written in Hebrew and in Aramaic. Hermes then turns out to pervade the whole Mediterranean, walking in the company of new sages who are in truth the most ancient ones of all, next to whom the Seven Sages of the past look like children. These were Eastern sages, magi, Chaldeans, brahmins and Jews, with names such as Zoroaster, Otanes, Hystaspes and Moses. And there was an attempt to make Pythagoras join them and compete with them, if – that is – we are to believe the edifying story recounted by Philostratus, who tells of Apollonius, his Greek champion imbued with the presence of Pythagoras, travelling the world and, of course, taking in Egypt, just as Pythagoras and Plato did. However, Numenius of Apamea, already mentioned above several times, was concerned to underline both distances and hierarchies. One moves from Moses on to Plato, not the other way around, for it is generally accepted that Plato was an Athenian version of Moses.[116]

Porphyry, who was an experienced philological critic was, even in his day, already questioning the authenticity of these texts circulating under the name of Hermes, which were reputed to contain hermetic theses despite being written in the "language of the philosophers", that is to say Greek. What could be the explanation for such contamination? Iamblichus' reply was: "It is because they were translated from Egyptian [into Greek] by men who were not unacquainted with philosophy".[117] Accepted as authentic, the *Corpus* survived the Byzantine period and, upon reaching Florence in about 1460, delighted its earliest readers there. It was backed by the authority of Church Fathers such as Lactantius and even Augustine, who accepted that its wisdom antedated that of the Greeks. Marsilio Ficino was obliged to defer his translation of Plato in order to launch himself, at the express request of his patron Cosimo de' Medici, into translating the books of Hermes into Latin. From this point onward, for Ficino, Hermes, along with Zoroaster, or closely following on his heels, ranked as the founder of wisdom. His translation, which was first published in 1471, had run to no fewer than sixteen editions by the late sixteenth century.[118] A short text inserted into the first edition (in between the fourth covering page and the publishing house details) ran as follows: "Whoever you may be reading this book, whether a grammarian, an orator, or a philosopher, you should know that I am Mercury Trismegistus. It will be to your advantage to buy me, for at very little cost I shall bring you great pleasure and be of great use". For over a century, everybody – theologians, scholars and astrologers alike – considered this literature to be a rich source of information on the magic and natural theology of ancient Egypt.[119] The other text that promoted speculation on hieroglyphics was a treatise by Horapollo. It was the only ancient work on hieroglyphics (generally dated to the fourth century AD) and was eagerly read in the Renaissance. At first it circulated in Florence, in manuscript form, but in 1505 it was published in Venice; a Latin translation followed in 1515.[120] This text, considered authoritative on the subject of hieroglyphics, provided encouragement for symbolic readings, in the manner of Greek or Platonic interpretations. As Plotinus said: "Every image is a kind of knowledge and wisdom, a real thing, altogether in one".[121]

Then along came Isaac Casaubon. He was born in Geneva to Protestant parents, and was reckoned by his friend Scaliger to be the best scholar in Europe. He came across the *Corpus* while engaged in an exhaustive refutation of Baronius' *Ecclesiastical Annals*, themselves Catholic ripostes to the *Centuries of Magdeburg*, produced by the reformed Flavius Illyricus.[122] Casaubon died in 1614, before completing his project. It was primarily concerned with the pope and his spiritual and temporal power, rather than with Hermes himself, who seems to have represented no more than a scholarly "excursus" in Casaubon's work. Nevertheless, there was a clear link between the two subjects. Catholics referred back to pagan prophets – the Pythia, the Sybil, Hermes – who, in an indirect and veiled way, had "foretold" the coming of Christ. The best of the pagans had somehow *known* that they were preparing for a better world. What was such a thesis worth as purveyed by the Church Fathers? Casaubon now set himself to read the *Corpus*, pen in hand. His knowledge of Greek literature and his experience with textual criticism confirmed his doubts as to the antiquity and authenticity of the *Corpus*. Hermes was not earlier but later than Plato, Aristotle and the Scriptures. The *Corpus* was influenced by the *Timaeus*, Genesis and the Gospel of Saint John. Many of the Greek words used did not antedate the state of the language at the time of Christ. The correspondences with the Bible, which had enchanted the Renaissance readers and showed them that pagans too had been vouchsafed Revelation, became for Casaubon so many proofs of plagiarism. There had been only one Revelation, and it had been mediated by Moses. Boundaries needed to be clearly drawn. Hermes was "an impostor who delights in purloining not only Holy Doctrine, but even the very words of the holy Scriptures".[123]

Porphyry who, in his own guise as a pagan philosopher, had been equally anxious to establish boundaries, had also wondered about these "Egyptian" texts that were, however, written in Greek. Iamblichus had dismissed such doubts on the strength of the training and cast of mind of the translators, who, through their work, had preserved what had originally existed in Egyptian. Now, the *Corpus* had itself raised (in Greek) the question of its translation into Greek, which would, Hermes declared, result in "a complete distortion (*diastrophê*) of the text and complete obscurity", whereas "expressed in the original language, this discourse preserves the meaning of the words with perfect clarity; indeed, the very particularity of the sounds and the very intonation of the Egyptian words in themselves retain the energy of what is said".[124] When Casaubon came upon this passage he frankly ridiculed this subterfuge, noting in the margin of his copy of the *Corpus*, "What a play-actor whoever wrote that is!".[125] To his mind the *Corpus* had been written in Greek, and only in Greek.[126] As an erudite Protestant, Casaubon set out to solve the question of authenticity or forgery. His task was to list and sift, tirelessly read, edit, annotate, reject, criticize. His first concern was not the relations between Egypt and Greece, but the false claim to have discovered, ready formulated, a more ancient and clearer revelation than the Judaeo-Christian Revelation.[127] His primary task was to refute that claim and reject it as a forgery. It was this scholarly and above all religious imperative to reveal the truth by eliminating what was false that inspired his general interpretation and method.

So *exit* Hermes? Of course not! The Reverend Father Athanasius Kircher, a scholar and unconditional zealot of Egyptian wisdom, for one, pressed on as before. For him, everything that existed simply constituted a manifestation of an omnipresent god. To somehow prove that truth, which first had to be discovered through divine inspiration, the Egyptians must have possessed esoteric knowledge, which their hieroglyphic writing was able to condense and deploy. Having placed himself resolutely in the current of Neoplatonic interpretations and Hermetic readings, he considered that to decipher hieroglyphics was simply to confirm what he already knew.[128]

On the basis of etymologies that were fantastical, albeit certainly taken over from Plutarch – such as Osiris being a compound of *Hosios* and *hieros* – he imagined he could prove that "there were no more differences between Greek and Egyptian than there were between Italian, Spanish, French, and Latin",[129] which was why it had been so easy for Greek philosophers to travel in Egypt and converse with the priests, and also why their information was so trustworthy. All the same, after Casaubon, Hermes was relegated to the margins of "standard" scholarship (whether it involved theology, philosophy or the natural sciences).

When the scholars of the Egyptian Expedition landed in Alexandria, they sought neither to rediscover nor to reanimate the wisdom of *the Egyptian*, but rather, with the distance afforded by the eye of an observer, set out to get the measure of every aspect of a land now in a state of abandonment, the most ancient museum in the world, crumbling into admirable ruins. From it they brought back the Rosetta Stone, along with a sense of the exoticism of "a voyage to the East". (Flaubert, in his *Dictionnaire des idées reçues*, was to define an "Orientalist" as "a man greatly travelled".) In 1824, this trilingual inscription (hieroglyphics, Demotic and Greek), discovered quite by chance in the little village of Rashid-Rosetta, became, thanks to Champollion, the touchstone of the burgeoning discipline of Egyptology. "Egypt seems forever to conceal beneath the veil of a mysterious language, the history, religion, graphic system and moral state of the people that Greek and Roman Antiquity recognized to be the first institutor of civilization".[130] He eventually arrived at the conclusion that in truth hieroglyphics represented "alphabetically, the sounds of the words of the spoken language", and so came to read the inscriptions that Greek eyes had fallen upon but never wished to see. However, the veil was by no means completely lifted yet, and the young discipline of Egyptology, caught between the dryness of philology and the incessant demands of esotericism, was still faced with an uphill struggle.

CHAPTER 3

The Invention of the Barbarian and an Inventory of the World

Having made that first journey to the land which, throughout the centuries, never ceased to figure in the Greeks' reflections on themselves and on their *sophia*, let us pause to consider the structure of their intellectual heterology, and the ways in which, depending on the circumstances, they established or revised the major categories of their anthropology. When Herodotus begins his *Histories*, the Barbarians are already there, forming an antonymic pair with the Greeks:

> In this account, the result of my enquiry, I hope to do two things: to preserve the memory of the past by putting on record the astonishing achievements both of the Greek and the non-Greek peoples; secondly, and more particularly, to show how they came into conflict.[1]

On the one side there are Greeks, on the other Asiatic peoples, that is Barbarians, and as they stand in opposition they define each other. Apparently no further explanation is called for: everyone knows this, everyone understands it. However it is worth noting straightaway that both sides need a historian to pick up the traces of the great things that they have accomplished, so as to perpetuate their memory. Antagonistic actors they may be, but together they nevertheless make up the history of mankind.

BARBARIANS AND GREEKS

Yet even in the eyes of the Greek historians, there had been an earlier time when that division did not operate. In his *Archaeology*, Thucydides observes that in the Homeric poems, which described the struggle between the Achaeans and the Trojans, there was no such division: "He [Homer] does not even use the term 'Barbarians' and this, in my opinion, is because in his time the Hellenes were not yet known by one name, and so marked off as something separate from the outside world".[2]

The only "Barbarians" mentioned by Homer are, one might say, the Carians, who are described as "barbarophone".[3] This was a term that attracted the attention of Strabo, the scholiasts and also the moderns.[4] Were these "barbarophone" Carians Barbarians, who therefore spoke a Barbarian language, or did they simply have "a Barbarian way of speaking"? According to the etymology of the word (with its repetition of the *barbar* sequence, a kind of onomatopoeia), to be a Barbarian was to have elocution and pronunciation difficulties, to stutter, to have an uncouth way of speaking.[5] The adjective is clearly not complimentary, but even if the Carians "have a Barbarian way of speaking", they are not Barbarians. Theirs is not a Barbarian nature.

Without Greeks there would be no Barbarians, but equally without Barbarians there would be no Greeks. For Thucydides, that is a logical postulate. Yet there was a time, the time of the early beginnings, when Greeks (but not Dorians, the descendants of Hellen), or rather future Greeks, arose out of Barbarian emigrations: first and foremost the Athenians. For they belonged to the Pelasgian people. And the Pelasgians, Herodotus "concluded", were "Barbarian" and spoke a "Barbarian language": "The Athenians, being themselves Pelasgian, changed their language when they were absorbed into the Greek family of nations".[6] Hecataeus of Miletus had an even more cut-and-dried view of the situation: the Peloponnese and virtually the whole of Greece had in the past been inhabited by Barbarians.[7] Greekness was thus something that could be acquired, following a period of apprenticeship, at least in those early periods when the divisions between peoples, spaces and customs were, so to speak, still in gestation. In those days, cultures were still very flexible and adaptable. It was a time of borrowings, migrations and voyages. This historicized version of the origins of the Athenians, which is not at all compatible with other, more mythical, ones, at least demonstrates what could be gained, in terms of explanations, by appealing to those two (as yet unestablished) categories: Greeks and Barbarians. The two could be conceived as a succession: first Barbarians, then Greeks. The Peloponnese similarly presents an example of transformation and intervention by the time factor. Of the seven peoples living in the Peloponnese, only two, according to Herodotus, were autochthonous: the Arcadians (to whom we shall be returning) and the Cynurians. The Cynurians were distinctive in two respects: they were apparently the only autochthonous Ionians and, furthermore, "they too have become Dorian *during the long time* that they have been subject to Argos".[8]

But those times were seemingly gone forever, in particular the possibility of the transformation of Barbarians into Greeks. The Greeks, once they had become Greeks, had, as we have glimpsed, increased mightily, whereas the Barbarians who had remained Barbarians "never became very numerous or powerful".[9] Thucydides, for his part, soon found a solution. On the basis of a number of indications, such as the practice of piracy and the carrying of arms, he concluded that "the ancient Greek world lived according to similar customs (*homoiotropa*) to those current in the Barbarian World".[10] Their way of life was Barbarian. Then the Greeks, in the first place the Athenians, became fully Greek, while the Barbarians remained Barbarian. Here again it was time that divided them and discriminated between them. Greekness detached itself from a background of "Barbarity", as if two temporalities, or two different kinds of relation to time, at one point existed in parallel, thereby illustrating the Lévi-Straussian paradigm of "hot" societies and "cold" societies. The Greeks were Barbarians but had become Greeks, the Barbarians were Barbarians and had remained Barbarians. They remained a "cold" society, while the Greeks, for their part, became "hot", manifesting their Greek character by their ability to "grow".

At any rate, it was between the sixth and the fifth century BC that "Barbarian", in the sense of non-Greek, came, in association with "Greek", to form an antonymous and asymmetrical concept in which a proper noun, *Hellenes*, was coupled with a generic designation, *Barbaroi*. The Persian Wars without a doubt acted as a catalyst. Around this new polarity the field of otherness was now reorganized and fixed for a long time to come.[11] The Greeks, on one side, confronted the others, *all* the others, who were lumped together simply by reason of not being Greeks. It goes without saying that this binary and strongly asymmetrical classification, conceived by and for the Greeks themselves, could be handled only by them and operated only for them. But before eventually becoming a ready-made expression, in which it was difficult to find a place for the Romans,[12] there can be no doubt that the Persian Wars conferred upon it a precise meaning, by providing the antonym with a face: that of a Persian. The Barbarian *par excellence* thus became the Great King, the embodiment of despotic *hubris*. Such was Xerxes, who, in his folly, believed that he could fetter the Hellespont.[13]

The wars against the Persians moreover led to a territorialization of the Barbarian: his domain was Asia, which he claimed, or was said to claim, as his own. Atossa, queen of the Persians, declares: "Two women as an apparition came, / One in Persian robes instructed well, / the other Doric, both in splendour dressed, / ... sisters they, who casting for their father's land, / She Greece received, she Asia, where to dwell. / And my son tries to check and soothe them; he yokes them to a chariot, / Bridles their necks; and one, so arrayed, towers proud, her mouth obedient to the reins. / But the other stamps, annoyed, and rends apart / Her trappings".[14] Now the opposition between Europe and Asia, represented by the image of the enemy sisters, was fitted almost exactly over the opposition between the Greek and the Barbarian, to such a point that this new vision was projected retroactively on to the Trojan War, turning the Trojans into Asiatics and Barbarians – thereby providing an added and *a contrario* proof that this was not how Homer had depicted them.

In connection with the epic poem, Hegel too was to speak of "The *Iliad*, which shows us the Greeks setting out on a campaign against Asiatics, in which the first legendary battles were to be fought in a formidable opposition between two civilizations, the outcome of which was to constitute a decisive turning point in the history of Greece". "In all great epics", he then proceeded to remark, "we see confrontations between peoples that differ from each other in customs, religion, and language ... and we are reassured by seeing the superior principle, justified by universal history, triumphing over the inferior". Hegel then concludes that "the Greek victories saved civilization and removed all vigour from the Asiatic principle"![15]

At any rate, Herodotus describes Xerxes, on the point of crossing over into Europe, making the trip to Priam's Pergamum, which "he desired greatly to see". There, he offered a great sacrifice to Athena Ilias, while his magi poured libations in honour of the heroes.[16] Xerxes may not have claimed to be a Trojan, but he did make that pilgrimage and assume the "Asiatic" heritage of Troy, inscribing his endeavour within the long history of confrontations between the Greeks and the Barbarians. Later, at the height of the Peloponnesian War, Euripides' *Trojan Women*, *Hecuba* and *Andromache* all set on stage Trojan characters who correspond, detail for detail, to the typical image of Barbarians, although in truth the "barbarity" may well lie on the side of the Greeks.[17]

"[The Persians believe that] Asia, with its various foreign-speaking peoples, belongs to the Persians, Europe and the Greek States being, in their opinion, quite separate and distinct from them (*kechôristhai*)". Those words, which were not pronounced by a Persian, but were written by Herodotus to convey to his Greek public how the Persians should be regarded (and what he considered their view of the world to be, or at least what it ought to be, given the division between the Greeks and the Barbarians), are altogether symptomatic.[18]

The point is made even more clearly by the fact that the *Histories* end with the punishment of the Persian Artaÿctes, the governor of Sestus. He is crucified on the very spot where Xerxes' bridge across the straits ended. Now, Herodotus had already foretold this ending at the point where he was describing Xerxes' construction of his bridges.[19] So Artaÿctes' fate is clearly an expiatory sacrifice, supposed to answer for the transgression committed by Xerxes when he overstepped the boundaries of "his" domain. But why such a vengeance, and why is it wreaked upon this particular man? Artaÿctes was not simply a Barbarian in the service of the king; he was "a hard and impious" man who, among other misdemeanours, had appropriated the possessions of the sanctuary of Protesilaus, to which, moreover, he was in the habit of taking women. On top of all this, he had deceived the king, telling him, "Master, there is the house of a Greek here who made war on your country and met the death that he deserved. Give me his house – it will be a lesson to men hereafter not to do as he did".[20]

Had the offence taken place recently? Who was this Protesilaus? Just "a Greek", as Artaÿctes represents him? In reality, he was famous because, according to Homer, he was the first man to fall in the Trojan War, killed at the very moment when, leaping from his ship, he first set foot upon the soil of the Troad. According to a later version, he was killed by the hand of Hector.[21] At any rate, Artaÿctes is crucified alive, while his son is stoned to death before his very eyes, and this "excessive" punishment, more Barbarian than Greek, is carried out by the Athenians, led by Xanthippus, the father of Pericles!

You can see how Herodotus makes the most of a retrospective identification: Protesilaus is a Greek, the Trojans are Barbarians, and Xerxes behaves as a "descendant" of Priam. The death of Artaÿctes, at the exact spot where the bridge ended on the European shore, thus corresponds to the death of Protesilaus on the Asiatic shore of the Troad. Both are *threshold* deaths. The correspondence, so long deferred, symbolically brings the war to an end, and likewise the *Histories*, which had been planned so as to tell of this confrontation. The sequence of events had run full circle. What is not clear is to whom this lesson was addressed at the time when Herodotus produced it, or even if it was intended as a lesson for the then present time. He chose to end his account in 479, precisely at the end of the period when the Athenians had acted as "the saviours of Greece" and at the point when the hegemony, followed by the empire, of Athens was about to begin. Was it inevitable that the former should lead to the latter? Herodotus, unlike Thucydides, does not say so. At any rate, Protesilaus was to make a come-back when Alexander, in his turn, would launch himself from Europe into Asia.[22]

Many centuries on, we find a surprising and amusing echo of the "great Event" that the Persian Wars were held to be, in John Stuart Mill. He writes as follows: "Even as an event in English history, the Battle of Marathon is more important than the Battle of Hastings. Had the outcome of that day been different, the Britons and the Saxons might still be roaming the woods!"[23]

The Persian Wars, and the monument that bears witness to them, that is to say Herodotus' *Histories*, territorialize the Barbarian and assign him his most common face, that of a Persian. But they also create a political image of the division between the Greeks and the Barbarians. Herodotus' work clearly conveys the message that Barbarian does not primarily or necessarily signify barbarity (cruelty, excess, softness ...), and that the fundamental cleavage is of a "political" nature: it separates those who know the *polis* and those who, being ignorant of it, live – can only live – in subjection to kings. A Greek is "political", that is to say free, and a Barbarian is "royal", subjected to a master (*despotês*). Barbarians cannot escape royalty, or not for long. Thus, it is said of the Egyptians that, although given liberty for a while, they could not wait to recreate kings for themselves, for they were "*unable ...* to do without a king for long".[24] Despite being "others" of great antiquity and great knowledge, the Egyptians have to be classified among the Barbarians. The same goes for the peoples of Asia who, by fighting against the domination of the Assyrians, threw off their "servitude" and made themselves "free". But after being "autonomous" for a while, they soon gave themselves a new "master" in the person of Deiokes, who, from being a judge, became a king.[25] The division between the Greeks and the Barbarians (together with its "political" elaboration) is not in doubt. But other divisions are also detectable, such as that which, setting in opposition conquerors and those resisting them, wars of conquest and wars of resistance, do not altogether overlap with that first opposition. All parties, Greeks and Barbarians alike, at one time or another were carried away by a "desire" to conquer, which eventually led them all to their destruction.[26]

In between the Barbarian world and the city, and a king and an assembly of citizens, there was the tyrant. The tyrant was a Greek figure of power characteristic of the late archaic period, and it was in reaction to that figure that the isonomic cities were to establish themselves. Herodotus' *Histories* weaves links between the king and the tyrant. Where their respective images (each of which borrows from the other) intersect, the representation of despotic or Barbarian power takes shape.[27] A king is a Barbarian, a tyrant is a king, so a tyrant is a Barbarian, or at least on the side of the Barbarians.

To overthrow a tyranny (the power of a single individual) is, strictly speaking, "to place the power in the middle", to transfer it from the royal palace to the *agora* so that it becomes the property of all those who are equal (*homoioi*); it is to replace secrecy by open debate, which presupposes equal freedom of speech (*isêgoria*) and the use of persuasion. *Isonomia* establishes the rule of *nomos*, law. Learning from the liberation of Athens, which ejected the Pisistratids, Herodotus is careful to point out:

> Athens went from strength to strength, and proved, if proof were needed, how noble a thing freedom is, not in one respect only but in all; for while they were oppressed under a despotic government, they had no better success in war than any of their neighbours, yet, once the yoke was flung off, they proved the finest fighters in the world. This clearly shows that, so long as they were held down by authority, they deliberately shirked their duty in the field, as slaves shirk working for their masters; but when freedom was won, then every man amongst them longed to distinguish himself.[28]

In his *History of Art*, J. J. Winckelmann recalled this passage to explain the transfer of the sciences and arts from Ionia to Athens: the coincidence of the Persian domination in Ionia and, conversely, Athens' expulsion of its tyrants, which created the necessary favourable conditions. In similar fashion, the French revolutionaries were to declare that, once Paris was liberated from the monarchy, it would surely be a new Athens.

The isonomic *polis*, which was a circular and centred space, organized by notions of symmetry, parity and reversibility, created and circumscribed a public space in which the communal affairs of the *dêmos* were regulated. And this geometric model was to provide the Greeks with a paradigm with which to envisage the world (whether to define health as an *isonomia* between antagonistic elements, or to conceive of the world, as Anaximander did, as immobile at the centre of a perfectly circular universe, or to construct representations of the *oikoumenê*, where the centre was the most highly prized point).[29]

In contrast, the despot (whether king or tyrant) exerts excessive power. So he is a prey to *hubris*, a concept imported by Herodotus from the field of tragedy. Incapable of moderation, he abandons himself to every kind of excess and indulges in every kind of transgression. In the first place, spatial transgression: a king leaves *his* space to foray further afield, to go too far. Cyrus, the founder of the dynasty, the father of the Persians, threw a bridge across the Araxus river in order to subjugate the distant Massagetae; and he perished. The mad Cambyses lost his armies in the sands of the deserts, in an attempt to overcome the long-lived Ethiopians, despite their being situated at the far edge of the world. Darius crossed both the Bosphorus and the Istrus (Danube), to attack another people of the outermost borders, the nomadic Scythians. He barely escaped with his skin from that escapade. Xerxes did a repeat performance, passing from Asia into Europe, but he had to make two attempts at it, for his first bridge was no sooner set in place than destroyed by a storm.[30] His transgression was also an aggression against the order established by the gods, as Themistocles declared: "God and our divine protectors ... were jealous that one man in his godless pride should be king of Asia and Europe too".[31]

In similar fashion, a despot cannot restrain himself from violating the *nomoi*, the body of laws, customs and rules that exist, whether in his own or in any other society. That is clearly a Barbarian way of behaving. This gallery of despots includes Greek despots alongside the Great Kings, but also a figure such as Candaules who, by obliging his adviser Gyges to view his wife when she was naked, forced him into an action that defied the rule (*anomos*), for among the Barbarians it was not done to be seen naked.[32] This tale, in which sight and transgression are associated, is an intriguing one. Gyges, who was, albeit unwillingly, a voyeur, was spotted by the queen and so had either to die or else to kill the king and marry his queen. It certainly indicates the power and primacy of sight: to have seen the queen was tantamount to having known her, having taken her by surprise, in fact having already taken her.

However, three figures head the list of despots. Cambyses is represented by Herodotus as the violator of rules *par excellence*, who carries his excesses to the point of madness. While in Egypt, he shows no more respect for the Egyptian *nomoi* (which he derides) than for the Persian, all of which he overturns. Periander, the tyrant of Corinth, is a man whose reputation as a transgressor is already well known.[33] Finally, Cleomenes, the king of Sparta, is a madman, or becomes one. After committing a whole series of acts of impiety and no longer knowing who he is (he pokes his sceptre in the faces of the Spartans), he ends his life by cutting himself to pieces with a knife, while chained up.[34] It is interesting to pause for a moment and compare these three figures, as they emerge from Herodotus' text, for while one is a Persian, the other two are Greeks, Greeks through and through. Should we conclude that the cleavage between Greeks and Barbarians is not operational? Not at all. Great Kings, tyrants and kings (such as the kings of Sparta) all have traits in common which, combined, make it possible to define the power that is committed to one single individual as despotic power: the king explains the tyrant and the tyrant explains the king. These too are figures situated at the limit or on the boundaries. Below them Herodotus positioned others, slightly less extreme, who might at one time or another swing over on to the "bad" side: figures such as Miltiades and Themistocles, who are ambiguous.

It was in opposition to this world of elsewhere and also of the past that the isonomic city established itself. The frontier between Greeks and the rest was from now on above all political, or so the *Histories* suggest. But the frontier does not simply separate Asia and Europe; it runs right through Greece itself, where it marks out and renders intelligible the period of tyrannies and the rise of isonomic cities (in fact, it even stigmatizes the one which, in the 430s, came to be reviled as the "tyrannical city": namely Athens). Now deemed alien to the city, and excluded from the common space, "outside the city" (*apolis*) in the strictest sense, the tyrant and the king are, in a way, Barbarians, or at least incline to the Barbarian side. Aristotle was to make this very point at the beginning of his *Politics*: if a man is a political animal, anyone who is by nature *apolis* is either considerably less than a man or else considerably more. Whoever cannot live in a community "is either low in the scale of humanity or above it".[35] Clearly, the fundamental divisions of the earliest anthropology (beast, man, god) are still in play here, but taken over and "politicized" by the city, they, together with the Greek/Barbarian pair, now present a political view of otherness.

In response to the Spartan representatives who, in 479, feared that the Athenians might come to an agreement with the Persians, the Athenians declared that there could be no question of their doing so, on account of their common "Greekness" (*to Hellênikon*), which they defined as the fact of "common blood, common language, the sanctuaries and the sacrifices we celebrate in common (*koina*), the whole way of life we understand and share together (*homotropa*)".[36] What they were invoking was clearly not Greece, as a land, but a collection of cultural characteristics that defined the Greek identity: that of all Greeks who shared a common city life.

REPRESENTING THE WORLD

The isonomic city's invention of the Barbarian, within the context of the clashes with the Persians first in Ionia, then in mainland Greece, was more or less contemporary with the development of Greek science, primarily in Ionia. Its concern was to collect knowledge and organize it, to investigate, make inventories, and also, perhaps most importantly, to apprehend the world, seize upon its principles, and represent it as it should be, if not as it was, in short to produce a kind of *a priori* inventory. Its practitioners, the Ionian *phusikoi*, natural philosophers, strode across large swathes of knowledge, relying on their powers of reasoning and setting the greatest value on geometric demonstration. Others, or possibly the same men, were also concerned to record traditions and organize the past. One such was Hecataeus of Miletus, who set about transcribing the many genealogical accounts of the Greeks. This appetite for knowledge was indissociable from writing, the very exercise of which affected knowledge.[37]

From the point of view of the treatment of space, the inventory took the form of *Periploi* and the production of the first maps. The term *geographos* appears to have been introduced by Eratosthenes in the third century BC, signifying one who drew or described the earth, the author of a treatise on geography or cartography.[38] Up until this point such a man, the author of an account of a journey or a tour through the inhabited world (*periêgêsis* or *periodos gês*) had been called a *periêgêtês*. Hecataeus, mentioned above, produced either one or the other, if not both (a description of the world and a map). Only a few fragments of these *Periploi* have come down to us, but we know the principles on which they were based. They were keen on measurements (the distance between two points, the number of days it took to sail from one to the other), and they involved circumnavigating the Mediterranean. A *periplous* would begin at the Pillars of Hercules, then sail round the sea from west to east, continuing until it returned to its point of departure, after hugging the African coast. It produced, in the first place, navigational aids for seafarers, but was also committed to identify, locate and name places (stopping-off points, towns, peoples) and to link them together within the time of the round trip. Designed as it was to produce an inventory, a *periplous* held the void (blank spaces) in horror. It advanced, by trial and error, from one point to the next, thereby constructing the space of the round trip. This explored space, organized by the drawing up of lists, constituted a magnet for works of compilation and rectification. It was no longer the space bequeathed by epic (although that information continued to be mobilized), a combination of a number of spaces that were qualitatively different – such as those through which Odysseus passed; nor was it the abstract, purified space that resulted from the postulates of the earliest cartography.[39]

The *Tour* or *Journey over the Earth* had totalizing pretensions. Strabo and the Hellenistic geographers continued to use that title to indicate the encyclopaedic nature of the ambitions of their treatises: a world tour and a study of the earth as a whole.[40] But, to concentrate on the early days, it was said that "Anaximander of Miletus, a disciple of Thales, was the first to draw on a tablet the outline of land and sea".[41] We do not know what this map looked like, but doubtless it was scrupulously geometric and tallied with the cosmology (referred to above) that conceived of the universe as a sphere, with the earth balanced at its centre. That inaugural map, more of a theoretical matrix than an empirical construction, was taken over and modified, possibly already by Hecataeus, who followed Anaximander. At any rate, when Aristagoras, the tyrant of Miletus, went to Sparta in 499 to ask for its help against the Persians, he took with him "a map of the world engraved on bronze, showing all the seas and rivers", to "show" that a military operation would present no problems. In the end, King Cleomenes was not won over; and did not "march".[42] But that episode shows that at the beginning of the fifth century, a map was both a rare object and at the same time one that might be of use and to which one might resort even outside scholarly circles, in order to impress.

But that excessive geometrization of the earth made Herodotus, at least, laugh. He mocked the already many people "who show Ocean running like a river round a perfectly circular earth, with Asia and Europe of the same size".[43] That perfectly circular earth was a geometrical reworking of epic geography, which described the earth as a disk surrounded by the river Ocean. Nor did relations of time escape his ironical criticisms. He pours scorn upon Hecataeus of Miletus, who, reciting his genealogy in Egypt, in sixteen generations worked his way back to a divine ancestor. Just imagine! The priests of Thebes, for their part, did not even need to search their memories. All they had to do was lead Hecataeus past the row of 346 statues of priests, which represented that number of human, and only human, generations, working back from the death of the most recent one![44] Between their archives of stone and Hecataeus' scholarly memories there was a difference of scale. And the person at whom this lesson was aimed was not a mere nobody, but Hecataeus himself, the scholarly genealogist who, clutching his reed-pen, could hardly forbear to scoff at all the far-fetched stories that the Greeks told themselves. On this occasion, though, it was he himself who was the naive simpleton.

Herodotus firmly divides this massive extension of the time of men into two parts, separating the time of the gods from the time of human beings, what can be known from what cannot, the thalassocracy of Polycrates, the tyrant of Samos, which can be dated and grasped, and that of Minos, which cannot.[45] That deliberate act of distancing oneself from a "mythical" past (the existence of which is never questioned, only the possibility of really knowing about it) is clearly an important element in the new form of self-knowledge that historiography was about to propose for the Greeks. Before weaving a line of continuity in its account of what had happened in the past, it would start off by marking thresholds and indicating breaks in the thread. Only then, within the space thereby circumscribed, would it address the traces and marks left by the activities of men, in order to prevent their being forgotten. "So much for what Persians and Phoenicians say; and I have no intention of passing judgement on its truth or falsity. I prefer to rely on *my own knowledge* and to point out who it was in actual fact that first injured the Greeks".[46]

One of the words of the time that best expresses this attitude to the world is *theôria*: travelling in order to see. According to Herodotus, there were three reasons for a Greek to travel to Egypt: trade, warfare and a desire to see.[47] When Pythagoras, the great traveller in both the East and the West, was asked to define a "philosopher", he compared life to the great Panhellenic Games to which people went in order to compete and win, to engage in trade and grow rich, or simply to see (*theas heneka*). A philosopher belonged to the last category.[48] He was a man who went to see: to see the games, to see Egypt, that is to say to see the world. In order to learn, or because he already knew? Both. He knew that one learns by seeing, for he understood what he saw and could make sense of it. Solon is another figure who is represented as a seasoned traveller for whom "to see" the world and "to philosophize" are linked. But he went to Egypt only after he had given the Athenians his laws. For Croesus, who received him with great pomp in his palace, the link between travel and knowledge went without question; and it was for that reason that he presented Solon with a question, saying: "Well, my Athenian friend, I have heard a great deal about your wisdom, and how widely you have travelled in the pursuit of knowledge. I cannot resist my desire to ask you a question: who is the happiest man you have ever seen?"[49] To which Solon, to

Croesus' mortification, replied that it was impossible to pronounce on the matter until death had the last word, for man was merely "vicissitude".

More generally, sages travelled, in particular the brotherhood of the Seven Sages, to which Solon belonged, but they did so more in order to give lessons than to receive them, more to display their own *sophia* than to question it, more to teach than to learn. They may have been observers, but they were certainly not participant ones. According to Herodotus at any rate, even Anacharsis the Scythian, "a man of great and varied knowledge", travelled and saw the great world.[50] The problem for him was that travelling could still not reconcile him to his condition as a Scythian. As a general rule, voyages may have provided these sages with food for thought, but only on the express condition that it did not challenge their own way of thinking!

In that respect, Herodotus the traveller is not very different from the Solon about whom he writes: his travels served him not so much to construct his representation of the world as to confirm and complete it. Like a Lévi-Strauss of antiquity, Herodotus proposes a picture of the various cultures: they are systematically organized[51] and outline a representation of the world in which the initial categories of Greek anthropology always remain operational, but always, so to speak, *more geometrico*. They provide the framework on to which he adds his observations relating to various ways of life (*diaita*), ways of being (*ethea*), customs (*nomoi*) and marvels (*thaumata*). It is on the basis of the knowledgeable standpoint of the "I" who is the traveller, all eyes and ears, that an interpretation of the world and its history comes to be evolved.

Thus the Egyptian space, which is so remarkable that Herodotus devotes one entire book to it, is not treated as an exception or aberration. It slots into place in the picture of the world that the *Histories* produces, in accordance with the schemata that engendered that picture. The two basic operative principles are firstly symmetry and inversion on either side of an "equator" running through the Mediterranean, and secondly the furthest latitudes struck by the sun, or "tropics", which are marked by the upper reaches of the Istrus (Danube) to the north, and the Nile to the south. Upon this canvas, the travelling geographer then deploys an analogy which, solely through *logos*, allows him to invent the sources of the Nile.[52] In this way, he is able to position Egypt in what seems to be its rightful place. Symmetrical to Egypt, but on the colder side, lies Scythia. And between those two spaces, which at once stand in opposition and also correspond, Herodotus' *Histories* brings into play a series of oppositions, which constitute so many points of reference or coordinates which, if necessary, can give rise to further descriptions.[53] It is always possible to move from the macro–system to a micro–system and to construct local oppositions, meanwhile retaining the general operational categories.

The enquirer is, furthermore, manifestly very preoccupied by boundaries. He intends his knowledge to extend right to the limit, to the point where his *logos*, reaching either a sea or a desert, devoid of all life, must come to an end. In contrast to the appetite for knowledge of Herodotus the observer, Strabo confines the geographer solely to an investigation of the "inhabited world", to wit the space dominated by Rome. Herodotus sets out to get to grips with the world, Strabo is more concerned with its administration. This preoccupation with limits, which is inclined to push blank spaces on the map as far away as possible, goes hand in hand with a mania for inventories: the ability to reel off the names of all the different peoples inhabiting a particular region, starting with the closest and ending with the most distant. That is the method adopted in the Scythian and Libyan *logoi*, which enumerate whole series of peoples, ranging as far afield as possible, all the way to the Arimaspes, the Griffons and other Fish–Eaters: list after list, name after name. Inevitably, Herodotus tends to geometricize the spaces that he delimits, measures, peoples, "sews" together, as he inscribes them in his world system. It is striking that Scythia, which Herodotus first tackles by listing its rivers and its tribes, is later described as taking the form of a square.[54]

Climate is another explanatory factor. Everything to the North is explained by the cold, everything to the South by the heat. Where the climate is soft, so are its inhabitants. But a law of compensation also operates. While Greece (Ionia) has received the most temperate climate, the extremities of the world (which are either very cold or too hot) have received the most beautiful and rarest of things (gold and spices). "It does seem to be true that the countries which lie on the circumference of the inhabited world produce the things which we believe to be most rare and beautiful",[55] just as Greece has received by far the most temperate climate. This perfectly "mixed" (*kekrêmenas*) climate is also said to be the "finest". So the finest or the "most rare and beautiful" (*kallista*) that is associated with the extremities corresponds to the "finest" character of the Ionian climate, which is precisely its mixed nature. This sets up a kind of equivalence that makes it possible to relate the excellence of the extremities to the excellence of the centre. Each has an excellence of its own and *nomoi* of its own, even if some kinds of excellence are richer than others, just as some *nomoi* are superior to others. This climatic theory, never spelt out by Herodotus but simply applied as a self–evident grid, features in his narrative at a number of points. It operates even in the logic behind the narrative, for instance where softness is associated with wealth, hardness with poverty. And it punctuates, or is even to some extent used to explain, the behaviour of the Persian sovereigns.

Indeed, the *Histories* closes with what is certainly an ironic reminder of that theory, placed in the mouth of Cyrus. When, after the victory over the Medes, one Persian advises him to leave their own poor country, Cyrus replies that it is an excellent idea but would make it necessary for the Persians to prepare themselves "to rule no longer and be ruled by others. 'Soft countries', he said, 'breed soft men. It is not the property of any one soil to produce fine fruits and good soldiers too'. The Persians had to admit that this was true ... and chose rather to live in a rugged land and rule than to cultivate rich plains and be slaves".[56]

The interpretation of the details of this text is a delicate matter. However, we may register its general gist, which is all the clearer given that it overlaps with other contemporary reflections on the role played by climate. One example is provided by the Hippocratic treatise, *Airs, Waters, Places*, a text of capital importance which, centuries later, was still exerting its influence as the basis for Montesquieu's climatic theory and in the background of Winckelmann's reflections on art. The first part of the treatise studies the effects of the environment on the state of a particular population, concentrating principally on the effects of the seasons and their changes (*metabolai*). Those variable, external factors are related to the internal humours of the organism, in which the right mixture produces a state of health. This medical textbook was intended to help an itinerant doctor rapidly to acquire the knowledge that he needed, when he arrived in a town with which he was not yet familiar. The second (unfinished) part comments in general terms upon the local climatic theory in relation to the *oikoumenê* as a whole. By applying the notion of change, the author is able to show how Europe and Asia "differ in every respect, and how the nations of the one differ entirely in physique from those of the other".[57] In Asia, the absence of violent climatic changes produces a soft people, short on virility and warlike aggression, and given to indulging in pleasure. But in compensation Asia benefits from certain advantages: everything there is finer and bigger, and the fruits of the earth are better. For "Asia", we should read first and foremost Ionia, the central land situated "in the middle" of the summer and the winter solstices.

This strongly ethnocentric, if not racist text is, however, more complex than that first characterization might suggest,[58] and for several reasons: because uniformity is no more the rule in Asia than it is in Europe. Ionia, with its constant springtime, is different from the rest of Asia. Furthermore, that first line of division is complemented by the major North–South opposition. As in Herodotus, the Scythians are said to correspond to the Egyptians. Thirdly, the climate does not account for everything. At several points the text encounters the problem of the articulation of "nature" and *nomos*, and is brought up short by this thorny epistemological problem. The Asiatic people (*genos*) is characterized as weak (*analkês*), clearly partly as a result of the absence of marked climatic changes, but also as a result of the Asiatic *nomoi*: most Asiatics are ruled by kings.[59] The association between royalty and Barbarianism reappears in a new guise.

So how far is nature responsible and how far is custom? And what part does nature play in customs? What was "initially an effect of custom eventually became a fact of nature", we read, in connection with the oblong skull of the Macrocephaloi, who initially manipulated the shape of the malleable skulls of children by swathing them tightly in bandages. And the position of the Ionians is ambiguous: they are Greek, yet live in Asia, so are they Asiatic Greeks or Greeks in between Europe and Asia?[60] Herodotus himself, a native of Halicarnassus, a Dorian city, manifests an ambivalent attitude towards the Ionians. He reminds us baldly that the Great Kings vaunted the servile disposition of the Ionians.[61] So have the Ionians become "Asianized"? Yet they never knuckled under to kings, so surely they are not "weak". The *Histories* closes with a final, reiterated apology that sets in opposition the absence of energy in Asia and the hardiness and warrior prowess of Europe.

One other idea, the history of which it would be interesting to trace, is the concept of mixture. Is it positive or negative? A mark of excellence or a sign of decadence? For the Hippocratic treatise, the causes of the advantages enjoyed by Ionia are the mixture (*krêsis*) of the seasons and their moderation (*metriotês*), and the fact that it is situated "in the middle" (*en mesôi*) between the summer and the winter solstices, so that nothing predominates violently and everything is distributed equally (*isomoiriê*).[62] Mixture, moderation, middle, egalitarian distribution: the interpenetration of a whole set of vocabularies is immediately detectable. Climatic, medical, geometric and political terminologies combine to set a high value upon the centre, as the product of a balanced mixture. More precisely, one and the same imagistic notion operates in fields of knowledge not yet clearly separate. The concept of a mixture, ranging from the mixture of seasons or of humours through to the theme of a "mixed constitution", had a long future before it, first in Greece itself, and later well beyond it. Would not Alexander soon be said to plan to "fuse" the Barbarian and the Greek worlds?[63]

In Herodotus' *Histories*, the most distant peoples are the ones said to resist borrowings from other cultures the most adamantly. Neither the Scythians nor the Egyptians wish to have anything to do with foreign customs, whereas the Persians, like the Greeks, are perfectly willing to adopt them, and Ionia, in this respect too, appears as a land of mixtures.[64] The importance that Herodotus attaches to *nomoi* in his world system is well known. They are the criterion of humanity. To have no *nomoi*, as in the sole case of the *Androphagoi*, whose name is enough to convey their nature, is definitely to be excluded from the human race.[65] When Anacharsis, on his return from his travels, seeks to introduce the cult of Cybele in Scythia, his compatriots immediately wipe it out.[66] Anacharsis has transgressed a prohibition and overlooked a frontier that separates the Scythians from the rest. Anacharsis is an interesting figure in the history of Greek otherness. At this point he is neither the martyr of Hellenism, punished for having learnt from the Greeks, nor a model of the natural or good savage. What he tragically illustrates is the great law to which Herodotus, citing Pindar, draws attention: custom rules the world.[67]

However, this relativist view (to each his own customs) does not have the last word in the *Histories* for, in the last analysis, it is not the case that one set of *nomoi* is as good as the next (the categories of anthropology make it possible, precisely, to classify them), for the Greeks alone have made *nomos* their sovereign, by placing it at the centre. In the famous scene between Xerxes and Demaratus, the former king of Sparta, now in exile, explains to the incredulous Persian that the Spartans too have a master, namely their *nomos*.[68] Whereas the Persians have a master who sometimes attacks the customs of others or even their own (as did Cambyses, the king reputed to be mad), the Spartans, for their part, have no master other than the law. The Greeks alone politicized their *nomos*, making the *law* the sign and instrument of their "auto-institution" (to borrow the expression of Cornelius Castoriadis). All in all, it is this matter of a frontier and *nomoi* that determines the cleavage between the Greeks and the Barbarians, and between Asia and Europe.

CENTRE AND EXTREMITIES

The Peloponnesian War (431–404 BC) indubitably opens a period of crisis in which many assumptions are brought into question and openness gives way to closure. Thucydides declares this war between Greeks to be the greatest ever. He dismisses both the history of the past and the history of non-Greeks when, as we have noted above, he declares that "the fact that [present Barbarian people] still live in this way is evidence that once this was the general rule among all Hellenes".[69] It is more a way of devaluing the past than of casting an anthropologized eye over it. The present alone deserves that one should truly strive to know it and understand it, with the aim of providing posterity with a model of intelligibility that it can usefully turn to if ever it finds itself faced with analogous crises. But the misfortunes of warfare (the episode of the civil war in Corcyra plays an emblematic role here) make one realize that a city, too, is mortal.[70]

The optimism of the fifth century, which trained a curious but self-confident eye on the world, was succeeded by anxious cities, nostalgic for the past, bent, like Athens, upon finding an ever-elusive "ancestral constitution" that all sides, whether they championed or opposed democracy, claimed to reflect. These were cities that inscribed (or rather rewrote) their past on their walls, publishing endless lists of magistrates which, it was claimed, went right back to the very origins of the town.[71] That adulation of the past, which in all probability went hand in hand with recognition of its irremediably unrepeatable nature, was also expressed by a spate of local histories that traced the cities' pasts from their origins down to the then present day. Their greatest concern was not the present, nor breaks with the past, but the establishment of a line of continuity that stretched right back to the earliest beginnings. In Athens, following the first history of Athens written by a foreigner, Hellanicus of Lesbos, a whole series of histories of Attica and Athens was produced by Athenian authors. Each of them began with Cecrops and continued down to their own day. For these moderate or conservative citizens, who (with the exception of Androtion) were not themselves professional politicians, recapitulating the memories of Athens and writing its history were a way of engaging in politics or, at the very least, of demonstrating their patriotism.

With the advent of the fourth and third centuries, although the antonymous Greek–Barbarian pair remained operational for classification and making distinctions, its definition underwent modification: it became less political, with more emphasis laid on cultural aspects. For Herodotus, already, the Greek identity had been circumscribed by a set of cultural characteristics (along with the blood that Greeks had in common), but now Greekness was represented as something that could be acquired. As we have seen, in the distant past of the time of beginnings, it had been possible to change from a Barbarian into a Greek. That, in fact, was exactly what had happened to the former Pelasgians who became Athenians. But now Greekness definitely became a matter of education (*paideusis*). It could be taught. As Isocrates declares in his great panegyric of Athens, published in 380:

> So far has our city distanced the rest of mankind in thought and in speech that her pupils have become the teachers of the rest of the world; and she has brought it about that the name "Hellenes" suggests no longer a race (*genos*) but an intelligence (*dianoia*), and that the title "Hellenes" is applied rather to those who share our culture than to those who share a common blood (*phusis*).[72]

Ever since Thucydides at least, Athens had presented itself as the "school of Greece", and Isocrates certainly saw himself as the teacher of the teachers of teachers! Some people, to be sure, had a vocation to be more "Greek" than others. But all the same, such declarations heralded the cultural universe of the Hellenistic period.

The opposition between Greeks and Barbarians was at once fixed and brandished as a political slogan (conquer Barbarian Asia!), and at the same time sapped from within. The more so given that cities, unsure of themselves, tended to turn to the past, valuing antiquity simply because it was antiquity. So what happened when people discovered, rediscovered or noticed that Greek *sophia* was not as ancient as other wisdoms, and that it had borrowed from cultures assuredly more ancient than itself? To hold, as Herodotus blithely did, that the Egyptians were both ancestors from whom the Greeks had borrowed much, yet also Barbarians, was to become more problematical. Particularly if, in the meantime, the definition of Barbarian was "becoming depoliticized". Surely the ancient masters of Greek culture could not be Barbarians?

This change went hand in hand with a rehabilitation of kingship. This was initiated as early as the fourth century by Xenophon and Isocrates. In the fifth century a king had been synonymous with Barbarianism (with its double face of king and tyrant). But now the king was no longer seen as a radical negator of the values of the *polis* (except by Demosthenes and those who followed him in his campaign against Philip of Macedon). Rather, a king was seen as a man who, by the very reason of being apart, had some chance of putting an end to the *stasis* (the struggle for power) that sapped and paralysed the civic community. Isocrates spoke up for kingship, addressing first Nicocles, the king of Cyprus, then Philip of Macedon. And Xenophon, for his part, did not hesitate to make a Persian trip and represent Persia through Cyrus the Younger (who was truly royal, even if he never got to reign) and, above all, his forebear Cyrus the Elder, the founder of the Persian empire, to whom he devoted a long fictitious biography, entitled the *Cyropaedia*. This turn of events is somewhat surprising. The man who was now promoted to the status of a model was the very same who, one century earlier, had been anathema: then, a king had been a Barbarian, not only a threat to the city, but also a negator of its political order.

One of the conditions of this revaluation of the idea of monarchy was precisely that the former equivalence between monarchy and tyranny should be rejected. Once that happened, it became possible to consider more than one concept of kingship: that in which the king was controlled by the law, as well as that in which the king himself became a "living law".[73] But whatever the concept, as a consequence the (political) distance between the Greeks and the Barbarians was reduced. After all, Busiris, a pharaoh who in Greece had the detestable reputation of a man who murdered foreigners in order to sacrifice them, was presented, by (once again) Isocrates, in the guise of the first civilizing king, a model for a just monarchy which remained within the bounds of the law. Even if his treatise was simply a rhetorical fiction, it was surely significant that the author felt able to turn Busiris into the initiator of Egyptian excellence.[74] Moreover, we should also remember that many other treatises on kingship (today lost) circulated between the fourth and the third centuries BC; and also the fact that the Hellenistic sovereigns, both the Ptolemies and the Seleucids, were to strive hard to insert themselves into a continuous sequence of prestigious and very ancient royal histories.

More generally, Greek intellectuals now developed the theme of "alien wisdom", as the felicitous title of Momigliano's book on the subject has it. Herodotus had set in opposition the South's association with antiquity and knowledge (Egypt) and the North's with youth and ignorance (the Scythian Anacharsis being the exception that proved the rule). But that system of oppositions no longer seemed operational and was tending to be replaced by another, which systematically set a higher value on the far-flung extremities than on the centre, and on primitive ways of life rather than "civilization". The Cynics were bent on producing that reversal. When he raised the cry "Let us primitivize life", Diogenes was intent upon dislodging the real Barbarian who lurked at the very heart of the city. He proposed that music, geometry and astronomy should be discounted, and saw nothing untoward in the idea of eating human flesh. Antisthenes, for his part, considered that a sage should not learn to read.[75]

In accordance with the logic that such figures adopted, blood-sacrifice, the pivot of the definition of humanity ever since Homer and Hesiod, was now denounced as "murder", for a truly civilized person "would abstain from all living creatures". All this involved a veritable subversion of the canonical Greek identity and radically called into question the way that shares had been allotted.[76]

Ephorus of Cyme (405–330 BC) discovered, alongside cannibalistic Scythians, good Scythians who were *galaktophagoi* (consumers of milk products), whose primitivism was the sign of a just and pure life, close to that of the gods.[77] Ephorus, who is known to have studied under Isocrates, was the author of a number of books. Apart from his great *History* in thirty books, which covered the period from the Return of the Heraclidae down to the then present day, he produced a local history of Cyme, a treatise on *Inventions* (who had invented what), and another on *Style*. He was already one of those prolific intellectuals who were certainly historians but who worked from the texts of others: a compiler. Diodorus Siculus expressly attributes to him the opinion that Barbarians were more ancient than Greeks. He is also said to be the writer who introduced Anacharsis into the list of the Seven Sages.[78] When assembled together, such propositions take on their full significance, sketching in a theory of culture that tended to give priority to the Barbarians.

Similarly, Dicaearchus, a direct pupil of Aristotle's and the author of a *Life of Greece*, advanced analogous observations on the practices of those Northern peoples as opposed to blood-sacrifice. Meanwhile, Theophrastus, who had taken over from Aristotle as head of the Lyceum, praised the same kind of attitude, but this time in the South, where it prevailed among the Egyptians, "the most knowledgeable people in the world, who live in the most sacred land", who also abstained from living creatures.[79] His treatise *On piety* declared that animal sacrifices were neither natural nor just. Distant and frontier lands showed far more piety.

Dicaearchus, who hailed from Messina, is believed to have frequented the Pythagorean circles of Magna Graecia before returning to the Lyceum. The philosophical orientation of his works is not in doubt, but he too was a prolific author. He wrote, for example, a treatise on the soul, a number of biographies – the Seven Sages, Pythagoras, Socrates, Plato – a collection of proverbs, several *Constitutions*, a commentary on Homer, and a *Description of the Earth*, as well as the above-mentioned *Life of Greece*, a cultural history in three books.[80]

Taking as his starting point a citation from Hesiod, he reckons that, compared with the present day, the Greeks of the past represented a golden age. They lived a life unacquainted with warfare and conflict, unafflicted by labour or disease; or by murder: in other words, without blood-sacrifice:

> Everything grew spontaneously ... They as yet knew nothing of skills, the skill of agriculture, of any arts... There was no warfare and no sedition, for no important goal was set before them that was worth engaging in a quarrel. So the greatest part of their life was made up of leisure, freedom from worry concerning necessary needs, health, peace, friendship ... It is clear from the declaration "enough of acorns" that was subsequently pronounced, in all likelihood by the man who was the first to seek to introduce changes, that the food of these early men was frugal and unsophisticated. Later, a nomadic style of life made its appearance, in which, already surrounded by superfluous goods, people sought to acquire yet more. They seized upon animals, noticing that some were harmless, others dangerous and cruel. Thus they tamed some and hunted the rest, and warfare made its appearance in life at about the same time... For already considerable goods were to be found which some people were bent upon winning, banding together to do so and urging one another on, while others were determined to defend them.[81]

Next, with the third way of life, agriculture, things went from bad to worse. This pessimistic view of the successive ways of life certainly stands in opposition to the schema that underpinned the reflections of a man such as Thucydides. For Dicaearchus, history revealed that softness, war and injustice had appeared "at the same time as the murder of animals". The passing of time may have brought "useful" things into life, but it also destroyed that initial harmony.

Ethnography thus took a definitely philosophical turn. But that did not in the least prevent it from cherishing exoticism. As it listed different ways of life, it invariably, more or less explicitly, compared uncivilized to civilized ways, and pondered the role played by *phusis* and that played by *nomos*. So much is testified by Agatharchides of Cnidus (second century BC), who was not himself a traveller but rather a library-based philosopher or ethnographer who reflected deeply upon the limits of the inhabited world. Like Hecataeus of Abdera before him, who devoted a work to a people of the extreme North, the Hyperboreans, he concentrated on a strange and impoverished way of life, in his case that of the tribes of the distant far South. In particular, he noted that the "Fish-Eaters" of the Red Sea lived in accordance with nature. Poor as their life was, they were nevertheless provided with the bare necessities of life, and were content with them: "Whereas the regime that we follow includes as many superfluities as necessities, the tribes of Fish-eaters exclude all that is useless, and do not lack what is necessary. They are guided by the gods in their way of life and not by men's sophisticated ideas about Nature".[82] With no appetite for power, no desire for riches, no quarrels or consuming hatreds, it was possible to lead a life in accordance with the laws of nature. In contrast, in civilized life, one finds many things that are of no conceivable use (*achrêsta*).

In similar fashion, Posidonius of Apamea, the great intellectual of the first century BC, a Stoic philosopher, geographer and ethnographer, who travelled in Gaul, represented the Celts certainly as excessive and excitable Barbarians, but also as "a simple race, free from vice".[83] Such sentiments were attuned to the same vast trend that inclined first to rehabilitate, then to set a high value upon, a certain primitivism, not unconditionally but reckoning that it at least offered a simplicity, an immediate rapport to oneself and to others, that civilized peoples had long since lost. It was but a step to move from philosophical ethnography to utopias which, precisely, presented themselves as travellers' tales, and it was a step that was taken by Iambulus, who told of his visit to the Isle of the Sun, to the south of Ethiopia. In that Golden-Age land, comparable in many respects to the orchard of King Alcinous, the inhabitants led a regulated life, imbued with "simplicity". However, after welcoming Iambulus and his companion, they eventually ejected them, claiming that they were "harmful beings, raised in bad habits".[84] Those modern Phaeacians, no longer go-between ferrymen, were in no doubt about those who were shipwrecked on their shores. It never entered their heads to make them their sons-in-law.

In terms of *sophia*, the centre or middle and the present were now undervalued compared to the ancient simplicity and purity of the far extremities. The Seven Sages may have journeyed afar with their knowledge, but they came from the "centre". Also noticeable, where time is concerned, is a depreciation of the present in favour of a mythical time (a Golden Age of the past or yet to come) that the noble savages and the ancient sages knew either how to preserve or how to rediscover. As for *theôria*, that too acquired a new meaning and was soon associated no longer with travelling and knowledge but, on the contrary, with a retreat from the world and a contemplative life.[85] A sage would no longer travel "to see".

The Greeks were naturally not seized overnight with doubt about their civilization, and the reversal of views on space and time was neither abrupt nor general. It resulted from a long-term cultural movement. Considerations relating to the environment and observations to do with the climate sometimes offered a different line of reasoning. In the *Epinomis*, a treatise (attributed to Plato) which, as its title indicates, is later than the *Laws*, a capacity for excellence (*aretê*) is directly associated with the climate. The three figures in this dialogue wonder what kind of knowledge a mortal needs in order to be designated as a sage (*sophos*). If it is true that the Barbarians were the first to observe the heavenly bodies, they must have owed that to the clarity of the Egyptian or Syrian sky. But, the Athenian interlocutor insists, "of all Greeks, we have a situation which is about the most favourable to human excellence", for it is placed in the middle (*mesos*) between the cold and the hot, so that "whatever Greeks acquire from foreigners is embellished by them and carried to perfection".[86] So they will indubitably be able to carry knowledge and worship of the celestial gods to their perfect peak.

The typology used by Aristotle, when reflecting on the ideal state, tends toward a similar conclusion:

> The nations inhabiting the cold places and those of Europe are full of spirit but somewhat deficient in intelligence and skill, so that they continue comparatively free, but lacking in political organization and capacity to rule their neighbours. The peoples of Asia on the other hand are intelligent and skilful in temperament, but lack spirit, so that they are in continuous subjection and slavery. But the Greek race participates in both characters, just as it occupies the middle position geographically, for it is both spirited and intelligent; hence it continues to be free and to have very good political institutions, and to be capable of ruling all mankind if it attains constitutional unity.[87]

A clear echo of the Hippocratic treatise is detectable here, although a few shifts are introduced. It is no longer just Ionia (Asiatic Greece) that occupies the central position, but the whole of the Greek "race" (*genos*), which is represented as being positioned at equal distance from both Asia and Europe. The Greeks thus manage to be both courageous *and* intelligent, to live in freedom with excellent institutions rather than in subjection, and even to rule others, whereas European peoples are incapable of doing so. Situated as it is in between Asia and Europe, the *genos* of the Greeks (Aristotle does not say "Greece") combines the good qualities of both, cancelling out their respective failings. No law of compensation, as in Herodotus, is now needed. The centre prevails over the extremities because it is where the mixture takes place.

When he associates slavery and Asia, Aristotle is both repeating a *topos* and also chiming with the preoccupations of Alexander's contemporaries. In the same vein, he is logically said to have advised his pupil to treat the Greeks as friends and the Barbarians as enemies: in total contrast to the policy of mixing peoples for which Plutarch was later to praise Alexander. On the other hand, Eratosthenes, the great Alexandrian scholar of the third century BC, rejects such a bipartition of the human race. In his view, the only worthwhile criteria are "virtue" (*aretê*) and "vileness" (*kakia*), for many Greeks are "wicked", while plenty of Barbarians are civilized (*asteioi*) (he cites in particular the Indians, the Romans and the Carthaginians).[88]

VIEWING THE WORLD FROM ALEXANDRIA

Soon the world would be seen not from Athens (or from an Athens looking at itself in the mirror of Sparta), or even from Greece, but from Alexandria (and later from Rome): from "Alexandria of Egypt", or rather "by Egypt" (*ad Aegyptum*), as the future capital, initially chosen by Alexander, was to be called (there would always be a certain distance between it and Egypt proper). So to see the world from Alexandria would not be to see it from the old Egypt. Founded in 331 BC, the town became the capital of the Ptolemies and the great centre of Hellenism, thanks to its exceptional institutions, the Museum and the Library, not forgetting the tomb of its founder.[89] For a while, a visit to Alexandria was an obligatory cultural duty. For it was in Alexandria that a whole compendium of knowledge about Greece, its culture and its past, and also about the world, was to be elaborated. A Greece stored in a library. Alexandria had a point of view to offer on Greece as a culture.

Here, past and present knowledge was collected, collated and compiled. In the domain of culture, "Hellenistic" meant first and foremost a period of recapitulation, of sifting, of setting in order and labelling, of producing second-order knowledge, which went hand in hand with a honing of the tools of criticism. Books were sent for, and were copied. Books travelled, and through books people travelled. For a seeker of knowledge, to see was to read, to know was to correct. A new figure appeared on the scene: the scholar who devoted himself to producing critical editions of texts and commentaries on them. He was called a *grammatikos*, a specialist of *grammata*, or a *diorthôtês*, a corrector or editor. One such was Zenodotus, the first librarian, whom King Ptolemy entrusted with the task of editing Homer. A whole succession of editions of Homer then followed, one after another, leading up to that produced by Aristarchus, who was to remain the Homer expert *par excellence* at least until F. A. Wolf produced his *Prolegomena to Homer* in 1795. The third century BC was a time of intense investment in the Homeric epic. It marked a high point in the monumentalization of an authenticated text and the establishment of Homer as the *archêgetês* of (Greek) knowledge. Callimachus, who also became Librarian, was not so much an editor as a compiler. He devoted himself to elaborating knowledge about knowledge, books on books, which took the form of catalogues and articles. He was the author of *Tables (Pinakes)* – *Tables of authors who proved themselves illustrious in all aspects of culture and in their writings* – in 108 volumes, and also of a *Collection of the marvels of the whole world, arranged in geographical order.*[90] The *poluplanês*, "he who has seen and seen much", had clearly been succeeded as a man of wide knowledge by the *poluhistôr*, "he who knows a great deal", that is to say a reader. Plato had already called Aristotle a "reader".

A scholar such as Eratosthenes provides a perfect representative of this period. When King Ptolemy III summoned him, in about 245, to take over the Library, he called himself a *philologist*. His training was that of a philosopher (he studied under Zeno) interested in a number of branches of knowledge: mathematics, geography, literature, history. He was the author, in particular, of *Chronographies*, chronological tables that made it possible to establish as precisely as possible the span (in years) of Greek *history*, all the way from the Trojan War down to the death of Alexander the Great. His aim was to incorporate, recapitulate, organize, in particular by fixing the limits of history and defining the domain of *muthos*. The critical inspiration behind this programme was similar to that which motivated the editors of texts.

Next, after history, geography was submitted to the same approach. According to Strabo, Eratosthenes set out to "rectify the ancient map of geography".[91] How? By taking into account both the information provided by Alexander's expedition and also the theorems of Euclidean geometry, he tried to combine more information with increased scientific rigour.[92] It was also Eratosthenes who calculated the circumference of the world on the basis of the measurement of an arc of the meridian. Bent on turning geography into a truly geometric science, he aimed to construct an exact representation of terrestrial space: the map was supposed to operate as a "geometrical device".[93] His attitude logically led him to reject Homer's so-called geography, to the great displeasure of first Polybius, then Strabo. It was a matter of de-magicalizing space. Homer's information was not trustworthy; he had not seen for himself and he did not know; he was a poet recounting fables, an author of fictions, not a geographer.

In reaction to such an attitude of incredulity in the name of scientific rationality, a number of theories were now produced which regarded *muthos* as an ancient way of telling the truth. This was precisely the position adopted by Strabo. He too aimed to operate a "critical" hermeneutics, but started with the assumption that Homer did speak the truth and that geography was an eminent form of philosophy.[94] Even so, Strabo, the resolute defender of a geographer-Odysseus and a traveller-Homer who with his own eyes had seen the world that he described, nevertheless, methodologically speaking, affirmed the superiority of the ear over the eye. "He who claims that only those have knowledge who have actually seen abolishes the criterion of the sense of hearing, though this sense is much more important than sight for the purposes of science".[95]

What can be the meaning of such a reversal? Not that only a man who remains secluded in his study can be called a really knowledgeable person, for Strabo is careful to draw attention to all the journeys that he himself has made. However, he does say that those whom he calls "scholars" (*philomatheis*), proceed just as "intelligence" (*dianoia*) does, on the basis of the evidence of the senses. It is on the basis of various data transmitted by the senses that the intelligence recomposes, for example, the concept of the apple. The same goes for "scholars", who work on the basis of all the data that they have managed to amass. Only a position such as theirs makes it possible to construct a general representation (*diagramma*) of the inhabited world. Autopsy can only ever be fragmentary; so what is needed are the link and filter of an "intelligence" (*dianoia*) to collect together, collate and correct all the many observations of travellers and relate them to the great organizing principles of the universe, in such a way that the general and the particular can be articulated together. The *philomatheis* constitute that "intelligence": and that in itself is no small mark of recognition on Strabo's part. Their work is of the same order as thought itself, but clearly it can be fully carried out only in a library. The cognitive superiority of the point of view of the reader over that of the mere observer is, in this way, established.

This triumphant "philological" moment imbued with an encyclopaedic ambition was not intrinsically motivated by doubt, nor did it foster anxiety.

The confrontation with Barbarian wisdoms was neither direct nor explicit. On the contrary, it took the form of an elaboration of investigatory protocols that aimed to authenticate the great traditional texts and first identify, then wherever possible eliminate the element of the *muthos* that so many ancient accounts, starting with the Homeric epic, had introduced. Viewing the world from the standpoint of the Library of Alexandria made it possible to take the measure of all that Greek culture had been, imparting visibility and legibility to it, in short confirming its legitimacy (and hence also that of the Greek monarchs, who, as newcomers to the East, needed that reassurance). The production of such an inventory made it possible to give to *to Hellênikon* a new definition, as a shared literary heritage. Hence all the questions which from that time onward have never ceased to be asked: how best to defend and transmit it? What is imitation? Is it possible to avoid a culture of imitation and commentaries?

CHAPTER 4

Greek Voyages

With his division between the Greeks on the one hand and the Barbarians on the other and, correlatively, the definition given to *to Hellênikon* (same blood, same language, common sanctuaries and sacrifices, similar *mores* and customs), Herodotus had provided the Greeks with an identity for times of crisis. Subsequently, the affirmation of the Greeks' superiority over the Barbarians served, in the eyes of Isocrates in particular, to justify the Greeks moving into Asia to free the Greeks there from subjection to the Great King.[1] Then Alexandria suggested a new definition of *to Hellênikon*, namely a shared literary heritage. But what was the day-to-day situation in Greece itself, when the frontier with foreigners coincided, as it did in Sparta, with that of the city, or when people entered a time in which the Persian Wars were no more than a glorious, piously nurtured memory? We have seen how the concept of the *Barbarian* was constructed and how that antinomy was fixed. But what of the figure of the *Greek*, on his own, once that definition by mutual exclusion was left behind?

To sketch in this second panel of Greek heterology, let us consider some of the images that the Greeks formed of themselves, always in a long-term perspective and concentrating on moments of change or reversal. As we pursue our quest for an always asymptotic Greek identity, we shall see how frontiers shift, re-form and are reformulated, and how the great fundamental divisions (man, beast, god) sometimes become destabilized. We shall seize upon some of the strategies used to create distances (the figure of the country yokel within the city) or to reduce them (Pausanias struggling with the strangeness of Arcadia). In Greece itself, in order to pass from one city to another, a traveller was bound to cross real frontiers which in some cases were visibly drawn by stelae or boundary-markers. However, in the present work we shall not be concerned with those delimitations.[2] Our principal travellers will be Anacharsis, Pausanias, Plutarch and Alexander, and we shall follow in their tracks for a while. But along with them, as if summoned up by them, and in their wake, we shall also encounter more modern "travellers", themselves readers of those ancient voyages, and likewise concerned to shift frontiers or suggest new ways of looking at history.

THE VOYAGES OF THE ELDER ANACHARSIS AND FRONTIERS FORGOTTEN

In Herodotus' system of the world, Egypt, situated in the South, corresponded symmetrically to Scythia, in the North. A traveller following the remarkable "meridian" leading from the Nile delta to the mouth of the Danube moved from heat to cold, from a land constantly surveyed and measured to nomadic empty spaces, from antiquity to youth (the Scythians were reputed to be the youngest of all races), from knowledge patiently accumulated over the centuries to ignorance with no memories. The Greeks could never be anything but children to the Egyptians, but what about the Scythians? However, as Herodotus, already, recognized, there was one exception: Anacharsis, a Scythian, yet a *sophos*.

According to Herodotus, the history of his life shows that, however opposed the Scythians and Egyptians appear to be, they do have one trait in common: both groups categorically refuse to adopt foreign customs, in particular Greek ones.[3] Anacharsis is not a Greek traveller, but a Scythian, a Barbarian, a nomad from Scythia visiting Greece. When he returns to his own land, he is assassinated. The relation between Egypt and Scythia is also set on stage, in a more literary vein, in Plutarch's *Banquet of the Seven Sages*. Anacharsis, the sage from the North, is present, a fully accepted member of the brotherhood, in which he plays an important role, but we also meet an Egyptian by the name of Niloxenus, a stranger from the Nile. He has been sent by the Egyptian king Amasis to interview the Sages, who have been brought together by Periander, the tyrant of Corinth. Egypt is really in need of enlightenment from Greece. The Sages perform as is expected of them, making pronouncements and solving riddles.

In the registers of Greek documentation, the official life of Anacharsis begins with Herodotus and continues until the third century AD at least. Lucian of Samosata assigns him a place of honour, and Diogenes Laertius includes him in the group of Sages and devotes a notice to him. After that, he had to wait until the late eighteenth century before enjoying another moment of fame, not in person admittedly, but through his descendant, the young Anacharsis. Abbé Barthélemy makes the latter say: "I am descended from Anacharsis the Sage, you know, who was so famous among the Greeks and so unworthily treated by the Scythians. Since my earliest childhood, the story of his life and death has inspired me with esteem for the nation that honoured his virtues and aloofness from the one that failed to recognize them".[4] That is primarily why he leaves the "nomadic life" that he has hitherto led. In 363 BC, accompanied by a former Greek slave whom he has freed, he begins his tour of Greece, setting out from the town of Panticapaeum on the Black Sea, and returns, regretfully, to his own country in 338, only after seeing Greek liberty "expire in the plain of Chaeronea".

For Herodotus, Anacharsis is first and foremost a traveller. Like Solon, he has travelled the world to see and, also like him, he has demonstrated his learning.[5] His character is founded upon the same combination of *theôria* and *sophia*. But his destiny takes a turn for the worse when, upon his return to Scythia, he celebrates the cult of the Great Mother Goddess (Cybele), in fulfilment of a vow. He does so in secret, but a Scythian surprises him and denounces him to the king, who, having seen for himself, kills him with an arrow. Once eliminated physically, Anacharsis is also wiped from the memory of the Scythians. Herodotus relates that if anybody asks about him he is told that "he is not known, for he went off to Greece and adopted foreign customs". So in truth he clearly is known, but as one whom it is better to forget. The formula recorded by Herodotus is remarkable, for the departure to Greece expresses both a euphemistic version of his assassination (he left on a voyage) and at the same time the very reason for his death (he chose Greece). His fate illustrates the deadly peril risked by anyone who, as a result of travelling the world, comes to "forget" its frontiers.[6] *Nomos* is the real "despot", and Anacharsis has transgressed the law. He must therefore disappear: *depart* and never return.

But according to another version "told by the Peloponnesians", Anacharsis was on an official mission, sent by the king of the Scythians. He had "learned about Greece" and declared upon his return that while all Greeks, except the Spartans, devoted their time to many studies, only the Spartans knew how to speak and listen modestly. "Nonsense", Herodotus declares, "that is pure fiction: he certainly died as I say he did". The other report is a story "forged" (*peplastai*) by the Greeks. However that may be, it at least illustrates the malleability of the figure of Anacharsis, a signifier travelling the world, through the centuries, charged willy-nilly with reflecting to the Greeks an image of themselves that they both do and do not want. Anacharsis was to be an observer–observed, fashioned by the Greeks for their own use.

Herodotus (unlike Abbé Barthélemy) does not interpret Anacharsis as a martyr of Hellenism who accepts death for the love of things Greek. But he does represent him as an itinerant purveyor of knowledge. Plato, for his part, without formally including him in the list of the Seven Sages, as he does later in the *Protagoras*, first cites him, along with Thales, as an example of the kind of sage whose characteristics and inventions were frequently invoked.[7] A number of such lists were circulating in the fourth and third centuries, some of them short, with fewer than seven names, others longer, with more than seven. It was most probably Ephorus who introduced Anacharsis into the list, on the grounds of his great wisdom and intelligence, as a replacement for Myson or Periander.[8] And in his *Histories*, Ephorus reflects the view that the Greeks had of themselves and others. As has been noted above, he is inclined to believe that the Barbarians antedated the Greeks, and seems ready to acknowledge that outlying lands are superior to the centre.

He points out that there are two traditions circulating on the Scythians. One represents them to be head–hunters and cannibals, while the other portrays them as a just people that "abstains from all living creatures". The latter is backed by the authority of Homer, for the Scythians are clearly the people whom Homer and Hesiod call the "Drinkers of Milk" (*Galaktophagoi*) or the "Distant Ones" (*Abioi*). On that basis, Ephorus concludes that there are two separate groups of Scythians, living in different places, the one made up of savages, the other of extremely just people, who practise a primitive kind of communism and who are invincible since they have nothing to lose. Anacharsis naturally belongs to the latter group.[9] The first consequence of Anacharsis' being accepted as a fully fledged sage was that he was accepted as having full access to speech and writing. It was not long before anecdotes, witty repartees, inventions (the two-headed anchor and the potter's wheel) and literary works were all being ascribed to him.

Ephorus' choice was not an isolated, discordant one. Dicaearchus includes Anacharsis in his more extensive list of Sages, as do Hermippus, a third-century BC Alexandrian biographer,[10] and also Hippobotus, another compiler of the same period, who was the author of a book on philosophers. Later, Plutarch and Diogenes Laertius were to establish their own portraits of Anacharsis on the basis of those sources. The case of Hermippus is interesting, as he was responsible for a dramatization of the first meeting of Anacharsis and Solon. As soon as Anacharsis arrives in Athens, he knocks on Solon's door, asking to see him and become his friend. Seeking to put him off, Solon replies that as a general rule one chooses one's own friends for oneself, "at home" (*oikoi*). To this Anacharsis slyly retorts that, since Solon is indeed "at home" (*oikoi*), he is in a position to welcome him, Anacharsis, as a friend. Impressed by the vivacity of his wit, Solon can do no less than oblige.[11] It is thus Anacharsis' intellectual qualities, his ability to indulge in Greek repartee, that enable him to cross Solon's threshold. Because he is already "at home" in the language, already on the inside, Anacharsis can cross this frontier (with Solon here of course standing for the whole of Greece).

Hermippus, for his part, was a Peripatetic, a pupil of Callimachus and, like him, very much a library man.[12] He was the author of numerous biographies: of the Seven Sages, or simply the Sages, of Aristotle, of Theophrastus, but also of Pythagoras (who took over precepts from both the Jews and the Thracians), and of course the magi. He may also have published a book on the Egyptians and the Ethiopians, and was reputed to have catalogued the works of Zoroaster. The fame of Zoroaster, who, according to Xanthos of Lydia, was born six thousand years earlier, grew steadily from the fourth century on, as did the length of the list of his works. Hermippus, who was a great reader and an unrepentant compiler, thus seems to have been a moving force in this orientalization or "Barbarization" of Greek wisdom. He may have played that role more through a desire to set straight the record on multiple traditions, by fixing accounts, tracing influences and establishing chronologies, than because of any conviction of the inferiority of Greek wisdom. In the late sixth-century BC world, Hecataeus of Miletus had tried to sort out the many stories of the Greeks, by recording them in writing. Once transcribed, their multiplicity became very apparent, to the point of becoming ridiculous. In the very much extended Alexandrian world, the philologists undertook to list and classify all the many stories and writings of the Greeks and others. But it was now no laughing matter! Although the authors of antiquity, for their part, made considerable use of Hermippus' work, modern (German) philologists, never at ease with his fragments, reckoned that he was either too credulous or, to put it bluntly, a forger.

Anacharsis' good fortune was that he was considered *doubly* wise – not only a sage in the ancient sense (as in the "Seven Sages", with whom he was from the start associated despite his Scythian "nationality"), but also in a new sense, this time thanks to that very "nationality", as a man from the outer regions, the representative of a simple life lived according to nature. That kind of non-scholarly wisdom, which had nothing to do with books, could well come from the North. This image of Anacharsis, the noble savage, was promoted and disseminated by the Cynics. He became the author of letters, dated by common consent to the third century BC, which were Cynical in both inspiration and tone.[13] In them, the Scythians are represented as quite naturally practising a Cynical way of life: dressing and eating simply, free in both their behaviour and their speech. The Scythians, Anacharsis tells the Athenians, did not make fine speeches but stated things forthrightly, just as they were. Writing to Solon, he rejects the idea that the Greeks are "wiser" than the Barbarians. Now that the Greeks are being urged to change and become *Barbarized*, they, the Scythians, who need only to persist in their way of being, may provide models for them to imitate. Anacharsis, the authorized spokesman for the primitive life, is a natural but less stark and provocative Diogenes. Diogenes himself had to *become* Diogenes, whereas all Anacharsis had to do was remain himself. The former, as an ascetic, had to repudiate his false civilization, whereas the latter simply needed to retain his outsider's attitude. Maximus of Tyre, an itinerant lecturer of the second century AD, portrays him as a sage who is not interested in spinning words. He travels to Greece, not to learn to be Greek, but to put its wisdom to the test, and to make a "tour of Greece". Apparently, only the little town of Chenaea, in the Peloponnese, presented him with a truly admirable man, namely Myson.[14] Lucian, too, was to speak of Anacharsis' intention to visit the whole of Greece.[15]

But Anacharsis was an outsider from inside, for he had long since crossed the threshold of Solon's home, so was in every respect qualified to play the role of a "Persian" in Athens (in the manner of the foreign visitors to eighteenth-century Paris in Montesquieu's *Lettres Persanes*). "Just as he finds our customs bizarre, he sometimes finds some parts of our dogmas strange, because he is unfamiliar with them, and he cannot understand them because he is unaware what links them together and the chain of which they form a part".[16] Later tradition was to make the most of this effect of inside-out exoticism. It portrays Anacharsis as at once astonished and amused. He mocks Solon, so busy drafting his laws, saying that laws are like spiders' webs, in which only the weak and the small get caught. And he is amazed by a meeting of the Assembly, where *sophoi* were to be found making speeches, yet left the decisions to the ignorant masses.[17]

Banquets also bemuse him. Given that they are merely pretexts for inebriation, why not be the first to get drunk and so win the first prize?[18] On this question of wine, the Scythians, it must be said, are somewhat confusing. Alongside the image of the abstemious, milk-drinking Scythians can be found another tradition that portrays them as inveterate boozers. They drink their wine neat, like Polyphemus, so they are savages. But wine itself comes to mean something different here: whereas in Homer it is a criterion of civilization for anyone who knows how to cultivate it and drink it, here it becomes an adulterated beverage. The Cynic philosopher is a drinker of water. When the king of the Getae decides to turn his subjects into a sovereign people, he makes them uproot their vines and stop drinking wine.[19] Anacharsis is thus caught between two concepts of wine: according to the one it is an indication of civilization, according to the other a sign of false civilization. When he is asked if there are flute-players in Scythia, "he answered on the spur of the moment, 'No, nor grape-vines either'".[20]

The gymnasium is the other central institution by which is defined the Greek identity that Anacharsis derides. Why on earth do young men spend their time rolling about in the mud and the dust, like pigs? This is the starting point for his conversation with Solon. Lucian delights in portraying him more than ever as a visiting "Persian". He is a nomad, a wanderer who has never lived in a town and has no idea what a political constitution is. How could he possibly appreciate that it goes back to an autochthonous people, and in particular to Solon, the legislator?[21] No more does he understand whatever can be the point of wrestling bouts "for fun". When you fight, you fight in earnest, against enemies. And he is shocked to learn that the prize for victory is nothing but an olive wreath: the concept of *agôn* is totally alien to him. He cannot see why on earth anyone should fight merely "for glory", that is to say to be someone of account, regarded by the spectators with respect. Likewise, the gymnasium as a place where the city trains and disciplines the bodies and minds of its future guardians remains a concept that is alien to him. He is amazed and bursts out laughing at the idea. When Solon warns him above all not to laugh if ever he sees youths in Sparta submitting to being whipped without making a sound, he replies that he is afraid he will be unable to contain himself, being quite convinced that a city that treats the flower of its youth in such a fashion is in need of a dose of hellebore, to calm it down.[22]

We shall never know how the Scythians trained their young men, as the conversation breaks off at that point, when Anacharsis defers talking about it until the next day. Lucian's ploy is understandable, as he never intended to produce a comparison between two educational systems, but instead prefers to set Anacharsis and Solon on stage in a new duet. Anacharsis the inside-outsider is definitely a part of the Greek heritage. He and Solon re-appear in another short treatise, *The Scythian or the Proxenus*. Here, Anacharsis has just landed in Piraeus. He is lost, a butt of mockery on account of his strange costume, and nobody speaks his language. He is already anxious to set sail again when a "good devil" comes to his rescue, in the person of Toxaris, a famous Scythian doctor who settled in Athens long ago. He recognizes Anacharsis from his costume and his air of bewilderment, and offers to be his guide. Toxaris, out of his great love of Greece, has left his country and his wife and children, and so becomes a model for Anacharsis, who is fired by a desire "to see Greece".[23] Toxaris tells him that the quickest way to do so is to meet Solon, an Athenian but also a traveller in Asia and Europe, for he in himself represents the whole of Greece.[24] At this point Solon happens to run into them, and so begins the whirlwind education of Anacharsis, who from then on never leaves his side. As a result Anacharsis received Athenian citizenship and became the only Barbarian ever to be initiated into the mysteries of Eleusis, which in this text represent the holy of holies in the Athenian or Greek identity. Had it not been for Solon's death, he would in all likelihood never have returned to Scythia.[25]

As can be seen, Lucian was quite prepared to portray two very different versions of Anacharsis. The first, the "Persian", laughs and speaks out as he sees fit, while the second, in total contrast, is a deferential pupil who keeps quiet and listens. This shows that Lucian was more interested in exploiting a *topos* and a situation – the meeting between Solon and Anacharsis – than in new thoughts on the variety of customs and the institutions of Greek polit-ical life. Furthermore, he also had a personal reason for laying emphasis on the second Anacharsis. Describing Anacharsis landing in Athens as a poor stranger was a way of writing about himself arriving in a Macedonian town "famous for its size and beauty".[26] Like Anacharsis, Lucian was a Barbarian, from not Scythia but Syria, and was likewise in need of a Toxaris, a patron. He found two, a father and son, the best of men by both birth and culture. For a man such as Lucian, earning his living as a sophist, that rapid evocation of the second version of Anacharsis operated as an ingenious way of intro-ducing himself and winning over his audience.

In his *Banquet of the Seven Sages*, Plutarch reactivates the circle of Sages of yesteryear. Periander is their host, but no longer a member of their brother-hood, which by then had no place for a tyrant. Anacharsis, a man of great wisdom and knowledge (*polumathês*) is there, and Egypt is also represented. Is he Scythian? Or is he Greek? To judge by his appearance he is still

Scythian, with long hair that a girl is engaged in combing so that, as Thales jokes, he does not alarm them, he who is in reality such a "civilized" man. But that is said with a wink. He is also Scythian in his knowledge of the rites of purification used for curing the sick, to which an allusion is made. And his experience of the nomadic life is mentioned by Aesop, who is also present at the banquet. A Scythian, whose only home is his wagon, is "free and autonomous": "homeless", *aoikos*, as he is, he is aware that what matters is not a construction of mud or wood, but one's inner dwelling, the possessions one carries within oneself.[27] But eventually, towards the end of the dialogue, when Anacharsis declares that "the body is the soul's instrument and the soul is God's instrument",[28] he is no longer at all Scythian, but purely a Platonist sage, with ideas that are close to those of Plutarch himself, or maybe even Plutarch's spokesman. If Plutarch sees Egypt as a great hieroglyphic of wisdom that one needs to know how to decipher (and a Greek can do so all the better given that he can read Greek into it), the name of Anacharsis has by now become an icon for Greek wisdom. Anacharsis seems to have completed his travels, and arrived.

Not quite, however, for Diogenes Laertius makes him return to Scythia, where he is assassinated by the king, his brother. Diogenes, who was a defender of the Greekness of *sophia*, not surprisingly presents Anacharsis as a victim of his own Hellenic zeal. In a letter to Croesus, Anacharsis declares that he has come to Greece to "be instructed" in its *mores* and customs, so that he will eventually return, a "better" man, to his own country.[29] Solon welcomes him for his wit. Then he goes home, where he is killed. Diogenes adds an interesting biographical detail: his mother was Greek, so Anacharsis grew up bilingual. Right from the start, then, he straddled the frontier, half-Greek, half-Scythian, but he seems to have overinclined towards the maternal side![30]

The biographies of Anacharsis tell of spaces, frontiers and death: death either real or symbolic, either negated or proclaimed. For Herodotus, clearly, he dies because he has forgotten about frontiers. One part of the tradition makes him die for having loved Greece too much; another part simply "forgets" the ending to the story: no mention is made of the return to Scythia. He truly does become the outsider inside. His portrait hangs in the gallery of ancestors. In the *Toxaris*, Lucian suggests a shift that may later have inspired Abbé Barthélemy. It is no longer Anacharsis who dies, but Solon; and had Solon not died, Anacharsis would probably never have returned to Scythia.

In *The Voyage of the Younger Anacharsis*, the hero decides to return to Scythia after the defeat of Chaeronea, which he senses to be the death of

Greek liberty. A single utopian space extends from the death of Solon to the death of the liberty of Greece, a space that is open just for a while, before closing upon itself forever. Neither the elder nor the younger Anacharsis would ever be able to return. The two "deaths" are homologous. The Athens of Solon and the Athens of Aristotle passed away forever. Lucian was obliged to exercise his profession as a sophist in Macedon, and the Abbé, who wrote in Paris, with Pausanias as his guide, never went to Greece at all.

The Voyage appeared in December 1788. In May 1789, Grimm reviewed the book, which had created a sensation:

> Just because once, five or six thousand years ago, at the very tip of a small peninsula, in one of the kindest climes in Europe, for a few centuries a democratic government was beheld to combine the elements of the stormiest ever system of liberty with the highest ever degree of culture, along with great wealth and power, is there any reason to think that it would be easy to reproduce the feat of such a moral and political phenomenon elsewhere?[31]

Jean-Baptiste Cloots, a German baron but one who lived in Paris and signed his earliest works "M. le Baron de Cloots du Val de Grâce", dreamed that the feat could indeed be "reproduced". In Paris, the new Athens, he took the name Anacharsis, and joined the Jacobin club. As "the Ambassador in France for foreigners in love with the Revolution", he took the title of "orator of the human race". Along with Paine, Washington, Schiller, Klopstock and a number of others, he was given French citizenship, and he was subsequently elected to the Convention as deputy for the Oise department. On 26 March 1794, he was guillotined in the company of Hébert. Three months earlier, the Convention had decided to expel from its midst all citizens born in foreign lands. After all, Robespierre decreed, this "cosmopolitan" was "only a German baron".[32] So it was that the last Anacharsis was assassinated, not in Scythia, but in "Athens", for having dreamed that there were no more frontiers.

FRONTIERS WITHIN, OR ORDINARY KINDS OF DISCRIMINATION

Are Greeks ever stupid? Given that Odysseus, that founding figure created by the Greeks themselves, catches our attention and that *métis* in its various forms has permeated and worked within the Greek culture for ten centuries at least, where does the path of cunning intelligence lead?[33] Is it a property peculiar to the Greeks? Are the monsters and savages encountered by Odysseus in the course of his wanderings and, later, the Barbarians who stand in opposition to the Greeks all, by nature, without it?

A famous, even emblematic pair provides one answer. Prometheus, the "Foresighted One", full of *mêtis*, stands in opposition to his brother Epimetheus, who is equally Greek but is totally devoid of *mêtis*. He "sees afterward", understands too late, is forgetful.[34] These two brothers provide an image of one way of allotting intelligence and stupidity. There are, quite clearly, savages who are capable of cunning, and one sometimes comes across clever (and deceitful) Barbarians. Unsurprisingly, the most stupid ones are probably one's closest neighbours (the Athenians certainly do not think highly of theirs), or alternatively the peoples situated on the extreme margins, in the *eschatiai* regions of the inhabited world. However, the "simplicity" of the outer limits may, as we have seen, sometimes be reversed and become superiority.

Where cunning is concerned what matters is not only its presence or absence, but also its quality: is it "good" or "bad"? Fair play or not? Odysseus himself sometimes swings over on to the bad side, in fact would fall squarely there if he were not "saved" by belonging to the race of heroes. As for Polyphemus, the savage of all savages, the bestial Cyclops, he is not "stupid". Before he is finally tricked by Odysseus, he indulges in a little black humour, accusing him of naivety: "You are a child (*nêpios*), my guest", he tells Odysseus when the latter demands the gift of hospitality that it is customary to offer a passing visitor.[35] But the tables are, of course, turned when Odysseus, through his trickery, manages to escape.[36] *Nêpios* means precisely *infans*, one who cannot speak, who does not understand words or know how to use them, the very opposite of Odysseus, who is a clever talker, never at a loss for words.

In the field governed by *mêtis*, "stupidity" is associated with the ignorance of childhood or infantile naivety: *nêpios* is the word for an innocent. In the world of human beings, Odysseus' companions are on more than one occasion described as *nêpioi*, a bunch of big kids. In contrast to Odysseus, who is always concerned to remember, they are fundamentally "forgetful": they forget that they are on a return journey, forget what they should and should not do, are ready to sacrifice any old how and to eat no matter what, just to satisfy their hunger pangs. And they pay for it with their lives. Before that though, thanks to Circe's magic, they are vouchsafed the dubious honour and advantage of experiencing the condition of beasts. So the question that arises is: were they always particularly disposed to stupidity? Is there a link between their "stupidity" and their transformation into pigs, never animals considered to be paragons of alertness? For as with human beings (and with gods too), certain animals are endowed with *mêtis*, while others are not.[37] So even if the *mêtis* of humans is superior to that of animals, it is certainly not a specific criterion of humanity. The fate of Odysseus' companions, those "poor fools" grunting in their pen (but all the same mindful that the bristles on their backs are only borrowed clothing), leads one to question the link (if such there be) between being a beast and being stupid. The French language conveys one: *bêtise*, or *bestise* as the sixteenth-century dictionaries spell it, designates a condition similar to that of beasts. But Greek, for its part, seems not to have followed that path, for *mêtis* is opposed by stupidity in the guise of "the state of infancy", in the original sense of the word.

A RETURN TO THE FRONTIER BETWEEN HUMAN BEINGS AND ANIMALS

Neither gods nor beasts. That was how the first anthropology put it. But within that initial division there was another that drew a distinction between wild animals and domesticated ones, as it did between cultivated space and uncultivated or wild space.[38] Whereas Odysseus strives always to maintain the distance between a man and an animal (without, however, overstepping the imperative boundary dividing men from the gods), his companions are constantly forgetting it. For that reason, their misadventure on Circe's island is not really surprising: they do indeed become (domesticated) animals. But what of the apparent neglect or at least metaphorical transgression of the dividing line that is implied by all those frequent animal comparisons in the Homeric poems? Achilles, Ajax and Hector are said to behave, respectively, like a mountain lion, a formidable wild boar, an eagle. Such comparisons introduce us into the aristocratic world of hunting. For in terms of "social" status, wild beasts and their hunters belong to the same world. Yet against the background of that culturally constructed proximity, the effect of the comparison is not to overstep or even to efface the original separation between man and beast. On the contrary, for the relevant features upon which the comparison fastens trace the image of a stylized animal, an image that conveys and translates the heroic sensibility and its particular values.[39] The animal becomes a blazon. When a hero is compared to a lion, he is more regal than animal. The comparison is a way of giving forceful expression to his

118

heroic nature and his nobility. On the other hand, when Diomedes, wearing a lion-skin, slaughters Dolon and the Thracians under Rhesus, he swings brutally over into savagery and bestiality.[40] Disguised as a nocturnal lion, in exile from heroic sociability, for the time being everything human becomes alien to him: he is no longer a man but a wild beast (which itself has "returned" to total savagery).

Outside the Homeric world and its system of heroic values, the threat of descents or redescents into animality was to reappear in Arcadia, in the highlands of the Peloponnese, where apparently the slightest oversight or failure to observe the correct dues of the gods risked punishment for such regressive behaviour.[41]

In the classical period the major divisions clearly continued to be observed, being regularly reactivated in the city through the regulatory repetition of the rite of animal sacrifice. But that certainly did not prevent man from being defined as an animal, as opposed to the inanimate beings.[42] However, even though he belonged to the group of living beings as a whole, he was distinguished from the rest as an "animal endowed with *logos*", "an animal with a share of the divine",[43] and eventually as a "political animal". Isocrates was to declare: "Because there has been implanted in us the power to persuade each other and to make it clear to each other whatever we desire, not only have we escaped the life of wild beasts (*thêriôdôs*), but we have come together and founded cities and made laws and invented arts; and, generally speaking, there is no institution devised by man which the power of speech (*logos*) has not helped to establish".[44]

Ever since the advent of the first sophists, it had been considered essential to conceive of the human community (*koinônia*) against that background of animality. The human community both antedated all forms of association and constituted the end (*telos*) of any human life, for which the ideal and imperative essential was "to live the good life". And, Aristotle declares, it was through and for the sake of that community that man, animal though he is, turned himself into a political animal.[45] As for the category of "wildness", this found a place in contemporary theories on the beginnings of the human race. The first men were believed to have existed as wild animals, and their lives were characterized by dispersion (*sporadên*) and an absence of all links (*ataktos*): hence their extreme vulnerability. But necessity (*chreia*), first and foremost that of defence against the murderous attacks of real wild beasts, prompted human beings to come together in groups for the first time. Then, gradually, socialization strengthened and spread. In all ancient Greek authors, the two expressions used to characterize that point of departure recur: "an animal way of life" and "dispersion". The wild beast evoked here is no longer the "civilized" animal of Homeric descriptions. To live *more ferarum* no doubt involved going naked and eating raw food, but above all it meant lacking any kind of social bond.[46]

This was precisely the question addressed by Protagoras in his myth of a social "contract": how and in what circumstances was the move made from dispersion to a truly viable community? In his view, mastery of the principal skills (fire, agriculture, weaving, etc.) did not suffice to put an end to the dispersion of the earliest days. The essential ingredient was still missing: namely, political skill (*politikê technê*). Because of that, human beings were still dying, incapable as yet of defending themselves altogether successfully against wild beasts (since warfare is defined as stemming from the art of politics). In similar fashion, successive attempts to form communities turned out to be short-lived. This continued until Zeus, who was worried about the situation, decided to present human beings with this necessary skill, in the form of an equal distribution to each of them of Respect and Justice. Echoing the first use of these terms, by Hesiod, *Aidôs* and *Dikê* now generated links of friendship (*philia*).[47] There can be no community without *philia* and no *philia* without a sense of justice and the recognition of humanity in others, with whom relations would, from now on, involve not violence but mediation by means of persuasive discourse. Politics is a "skill" and the city, which stems not from nature but from culture, is *artifice*. Protagoras' myth ends with the following caution: "Let whoever proves himself incapable of participating in Respect and Justice be put to death, like a disease (*nosos*) at the heart of the city".

When Aristotle, in his turn, reflected upon the individual incapable of living in a city, he concluded: "A man that is by nature and not merely by fortune citiless is either low in the scale of humanity or above it".[48] Such a schema made it possible, retrospectively, to assign to the historical figure of the tyrant the place of someone who was *apolis*. Given that he seized all the power for himself alone, he could easily take on the face or mask of a wild beast: hence his abnormal, if not *anomic* (from *anomia*, beyond the law) behaviour. From such interchanges between *thêrios*, *agrios* and *apolis*, there eventually emerged the idea of a "politicization" of the animality that is the mark of a pre-political state or of stepping outside (or even forgetting) politics. Through a series of operations effected on the frontier separating man from animal, these reflections on the nature of the social link thus led to the creation of a place (in the time of origins) for animality or wildness and also a function for it (particularly in the elaboration of the concept of *apolis*).

Still adopting the standpoint of the city, another distinction was soon introduced, a new separation set in place. *Agros* produced *agrios* and, later, also *agroikos*, to designate someone who lived in the countryside, among the fields. In Homer's Greek, *agros* designated pastureland, fields that were not cultivated, as opposed to *aroura*, ploughed land; and *agrios* meant "savage, ferocious". As Chantraine has shown, *agrios* took on the sense of ferocious as a result of the influence of hunting vocabulary (*agra* was the word for both the hunt and the game hunted). A boundary thus passed between the ploughed fields, on the one hand, and the outlying zone that was used for pasturage, but also for hunting. There, hunters crossed paths with shepherds, the normal occupants of these spaces. The appearance, in the fifth century BC, of the derivative *agroikos* (unknown to Homer) marked a shift in the boundary: now the division was between the town and all that lay outside it:[49] on the one hand there was the urban space, on the other all the rest. *Agroikos* not only circumscribed a space and an inhabited area; it also conveyed a way of life and, quite soon, came to stigmatize a way of being: that of country folk, rustics, yokels. To use the word *agroikos* was thus to speak of the countryside from the standpoint of the town, and to roll *aroura*, *agros* and *agrios* all into one. And it was also, from the point of view of literary genre, to move from epic to comedy.

The countryside was part of the city territory or, to be more precise, of what was called the "political land". In principle, it was inalienable, and it qualified whoever possessed a plot of it to be recognized as a citizen with full rights. Unlike the medieval republics, the city initially rejected any separation between the town and the countryside. The small-scale peasant landowner (*autourgos*) was admitted (although not immediately and not forever) as a full citizen. The appearance of the word *agroikos* and its subsequent evolution provides some clues as to the changes that altered relations between the town and the countryside in the course of the period stretching from the mid-fifth century down to the third century BC. The general trend is clear: it shows a growing distance developing between the two spaces, if not the two worlds, to a point where, in the name of "capacity", it called into question the civic qualifications of the country-dweller or at least implied that he was, or ought to be, no more than a second-grade citizen.

Eventually, *agroikos* came to take on a whole range of meanings, all of them negative, all of which were carefully registered by lexicographers of later periods (but most of which came from Attic comedy from Aristophanes down to Menander). An *agroikos* was described as "gauche", "brainless", "bad-tempered", "hard", "uneducated".[50] Clad in animal skins, the peasant of comedy was portrayed as being, himself, some kind of beast. The whole range of meanings of *agrios* tended to be applied to him. He knew nothing: neither the right words nor the right manners (that is to say those of the town). When Strepsiades, the peasant in the *Clouds*, comes to seek out Socrates, asking to be taken on as a disciple, he declares that he wishes to learn how "to speak".[51]

In Athens, a peasant (landowner) was a citizen but, more surprisingly, so too was an artisan. The former was rural (unless, perhaps, he was a large landowner), the latter generally a city-dweller. But the Peloponnesian War shifted that balance. In 431, Pericles' strategy was to turn Athens into an island: the countryside was abandoned to the raiding Spartans, and its population was invited to retreat, as if to an island, behind the Long Walls of the town.[52] Of course, there was a social and political dimension to that military decision, to the extent that it reflected a change in the relations between the countryside and the town, a change that favoured the democratic city. But above all it entailed the cramming of thousands of peasant refugees within the walls of Athens itself. Although this was initially supposed to be a temporary, tentative measure, it became increasingly permanent as the war itself did, following Attica's permanent occupation by the Spartans. The multiple consequences of this situation exerted a lasting influence on the relations between town and countryside. After the defeat, that enforced proximity of the two worlds resulted in an even wider rift between them.

In this slice of history, or at least in the history of the word *agroikos*, Aristophanes, whose plays were contemporary with the war, reflected an important – because ambiguous – situation. Although he did not take the side of the "town" (with its quintessential democratic products, the demagogue and the sycophant), quite the reverse, he nevertheless helped to fix the image of the *agroikos* as a country bumpkin. The Socrates of the *Clouds*, a pallid city-dweller, is certainly ridiculous (and dangerous). But Strepsiades, the peasant, who has mistakenly taken it into his head to marry a townswoman, and one who is moreover a stuck-up madam descended from a ruined great family,[53] fares no better. In a single line, Socrates calls Strepsiades both an imbecile as old-fashioned as Cronos and a man from pre-human times.[54] Like the Arcadians, he goes back to the age of Cronos. He is neither a beast nor bestial – simply an "imbecile" (*môros*), because he is archaic.

Aristophanes mocks his old-fashioned demeanour, but dwells even more on his ignorance, his primitive (or infantile) naivety, and on the fact that in the eyes of the subtle Socrates, he is irremediably limited and unfashionable. Everything, even the stage-set, is devised to make the most of the opposition between the "lightness", the airy subtlety, of Socrates, up there in his basket, and the "pre-lunar" lumpenness of the man of the soil, who can think only of duping his creditors. Epithets that seem so many extensions of the word *agroikos* rain down upon him: he is ignorant, Barbarian, clumsy, awkward, slow, incapable of remembering anything, old-fashioned, more archaic than Cronos or the moon.[55] The play was performed in 423, when the war was at its height. In its final twist, it does, it is true, end in confusion for the man whom the chorus have called "the pontificator of the most subtle nonsense". All the same, by then the image of the country bumpkin is already established.

In the New Comedy of the fourth and third centuries, he becomes a stock stage character.[56] Theophrastus' *Characters* (about 320 BC) honour him with a portrait that drives the point firmly home. His rusticity, every aspect of which is noted, is based upon his noisy (unconscious) ignorance of good manners: of how to dress, when to be surprised, when not to be surprised, etc. A bumpkin is ignorant, in other words "has not the least experience of things of the town".[57] That is the root of his *ethos*, in the eyes of Theophrastus, the city-dweller who was, we are told, a natty dresser, for whom the gardens of the Lyceum must have more than sufficed in the way of countryside. All the above-mentioned literature marked the beginnings of the folklorization of the figure of the country bumpkin.

As an owner of land, the *agroikos* was a citizen. Theophrastus portrays him as he is "going up" to town, to take part in a session of the Assembly.[58] This provides him with plenty of scope to exploit the contrast to the full, for the *agroikos* is both at home (as a citizen) and a stranger (in the eyes of those observing his behaviour). If his citizenship is not directly called into question, his lack of "political" savoir-faire is certainly lampooned. Here is a man who goes off and discusses public affairs out in the fields with a bunch of farm-labourers! It is a grotesque, if not shocking scene: what an orator, and what an audience! The arrival of the *agroikos*, a vessel of ignorant rusticity, heralded the death (feared by some and welcomed by others) of one particular representation of the city.

The above picture is not so much a hurried sketch or a genre painting as a brief recapitulation of a comic tradition, initiated by Aristophanes and then fostered as a result of the enforced period of cohabitation during the war. But apart from that comic representation of the country bumpkin, there also existed a philosophical elaboration of "rusticity" of which Theophrastus cannot have failed to be aware. After all, he had been the pupil of Aristotle, in whose ethical treatises the ignorant and stubborn *agroikos* is classified on the side of excess. He is wary of all pleasure, even the moderate and necessary kind, but he knows nothing of true temperance because he is completely "insensitive" (*anaisthêtos*). His total lack of a sense of humour where either himself or others are concerned also relegates him to the side of excess, way beyond the correct balance. At the same time, however, the city-dwelling wit who makes fun of absolutely everything is also judged to be excessive.[59]

Plato does not defend any theory of rusticity as such, but he does bandy about the word *agroikos*.[60] And quite often it is associated with uncouthness, baseness, stupidity, a lack of education of course, and behaviour unworthy of a free man.[61]

This rapid overview down to the time of Theophrastus reveals an increasing devaluation of the *agroikos* which can be interpreted as a sign and expression of the rift, which was to deepen, between the town and the countryside.[62] Furthermore, as the link between Greekness and education came to be increasingly underlined,[63] the *agroikos*, basically an uneducated man, was increasingly overtly pushed to the margins of civilization: a savage within (who could be excluded from citizenship as soon as he lost his land). He was represented as "gauche" in opposition to the city-dweller (*asteios*), who, for his part, was worthy of town life, elegant, intelligent, sophisticated, and also described as *dexios* (on the right side, adroit).[64] It is worth noting that those negative connotations were not only expressed but even strengthened by thinkers, above all Plato, who at the very same time were attempting to purvey the idea that it was crucial for the city to eliminate the rift between the town and the countryside. The *Laws*, for example, devises a complex system for dividing up the city territory in such a way that "each allotment ... contains a near piece [i.e. close to the city] and a distant piece".[65]

In this process of folklorization which tended to turn every peasant into a bumpkin and to rule out the possibility that any free man or citizen could possibly be clad in animal skins, Xenophon constitutes a remarkable exception. He was a gentleman farmer who had retired to his estate at Scillus in

Elis, where he tried to revive a more ancient concept according to which, on the contrary, the agricultural profession was the only activity that was truly worthy of a free man. Or rather not the agricultural *profession* – in the sense in which an artisan, confined to his workshop all day long and basically dependent upon it, practises a profession; for agriculture first and foremost expresses a fundamental accord between the individual and the earth.[66] Besides which, unsurprisingly, it produces the very best soldiers. He thus opposes one folklorization by another, which is traditionalist and nostalgic and which chooses to see the soldier-farmer as the citizen *par excellence*.

In complementary fashion, in Athens, the city's ejection of the *agroikos* to its margins was accompanied by the spread of the cult of Pan, the billy-goat and goatherd god, much revered in caves. But this was a country cult tailored to the use of city-dwellers.[67] Similarly, the development of bucolic poetry was also to be the work of city-dwellers. Shepherds, traditionally men of the *agros* and the outlying regions, on the margins of society, were to find that they were made welcome in town, but only provided they "played the part of shepherds", at least as the city-dwellers imagined this.[68] Meanwhile city-dwellers were making their way to the country, where they too could play at being shepherds.

It was in the *Idylls* of Theocritus, who had lived in Syracuse, Cos and Alexandria, that, in the third century, this readjustment of frontiers was most evident. "How sweet, goatherd, is the murmur of this pine tree, singing beside the spring, and the sound of your pipes is just as sweet", sings Thyrsis, who goes on to describe a pastoral and stylized landscape to which Virgil would later give the name Arcadia, transforming it for years to come into a utopia for Western art.[69] Here, one might now come across a Polyphemus, a Cyclops transformed into a shepherd in love with Galataea. The seventh *Idyll* interestingly sets on stage a poet from the city, who goes to the country to take part in a country festival. On the way he meets a shepherd-poet (or rather a poet disguised as a shepherd) whom he salutes as follows: "They say that you are a musician unrivalled among the shepherds and harvesters. I am delighted to hear it, but I fancy I can equal you". The other smiles, and hands him his shepherd's crook.[70] Whatever the significance of this scene, all this swapping of places and words indicates an exchange (if not a relaying process) between town and countryside, an exchange which, although it clearly acknowledges separation between the two, at the same time brings shepherds *and* peasants together.

BOEOTIAN SWINE

The Athenians were prone to "animalize" their immediate neighbours beyond the frontiers of Attica, who in many cases were also their enemies. A common enough ploy. Thus the stupidity of the Megarians was proverbial, and a "Megarian ruse" was quite the reverse of subtle.[71] However, the palm for lumpenness unquestionably went to the Boeotians (and continued to do so even for moderns), for everyone knew that a Boeotian was bound to be a lout. Abbé Barthélemy suggested that the difference between the "pure" air of Attica and the exceedingly "thick" air of Boeotia might have something to do with it, although it might be more a matter of education. If the Boeotians "seem heavy and stupid, that is because they are ignorant and uncouth: as they spend more time on physical exercises than on exercising their minds, they have neither a talent for speech, nor the graces of elocution, nor the enlightenment that stems from an acquaintance with literature, nor the attractive kind of appearance that is produced more by art than by nature".[72] So the cause must be their thick, stodgy nature (a matter quite different from leading a simple life in accordance with nature).

However, the ancient evidence for the stupidity of the Boeotians is neither very rich nor very full. Pausanias, in whose footsteps Barthélemy usually follows, says not a word about it. On the contrary, a visitor to the region is encouraged to imagine the erstwhile splendours of Orchomenus and the treasury of Minyas, to meditate before the statue of Epaminondas, which testifies to the lost autonomy and liberty of Greece, and to deplore the "savage" manoeuvres of Sulla at Thebes. Besides, Boeotia certainly did not produce solely imbeciles, for it was the native land of the like of Hesiod, Pindar and Plutarch, all men with impeccable credentials, not to mention the Theban Oedipus, a great solver of riddles if ever there was one, and quite a few others!

Herodotus, despite being taken to task by Plutarch for having systematically denigrated the Boeotians, does mention their "Medism" at the time of the Persian invasion of Greece, but never suggests that they are stupid. Polybius, a historian preoccupied with dates, makes the onset of their decadence coincide with their famous victory over the Spartans at Leuctra, in 371. From then on, "abandoning themselves to good cheer and strong drink sapped the energy not only of their bodies but of their minds".[73]

In Aristophanes' *Acharnians*, the Theban who arrives to do business in the private market opened by Dicaeopolis is addressed simply as "little Boeotian, eater of round barley loaves".[74] In truth he brings with him all kinds of victuals; but apparently only the eels from Lake Copais prove to be a sought-after delicacy. In exchange, Dicaeopolis provides him with a typically Athenian product that has not yet made its way to Boeotia: a sycophant, carefully packaged.[75] This particular scene is set within the limits of an honest rusticity!

Here and there however, more radical judgements are passed upon the IQ of the Boeotians. Plutarch reports: "It is a fact that the Athenians used to call us Boeotians beef-witted and insensitive and foolish, precisely because we stuffed ourselves".[76] That is also his explanation for the proverb that he goes on to cite, which refers to "Boeotian swine". The expression is attested in various collections of proverbs and appears in exactly the same form in the work of another Boeotian, Pindar: " ... if we escape the age-old taunt of 'Boeotian swine' ", he writes in the sixth *Olympian*.[77] A scholium to this line explains it as a pun on *hus* or *sus* (pig) and *Hyantes*, the name of an ancient people of Boeotia.[78] So this may have been an ancient joke that even Pindar no longer understood, reinterpreted in the light of history, the local diet, or the climate. " 'Boeotian swine' were people who were insensitive and uneducated" is the gloss provided in another corpus of texts.[79] As the embodiment of grunting stupidity, a pig (or sow) is present in another proverb, which is based on an association of two extremes: "The sow corrects Athena", it states.[80] Other proverbs, similarly founded upon the interplay of assonances, repeatedly stigmatized Boeotian stupidity: *Boiôtios nous*, "Boeotian wit"; *Boôn ôta echete*, "you have ox-ears" or, as we might say "cloth-ears", completely unreceptive.[81] References to pigs, it should be said, are widely dispersed: Apollonius of Tyana, when accused of sacrificing a newborn Arcadian child, would later jeer at the "pigs of Arcadia", to draw attention to the primitive way of life of the inhabitants of that region.[82]

As well as diet, the climate was sometimes blamed for the rusticity of the Boeotian peasant. As the treatise *Airs, Waters, Places* explains:

> Where the land is rich, soft and well-watered, and the water is very near the surface, so as to be hot in summer and cold in winter, and if the situation be favourable as regards the seasons, there the inhabitants are fleshy, ill-articulated, moist, lazy, and generally cowardly in character. Slackness and sleepiness can be observed in them, and as far as the arts are concerned, they are thick-witted, and neither subtle nor sharp.[83]

Reinterpreted by Michelet, no doubt via Abbé Barthélemy, this was to become: "Alongside the fertile but stupid Boeotia we find the sterile but brilliant Attica .... A Boeotian simply stepped from his hovel into his field. An

Athenian went off across the seas to find whatever was lacking to his needs".[84] Hence the lure, for Athenians, of the open sea and distant voyages!

FROM THE *IDIÔTÊS* TO THE IDIOT

While stupidity, embodied in the features of the country bumpkin, was becoming politicized, one other term sometimes crops up within the same field: *idiôtês*, which, via the Latin *idiota*, eventually produced the modern word "idiot". Initially *idiôtês* designated an ordinary individual as opposed to one who, within the city context, was elected to a responsible post or allocated it by lot. *Idiôtês* meant, not an inadequate man, but just an ordinary citizen, an unexceptional individual (or, equally, a private soldier as opposed to a general). To this first meaning of the word a second was later added: that of someone who was a layman and ignorant as opposed to a man with special skills who, thanks to learning and experience, *knew*.[85] In Menander's *Woman of Samos*, one character is insulted as a "wretched ignoramus" (*athlios idiôtês*).[86]

A number of shifts of meaning occurred between ignorance and "political simplicity", so that in the long run *idiôtês* came to express political and social inferiority.[87] And eventually the lexicographers defined the meaning as not just an ordinary citizen, but rather a man who was, quite simply, not a citizen at all.[88] The word "idiot" was now depoliticized. As to its other meaning, that of ignorance, this came to mean in particular ignorance of the field of letters. An *idiôtês* became someone who could neither read or write, an *illiteratus*, a meaning that medieval Latin was to retain, setting up an opposition between the cleric or clerk and the idiot.

However, that exclusion was on occasion reversed, at least in the Christian tradition: certain figures were described as the idiots (either male or female) or the friends or fools of God, such as those who appeared in Egypt in the fourth century AD. Faced with one such woman, who had been rejected by her convent, a passing holy man fell upon his knees.[89] Such stories of "idiots" or "fools" were to circulate and move northward, eventually setting on stage the figure of the *idiotus*, who was at once illiterate yet enlightened. Although never formally recognized theologically, he sometimes turned out to be the one person imbued with true knowledge.[90]

For obvious reasons, the Greek city was never able to engineer such a reversal. Nor, even temporarily or exceptionally, did it turn "idiocy" into knowledge that far exceeded that of the most learned of doctors. Even when the whole of knowledge was reduced to proving that those who think they know in reality do not, such reversals could take effect only starting from a position of *sophia*. At no point did the *agroikos* become the bearer of a message or the repository of a truth. The only *idiot* that the city did produce and set on stage was the Cynic philosopher. Anacharsis, the "Persian", the outsider who was inside, was to some degree able to play this role, being a *sophos* in the ancient meaning of the term, an itinerant purveyor of knowledge, and also in the new sense of the expression, a man from the margins and a man of nature.

The bearded Cynic philosopher, clad in a short cloak and equipped with a pouch and a staff, was represented as a beggar, living from hand to mouth, with no fixed abode or country: a traveller wishing to live "in accordance with nature".[91] Unlike Odysseus' companions, bewitched by Circe and enslaved by pleasure, such a man knew how to say no. Yet, for him, animals were a constant point of reference if not a model. Diogenes, setting himself to learn from such men, and gladly accepting "dog" as his nickname, relearned how to eat raw food and went so far as not to reject even the idea of cannibalism. He was said, purely to set an example and not without misgivings, even to have eaten a raw octopus. Plutarch ironically comments that "just like Pelopidas, for the liberty of the Thebans, or Harmodius and Aristogiton, for that of the Athenians, this philosopher risked his life struggling with a raw octopus, in order to 'brutalize' our lives".[92] Such were the grandeur and decadence of Greece!

The city had banished savagery to beyond its walls. By aping the beasts, the Cynics reintroduced it, but did so in the name of nature. It was no longer because, as in the world of Homeric epithets, animals were purely cultural and abstract concepts. On the contrary, it was because animals lived totally according to nature (even if this nature was no less a fiction than that culture had been). It was now not a matter of comparison and blazons, but rather of imitation. From a strategic point of view, the important thing was to challenge the city, its *nomoi* and the shares that it allotted: the "political animal" was portrayed as leading an artificial and depraved life. In the view of a Cynic, an animal was vastly superior to a man: it possessed nothing and knew how to be content with what nature provided. Yet at the same time it was close to the gods, for they likewise were not prey to any need. Not for a moment did this challenge in any way appeal to the attraction or appearance of the savage inside the city (the *agroikos*). Instead, it played the card of animality and publicized itself through the figure of the beggar, who, like Diogenes in his barrel, was rather part and parcel of the urban landscape. Occasionally it also claimed to be influenced by the "outsider inside", that convenient citizen-nomad, Anacharsis. The important thing was to keep the matter between citizens.

The *agroikos* was certainly ruled out as a model, given that, as was common knowledge, he was ignorant and lacking in any kind of education. The Cynic philosopher, in contrast, justified his position on the grounds of knowledge to which he overtly laid claim. He was the one who knew what to do and what to say in life.[93] He never tired of scoffing at the ignorance of the Greeks and criticizing the absence of any true education.[94] It was even in the name of his "knowledge" that he could rebut the accusation of madness that was frequently flung at him. Plato is said to have described Diogenes as "Socrates gone mad".[95] He was just the man to ignite the madness of all those little political animals, "drunken as they were and crazed by reason of ignorance (*agnoia*) and stupidity (*amathia*)".[96] He might act stupid and mad, the better to show up the madness and ignorance of the Greeks, but in truth he was neither stupid nor mad. The beggar's disguise, like that of Odysseus in the midst of the suitors, hid a veritable king.

THE REVENGE OF CIRCE'S PIG

In a prolongation of the Cynic movement, but reviewed and emended by the intellectual world of the Second Sophistic, the episode of Odysseus and Circe makes its last appearance. This time, the issue is not pleasures and how to master them, but rather involves a plea in favour of the animal condition. This might well have been entitled *The revenge of Circe's pig*! But the actual title of this treatise is *On the use of reason (logos) by brutish animals*. Opposing Aristotle, who had denied that animals had any access to *logos*, Plutarch the Platonist argues that the animal life is superior and suggests a (reversed) replay of the scene on Circe's island.[97] Before taking his leave, Odysseus, as ever preoccupied with his own reputation, tries to persuade Circe to return to their original condition the Greeks she has transformed. But the interested parties rebel: under no circumstances do they wish to follow Odysseus. Instead, they invite him to become a pig like themselves.

This first reversal is complemented by another. Mention has been made above of the proverbs featuring "Boeotian swine" and "the sow who wants to correct Athena". Plutarch now sets on stage three characters: Circe, Odysseus and Gryllus. Who on earth is Gryllus? A Boeotian, precisely, whose very name suggests "pig" (*grulos* or *grullos* means "pig")! So here is a *triple* Boeotian pig, arguing with and getting the better of the man whose *mêtis* owes so much to the vigilant protection of Athena. The lesson he teaches Athena could hardly be more direct. And through his revenge, the Boeotians as a whole get their own back on their detractors.

In this Platonic-style dialogue Odysseus is eventually overcome by the pig, who is by far the better "sophist". Although he starts off as the Odysseus who is so full of intelligence and knowledge, soon he is being treated with irony and condescension by his animal interlocutor and, towards the end of the dialogue, the tone of "*O Beltiste*", "my good fellow" (which any reader of Plato immediately recognizes), is not far off the Homeric *nêpios*, "poor fool". The treatise is a variation on the theme of the superiority of the animal condition over the human one, argued on the strength of the excellence of life lived according to nature. In every domain – be it courage, desire, temperance or even intelligence – *phusis* is always better than any learned, external rule, which human beings both need and yet are incapable of not transgressing. In the very face of Odysseus, who, by this time, must be feeling pretty "stupid", Gryllus-the-pig constructs his eulogy of animality.

SEVENTH-DAY TRAGEDIANS

While Boeotians, close neighbours of the Athenians, seem more or less stuck with the image of rusticity, a more distant population had the rare privilege of being associated with both stupidity and madness: the inhabitants of Abdera, a town situated in Thrace. The Abderites were not Thracians, a people never particularly noted for their cleverness, but Ionians who had emigrated from Teos in Asia Minor.[98] At first sight, Abdera does not look at all like a refuge for the mentally retarded, since it produced, among others, Democritus, Protagoras, his pupil, and, somewhat later, Hecataeus, whom we have repeatedly encountered in Egypt. Yet the Abderites possessed a well-established (if relatively meagrely attested) reputation for stupidity or madness, or both. Democritus is thus regarded as the exception who proves that it is not impossible for a great mind to be born in a land of fools under a "thick sky".[99] For Cicero, the very name "Abderites" signified stupidity.[100] An allusion in Demosthenes' works shows that it was a reputation that was already widely known in the fourth century BC.[101]

Six centuries later, Lucian paints a strange picture of the Abderites suffering from an unprecedented affliction:

> The people of Abdera were smitten by an epidemic. These were its symptoms: at first every one of them fell ill of a fever, violent and obstinate ...; about the seventh day it was broken ...; but their minds were left in a ridiculous state;

they all went mad with tragedy, shouting iambics and creating a din; and they mostly sang solos from Euripides' *Andromeda* ...; the city was full of these seventh-day tragedians, all pale and thin, roaring ... in a loud voice, hour after hour, day after day, until winter and a severe cold spell stopped their noise.[102]

Lucian attributed the responsibility for all this to a famous actor who had visited Abdera at the height of summer and had given a performance of *Andromeda*. Stupidity or madness? *Docti certant* (the learned dispute). Pierre Bayle thus comments as follows: "I am of the strong opinion that the ravages caused by the actor and the sun to the minds of the Abderites were not so much a mark of stupidity as of vivacity; but they were still a mark of weakness".

As is testified by Bayle's copious article, which recapitulates the interpretations produced by a whole string of other writers, the moderns were very interested in the Abderites, or rather in the question of whether they were stupid or mad, or more mad than stupid: Erasmus, (who even coined the expression *Abderitica mens*), Isaac Vossius (who produced a defence of the Abderites, maintaining that their madness was too sophisticated to have afflicted uncouth people), and Moreri, who raised the matter in his *Dictionary* (and whom Bayle criticized for having understood virtually nothing) were the leading figures in that list. And then there was Bayle himself, who reported, criticized and argued, but certainly took the case seriously.

The story of the Abderites then continued in Germany, under the pen of Christoph Martin Wieland, a good scholar of antiquity and a translator of, in particular, Lucian. In 1773, Wieland published a comic novel entitled *The Abderites*. Picking up the episode recounted by Lucian, the book made fun of the madness, stupidity, vanity and mediocrity of ordinary men. Abdera may have disappeared from the map, but the Abderites, or rather their descendants, are certainly still alive and are to be found wherever one turns, ever true to themselves. By virtue of the *de te fabula narratur* ("this story is about *you*"), their story presents a faithful mirror in which the moderns cannot fail to recognize themselves. To cure the epidemic unleashed by the *Andromeda*, they summon Hippocrates, who can do nothing for them, as there are no worse patients than those who refuse to accept that they are sick. He tells them that only the philosopher Democritus, whom they have long since ejected from their city, might be able to cure them if they placed themselves in his hands.

It was possibly via this philosophical tale that, in 1798, the behaviour of the Abderites, labelled *Abderitism*, found its way into a completely different kind of text: *The Conflict of the Faculties*, the last work published by Kant.

It appears in the second section of the book, which poses the question of whether the human race is making constant (moral) progress and is improving. One answer to that would be that, on the contrary, it is perpetually regressing and becoming worse and worse. Kant calls this "a terrorist conception of the history of the human race". According to a second (in truth, "indefensible") view, it is "constantly progressing toward the best possible end". Kant calls this "Eudaemonist". The third answer is "Abderitism". Since this concludes that, all in all, the state of the human race is stationary (a combination of advances and regressions) and expresses the "busy foolishness" that characterizes our species, Kant surmises that it may well win "the majority of votes". Not his, however:

> The entire interplay of mutual exchanges between members of our species should be considered purely as a game of puppets. So, from the point of view of reason, it confers no greater value upon the human race than upon other species of animals, which practise such amusements at lower cost and without expending any intelligence.[103]

Thanks to its story being transmitted by Lucian, distant Abdera becomes a signifier that raises the question of the respective lots of humans and animals, the frontier that separates them, and the general exercise of reason.

THE LIMITS OF ARCADIA

Arcadia was hard to reach, but a region that every traveller in search of a Greek identity was in duty bound to visit. For Pausanias, who undertook to explore it, it was to represent a key experience. In the first place, it meant travelling back through time almost as far as the very beginnings when frontiers and allotted roles were still undefined. The very ground seemed somehow to slip away beneath a walker's feet. Yet it was here that a way suddenly opened up to reach the most ancient, and hence the most authentic, Greece.

"Arcadia occupies the centre of the Peloponnese. Soaring above the regions that surround it, it bristles with mountains, some being of a prodigious height and almost all inhabited by wild animals and covered with forests". Those are the introductory words to the younger Anacharsis' tour of Arcadia. The narrator goes on as follows:

> This country is an endless series of pictures where nature has deployed its grandiose and fertile ideas and which it has put together haphazardly, with no

regard for genre differences ... How many times, upon reaching the top of a lowering mountain, have we seen lightning snaking away below! And how many times, pausing up there in the skies, have we suddenly beheld the daylight darkening, the air thickening and violently agitated, presenting us with a spectacle as beautiful as it was terrifying! Those torrents of mist swirling rapidly beneath our eyes and falling upon the deep valleys, those mountain torrents plunging and roaring into the abyss, those great mountain masses which, through the thick fluid that surrounded us, seemed draped in black, the funereal cries of the birds, the plaintive murmur of the wind and the trees: this was the underworld of Empedocles.[104]

The Abbé really does surpass himself – particularly considering that he himself had never visited Greece and his guide, Pausanias, was anything but a landscape artist. This Arcadia, already a romantic conception, proceeding from the picturesque to the sublime, in truth owes everything to the landscape theories of his own day.[105] As for the elder Anacharsis, he never did walk along the paths of Arcadia.

For the Greeks, mountainous, desolate Arcadia, at the heart of the Peloponnese, was above all an extremely ancient land, a world from before the present one.[106] Its inhabitants were commonly called "pre-lunar", the very epithet that Aristophanes uses for Strepsiades. People of the black night, before the world was set in place, before night was separated from day, close to the giants and antedating the order imposed by Zeus, they were there before time itself, since the moon is fundamental to its organization.

Not only were they very ancient; they were also autochthonous; born from the earth itself and always present in the same place, never, even for a short time, straying from their own land.[107] In Thucydides' picture of the earliest times in Greece, they, like the Athenians and for the same reasons, represented exceptions. Other populations were constantly on the move, prone to internal *stasis* and vulnerable to attacks from others, always seeking new lands and as yet incapable of accumulating and storing possessions. But meanwhile the Arcadians, because of the aridity of their territory, knew nothing of all those movements and migrations.[108] That was the Thucydidean version of autochthony. But from that moment on the destinies of the two groups of autochthonous people diverged. In the case of the Athenians, that initial poverty was converted into a strength, for Attica offered itself as a land that welcomed refugees, and the latter flocked to swell the number of its citizens.[109] Athenian autochthony was a sign of special election and a promise of power (*dunamis*). In contrast, at least in the view of other Greeks, autochthony never did anything for the Arcadians except perpetuate their poverty and isolation. They remained cut off, trapped in their mountains and in a *cold* time of stagnation: Greeks, but not really living in the time of the Greeks.

Pausanias, a rather uneasy archaeologist who, seven centuries later, explored this time-capsule of a world that the Greeks had long since lost, was told by the Arcadians that "Pelasgus was the first inhabitant of this land". As the poet Asius put it: "The godlike Pelasgus on the wooded mountains / Black earth gave up, that the race of mortals might exist".[110] Truly an autochthonous being and the ancestor of the future Arcadians, Pelasgus, according to the same tradition, was also a civilizing hero: he invented the hut, and clothing in the form of goat-skins, and changed his subjects from herbivores into acorn-eaters, *Balanêphagoi*, as they were frequently called.[111]

For Greek anthropology, the consumption of acorns implied a diet, a mode of life and a social and political state that antedated the invention of the "fruits of Demeter". The age of the oak tree was followed by the "life of milled wheat", which established the major features of the human condition and the divisions and lots apportioned to human beings, nature, the animals and the gods.[112] Of course, that change of diet could equally well be considered as a regression, and the slogan "Enough of the oak tree" as the end of the carefree frugality of the Golden Age and the beginning of the decadence of the human race. That is the position adopted by Dicaearchus in his work entitled *The Life of Greece* and also by the advocates of a return to the life "of the past" or according to nature. The pastoral way of life and then, even more, agriculture ushered in the misfortunes associated with human property, conflict and warfare.[113]

According to the tradition recorded by Pausanias, in Arcadia that switch occurred only in the fourth generation after Pelasgus. It was Arcas who "introduced the cultivation of crops, which he learnt from Triptolemus, and taught men to make bread, to weave clothes, and other things besides".[114] It was with him that the country, changing its name from Pelasgia to Arcadia, truly entered the world of "men who eat bread". However, in Arcadia, unlike elsewhere, that progress does not seem to have been irreversible. On the contrary, it remained tentative, virtually conditional, for any remissiveness or any transgression where the gods were concerned could, and sometimes did, call the whole existing situation into question.

Arcadia not only virtually preceded the rest of the world but was also a world apart, with its own divine and human genealogies. The whole space was saturated with vestiges, ruins, and the remains of *logoi* that were only linked together thanks to the enquiries of Pausanias, who, pressing indefatigably on from one stopping place to the next, assembled them all together. Divine, heroic and even funerary geographies were set alongside one another.

Most of all, Arcadia provided evidence of a world prior to the great dividing lines, when boundaries were still uncertain and unstable. Lycaon, the son of Pelasgus, was a civilizing hero. He founded the first town and organized the Lycaean Games. But he was also the first to have the idea of sacrificing a human being to Zeus Lykaios: "Lycaon brought a human baby to the altar of Lycaean Zeus, and sacrificed it, pouring out its blood upon the altar and, according to the legend, immediately after the sacrifice he was changed from a man to a wolf".[115] Meanwhile, according to Pausanias, Cecrops, his Athenian contemporary, was for his part deciding to honour Zeus on High not with the sacrifice of anything living, but with an offering of cakes. From those opposite sacrificial choices made, respectively, by two different but equally autochthonous figures, there then stemmed two completely divergent histories. The one had opted for "pure" sacrifice, the other for "murder" in a most extreme form. The Athenians subsequently became the civilized people *par excellence*, whereas the human identity of the Arcadians remained forever uncertain and threatened. Alongside the story of Lycaon, the wolf, who became exactly what his name proclaimed him to be, there were many other wolf stories. A certain Demaenetus, "after consuming the entrails of a sacrificed child, found himself changed into a wolf", but ten years later he recovered his human form. Another Arcadian, after being singled out by lot, was led to a lake. He hung his clothes on a tree, swam across it, and changed into a wolf. It was said that if he abstained from eating human beings for nine years, he would be able to return to the lake, swim back across it, and recover both his human form and his clothes.[116]

When Apollonius of Tyana was brought before Domitian, he was accused, among other crimes, of having slaughtered an Arcadian child and dabbled his hands in its blood, praying to the gods to reveal the truth to him – him who, as a disciple of Pythagoras and the Gymnosophists, had never before even approached an altar for blood-sacrifices! This story constitutes a distorted echo of Lycaon's sacrifice: it does not state that the Arcadians sacrificed children, but rather that, in the event of anyone wanting to sacrifice a child, he would choose an Arcadian one. Although Apollonius refutes the accusation, he nevertheless recalls to mind the traditional portrait of the Arcadians: "The Arcadians are not so much wiser than other Hellenes that their entrails should convey more bowel-lore than those of other people. On the contrary, they are the most boorish of men, and resemble hogs in other ways and especially in this, that they can stomach acorns".[117] This scene also shows that the Greeks continued to regard their Arcadia as a wild land, even though the Romans, ever since Virgil, had been imagining and celebrating a quite different Arcadia.

Lycaon, the Wolf, had a daughter, Callisto, the Most Beautiful One, who was marked by a similar instability. According to the tradition, because she was loved by Zeus, she was turned into a bear by Hera, was then killed by Artemis, and was finally changed into a constellation. Nevertheless, the Arcadians continued to show visitors her tomb, which Pausanias himself had seen.[118] Conversely, some Arcadian animals were possibly not completely animal. The famous birds of Lake Stymphalus, killed or hunted by Heracles, were said to be "man-eaters" and furthermore to possess beaks so hard that they could pierce bronze and to use their feathers as arrows, like so many archers.[119] As for the gods of Arcadia, they too sometimes made themselves known in animal forms: Pan, who reigned over the country's mountains, was half-goat, half-man; the Demeter of Phigalia was represented with the head of a horse; while Artemis Eurynome was half-woman, half-fish.[120]

In yet another register, in Arcadia the separation between earth and water did not appear to be either clear or definitive. A plain could be at one moment parched, the next transformed into a veritable lake. It is true that the karst hills of Arcadia contained a whole subterranean network of waterways that would collect in one spot, then disappear through a *chasma* or fissure, to resurface further on in the form of springs. One and the same space could change from being arid to being flooded – the Argon ("sterile") plain, for example, or the region of Pheneus, which was improved by Heracles.[121]

Finally, the division between the world Above and the world Below was not completely hard and fast, for close to the town of Nonacris there was a high cliff, from which flowed a deadly poisonous torrent of water, identified as water from the Styx.[122] This deadly water was counterbalanced, in the neighbourhood of Cynaetha, by a beneficent spring called Alyssus, the water that cured madness.[123]

When the Arcadians forgot the rites and neglected the Artemis of Stymphalus, she wasted no time in reminding them of herself, by allowing the plain to become a lake. And so it remained until a hunter in pursuit of his prey disappeared into the lake and unblocked the outflow channel (which was obstructed by a tree-trunk). Once the plain had dried out and the lesson had been well and truly learned, the Arcadians resumed the celebrations of the goddess's festival with much greater zeal. But Artemis, the goddess of wild space, who delights in mountains and marshes, was always prepared to cancel her concessions. Once again she turned this space from which she had withdrawn into a wilderness before finally resolving the crisis by accepting both animal and human sacrificial victims. Whether in a beneficent or a vengeful mood, she never hesitated to move the boundary lines where she exerted her control over the division between wildness and civilization.[124]

In symmetrical fashion, when those same Arcadians, who certainly were very unreliable and forgetful, neglected the black Demeter of Phigalia, she reacted, not by changing the very nature of the space, but by afflicting the region with barrenness (*akarpia*). Their mistake had been virtually to cease offering her the first fruits that were her due. In their distress, the Arcadians went to consult the Pythia, who appears to have relished underlining their peculiarly precarious position:

> Azanian Arcadians, acorn-eaters, who dwell
> In Phigaleia, the cave that hid Deo, who bore a horse,
> You have come to learn a cure for grievous famine,
> Who alone have twice been nomads, alone have twice lived on wild fruits.
> It was Deo who made you cease from pasturing, Deo who made you
> pasture again,
> After being binders of corn and eaters of cakes,
> Because she was deprived of privileges and ancient honours given by men
> of former times.
> And soon she will make you eat each other and feed on your children,
> Unless you appease her anger with many libations offered by all your
> people,
> And adorn with divine honours the nook of the cave.[125]

Needless to say, the people of Phigalia needed no second telling by this remarkably clear oracle, which warned them of a possible return to total savagery, and they hastened to honour the goddess as they should.

Despite the fact that the Arcadians are no longer acorn-eaters, as Demeter has turned them into eaters of cakes, they are constantly in peril of reverting to their former state and again being true to the name or nickname that the Pythia gives them. And just beyond such regression stalks the threat of cannibalism and feasts in which the shared flesh would be that of their children. For the age of acorns was also the age of the monstrous sacrifice perpetrated by Lycaon. If they revert to acorns, they will also repeat that murder, and once again will be wolves.

Savagery, in all its forms, is clearly a feature of the Arcadian scene, where it is forever lurking. That point is made, in the second century BC, by an authentic Arcadian, Polybius, a native of Megalopolis.[126] He provides us with a chance to see the Arcadians through Arcadian eyes. What this shows is that while the rest of the Greeks regard the Arcadians both as Greeks and as "others", the Arcadians see themselves as excellent Greeks who, however, in the north of their country themselves have to cope with their own others, savages, as neighbours: these are the Cynaetheans.

Polybius deems it indispensable to devote a digression to this undeniable problem. Among other Greeks, the Arcadians are well known for their *philoxenia* (hospitality), *philanthropia* (humanity) and *eusebeia* (piety). But the Cynaetheans, for their part, are – alas – famous for their "savagery" (*agriotês*) yet they are incontestably Arcadians. So the question is, how is this possible? Why is it that "they finally became so savage that in no city of Greece were greater and more frequent crimes committed"? The climatic theory and the interaction of the *phusis/nomos* pair provide a rational explanation. In respect of both its climate and its geography, Arcadia is a "harsh" (*sklêros*), "cold", "gloomy" country, so its inhabitants, through imitation (*sunexomoiousthai*), adapted to those conditions and naturally (*phusikôs*) have within them a hard, withdrawn, austere and at the same time touchy element. In particular, they are extremely attached to their liberty.

To cope with this situation, the Arcadians of the past had the idea of a *nomos* which would both adapt to and counteract that *phusis*: namely, music. While music is "useful" for all human beings, it is "essential" for all Arcadians. Conceived as an education, or even as a strict training (*agôgê*), it was obligatory for all young people up to the age of thirty.[127] Through practising it, they learnt not "softness", but the rhythm of military marches, the movements of dancing, and the asceticism of order (*taxis*). By disciplining their bodies, they made them supple, counteracting their natural stiffness and making them sociable. It also cultivated them by teaching them about the national gods and heroes. Through competitions, music replaced rivalry by emulation. It was thus a factor of sociability and created social bonds. It changed the Arcadian *autourgoi* into *politai*. In short, it politicized them. Basically, it made it possible for these "tamed" (*exêmeroun*) or "civilized" Arcadians to acknowledge themselves to be Arcadians, and so to be fully Greek.

Now, it was precisely those who lived in the harshest (*sklêrotaton*) climatic and geographic conditions who most imperatively needed music yet who neglected it. As a result, they soon regressed into savagery. Once the constraint of *nomos* was abolished, the social bond was broken; and the Cynaetheans no longer behaved as human beings but as beasts.[128] Polybius writes of "great massacres", cruelty and bestiality, and the worst acts of impiety ever seen in Greece.[129] The situation grew so bad that any Cynaethean became a walking defilement in the eyes of the other Arcadians: it was not even possible to receive their ambassadors, and wherever they had passed, the roads had to be purified.

The Cynaetheans who forgot that music was their very first need thus became the exception that proved the rule. By means of this digression, Polybius, who at a stroke exempted and rescued the rest of the Arcadians, confirmed their excellent Greek credentials. But even when an Arcadian spoke of other Arcadians, he could never avoid the theme of savagery, which was always there beneath the surface, repressed, but always ready to erupt again if his attention was relaxed. He coped with that threat by localizing it (in the North) and defused it by explaining it, not mythically (it was all the fault of Lycaon), but scientifically (a disruption of the *nomos/phusis* relationship).

IN THE STEPS OF PAUSANIAS

But Megalopolis, the Great City, was now reduced to a "great desert", and in the countryside laid waste by too many wars, horses and donkeys were left to graze. Strabo, whose tour of the Peloponnese ended with Arcadia, saluted it but then promptly departed: "The Arcadian peoples ... are reputed to be the most ancient tribes of the Greeks. But on account of the complete devastation of the country it would be inappropriate to speak at length about these peoples".[130] For an Augustan geographer who viewed the world from the standpoint of Rome, there was hardly anything left to see there and little to be said about it.

However, Pausanias, the Greek traveller of the Antonine period, found plenty there both to see and to say. And even more upon which to ponder. He was a Greek from Asia (from the region of Mount Sipylus, in Lydia), born in about 115 AD. He finished composing his *Periêgêsis* of Greece between 175 and 180. He had the financial means to travel (and in those days they had to be considerable) and visited Asia Minor, Rome and Southern Italy, and Egypt, to see its pyramids and the colossus of Memnon.[131] But his intellectual purpose was not to write a description of the world. The journey that mattered most to him was the voyage through Greece, which inevitably also became a voyage *about* Greece. For anyone who knows how to see the Cyclopean walls of Tiryns, now forgotten and in ruins, and how to make them speak, they have more to say than the pyramids of Egypt, which have so often been described but which represent only one half of the map of curiosities offered by the empire. The stones of Tiryns murmur of the history of a Greece long gone, which, however, had created Greece and once *was* Greece.

Herodotus declared, "I shall proceed in my history, telling the story as I go along of small cities no less than great". The expression "cities" was a direct echo of the *Odyssey*, in which Odysseus "wandered for many years, seeing many cities". But Herodotus had added two stipulations, which introduce us into a different intellectual world: he wanted to visit cities "small no less than great", and he wished to do so "*homoiôs*", respecting their parity, for those cities were no longer what once they were: the large ones had shrunk and those that were now great used to be small. To speak solely of those that were now great or solely of those that used to be great would not be to proceed *homoiôs*. Herodotus was an Odysseus fighting against time or striving to apprehend it, to render it visible, to arrest it by fixing it between those two boundaries of the "great" and the "small".[132]

Pausanias set himself the task of writing "a general description of Greece", paying attention to all things Greek.[133] The similarity of the terms used cannot be fortuitous, nor can the differences. Now it is a matter of visiting not the cities of men, but only the world of the Greeks. The element of time, whether connected with the distance between and reversal of what is great and what is small or not, has altogether disappeared. These "Greek things" are, it would seem, ageless: they were there yesterday and are still there today. However, two requirements are spelt out. One is the old, Herodotean insistence on proceeding even-handedly, *homoiôs*; the other, which is new, is exhaustivity. The aim is to say everything, describe everything, giving equal consideration to everything (*panta homoiôs*). But how can a traveller possibly reconcile those two requirements, exhaustivity and parity? He must not do things by halves, nor must he wander off into digressions, and above all he must exercise choice: record everything to do with Greece, yes, but only those things that "deserve to be remembered".

For this operation, Pausanias has at his disposal a category that had long since proved its usefulness, the category of what is "notable", with all its gradations, ranging from "what is worth recording" to "what is most worth recording".[134] Whatever is notable is also memorable. "Those, in my view, are the most famous things" is how Pausanias rounds off his description of Attica. In similar fashion, before embarking on his description of Sparta, he thinks it useful to remind the reader of the general rule by which he abides: only to record the traditions most worthy of being recorded.[135] In what does that which is most notable consist? In words that have been heard (or read) and things that have been seen: "There are many other things to be seen among the Greeks, and many others that deserve to be admired when one hears of them".[136] On the one hand there is that which is said (*logoi*), on the other that which the eye of a traveller may seize upon (*theôrêmata*). Clearly, in this Greek voyage, an eye without words would often be blind, possibly passing over what needed to be seen or not even realizing what it was that it was seeing. However, words on their own, digression after digression (*epeisodion*), would lead the traveller astray. Whatever catches his eye or requires his attention in the course of his travels functions as a recall to order, a principle of classification and for the selection of the right words, and also an incitement to respect the rule of "even-handedness" inherited from Herodotus.[137]

In Pausanias' *Journey through Greece*, Arcadia represents an important moment. It presents an opportunity not only for questioning a number of accepted beliefs, but also for acquiring a better understanding of Greek *sophia*. Up until this point, Pausanias had dismissed as "naive" a number of stories that had been reported to him. But here, in the heart of the Peloponnese, he became convinced that behind the obvious meaning there might lie a hidden second meaning which it was important to decipher. For "those who were called sages did not express themselves clearly, but only in riddles". The stories of Cronos devouring his own children belonged to this form of *sophia*.[138] All in all, there was no reason to believe that the ancient Greek wisdom was, structurally, any different from Barbarian, Egyptian or other wisdoms. In all cases, the revelation of meaning required some previous exegesis. Allegorization made it possible to transform what appeared to be naivety into profundity. Pausanias thus came to see Arcadia as a land that was not so much primitive or wild as primordial: an "enigmatic" land that needed to be deciphered, just as did the ancient *logoi* about it.

In the manner of a "road to Damascus" experience, Arcadia also convinced Pausanias that he should revise his "principle of things as they are".[139] Just because something is impossible today that does not mean that it was also impossible in the past. For example, the story of Lycaon turning into a wolf: "It has been a legend among Arcadians from of old and it has the additional merit of probability (*eikos*)". In those days frontiers were not altogether impassable: the gods and human beings could eat together; a good man could become a god or, on the contrary, if he committed an act of impiety, he might become an animal, as did Lycaon, or a stone, as did Niobe, the daughter of Tantalus. Everything happened quite openly. Today, however, Pausanias goes on to say, "wickedness" has increased so much and spread over the entire surface of the earth so that men no longer become gods (except according to the flatteries addressed to despots) and divine vengeance against criminals is not exercised until after their deaths.[140]

Strabo cited the ruined state of Megalopolis as an excuse for his not lingering there. But for Pausanias, who was passing through, it on the contrary inspired a meditation on the destiny of cities and the passing of time.

> Megalopolis was founded by the Arcadians with the utmost enthusiasm amidst the highest hopes of the Greeks, but it has lost all its beauty and its old prosperity, being today for the most part in ruins. I am not in the least surprised, as I know that heaven is always willing something new, and likewise that all things, strong or weak, increasing or decreasing, are being changed by Fortune, who drives them with imperious necessity according to her whim. For Mycenae, the leader of the Greeks in the Trojan War, and Nineveh, where was the royal palace of the Assyrians, are utterly ruined and desolate; while Boeotian Thebes, once deemed worthy to be the head of the Greek people, why, its name includes only the acropolis and its few inhabitants. Of the opulent places in the ancient world, Egyptian Thebes and Minyan Orchomenus are now less prosperous than a private individual of moderate means, while Delos, once the common market of Greece, has no Delian inhabitant, but only the men sent by the Athenians to guard the sanctuary. At Babylon the sanctuary of Belus is still left, but of Babylon that was the greatest city of its time under the sun nothing remains but the wall. The case of Tiryns in Argolis is the same. These places have been reduced by heaven to nothing. But the city of Alexander in Egypt, and that of Seleucus on the Orontes, that were founded but yesterday, have reached their present size and prosperity because fortune favours them . . . . So temporary and utterly weak are the fortunes of men.[141]

With these lines, which are unique in his work, Pausanias completes his reworking of Herodotus: this meditation on the ruins represents the latter's "cities great and small" and is Pausanias' way of introducing the element of time into "Greek things". The theme of the instability of all human things reappears, but whereas for Herodotus they changed from being great to being small and also from being small to being great, it would seem that now it was always a one-way change, from greatness to ruins. Pausanias was travelling through a landscape of ruins. He could almost be writing "Morea is deserted", as Chateaubriand was to in 1807. For Chateaubriand, the spectacle of solitude where "only dogs remain to greet you with their barking" distracted him from his "delightful memories". But Pausanias, for his part, concentrates all the harder on evoking and recording memories.[142] Minyas' Orchomenus and the walls of Tiryns, despite being represented as Greek "marvels" to rival the pyramids of Egypt, now offer the observer nothing but ruins to admire.[143] Without the stories about them, which enable the spectator to *see* them, they would be nothing but what they actually are: a few sections of tumbled-down walls.

By writing Greek stories down, Hecataeus of Miletus for the first time brought their multiplicity to light. The mirth that this occasioned pointed the way to sagacity, presenting a pressing invitation to sift and classify. Pausanias, for his part, found himself perpetually exposed to the multiplicity and variability of the same stories. Either he recorded the differences between one author and another, or he noted the inconsistencies between what he read in one or another author and what he was now being told. "The legends of Greece generally have different forms, and this is particularly true of genealogy".[144] But this observation does not imply any plan to reduce the differences or to choose between the variants. His book (described as a *suggraphê*) tends, on the contrary, to draw attention to this diversity. The traveller proceeds from one division (*moira*) to the next,[145] each time recording everything worth noting before moving on.

These inconsistencies or variants (*diaphorai*) possibly provide the most telling evidence of the Greek identity, a compound of commonly held culture and total autonomy. All the accounts feature the same gods, even the same stories about them, but each recounts them in its own particular way. Now (in Pausanias' day, that is) Greece was a province, but what was the basis of this administrative unification, if not its lost liberty? In the old days, as the inscription on the plinth of the statue of Epaminondas in Thebes proclaims, "the whole of Greece was autonomous in liberty".[146] In other words, it was full of conflicts. Autonomy and liberty went hand in hand: a city was truly free only if it was also autonomous. To try to turn a blind eye to the differences and reduce the inconsistencies between all these *logoi* would be to present a travesty of the real Greece of the past. That is why the *Periêgêsis* heads back in time, seeking a Greece long gone which, truth to tell, virtually never was, yet which, nevertheless, was Greece.

144

Like the voyage of the younger Anacharsis, that of Pausanias, the meticulous antiquarian, with his guidebook full of rather boring lists, incorporates a utopian dimension. From his tour of these places filled with memories, some of which live on for some people but which are deserted and forgotten by many others, and which the traveller sought to bring back to life, there sprang, at least within the space of time that it took to write about it, the utopia of the Greece which, enthusiastically and full of hope, founded Megalopolis and praised Epaminondas for restoring autonomy and liberty. In these nostalgia-filled pages, a utopian vision of classical Greece was formed, one which the moderns were to inherit.

Pausanias travelled "in order to see". He wanted to see what was no longer visible (now that Greece lay in ruins), but also to advance as far as the limits of visibility. Still in Arcadia, he pushed on to Phigalia, "above all for the sake of Demeter". But here there was no longer anything at all to see. The statue of the goddess no longer stood in the cave, and most of the Phigalians had never even heard of it. Only the very oldest of them remembered that, three generations before him, stones falling from the roof had crushed it. In fact, traces left by those fallen stones were still visible.[147] But in order to *see* that they were no longer in place, you had to have read the various relevant *logoi*, of which the *logos* of the old Phigalian was but the last link in the chain.

There are also things that one cannot see because they are reserved solely for initiates. In the sanctuary of Demeter on Mount Pron, not far from the town of Hermione, there was an annual sacrifice (in which old women acted as the sacrificers), which Pausanias describes. "But the thing itself that they worship more than all else, I never saw, nor yet has any other man, whether stranger or Hermionian".[148] Entering prohibited places, and seeing what it was forbidden to see, were as a general rule punished by the deity. Pausanias reports several such cases, in particular that of Aegyptus, who, having entered the forbidden sanctuary at Mantinea, lost his sight (and, later, his life).[149] Finally, there were the things that one had oneself seen, as an initiate, but that one could not talk about. For a non-initiate could not know of what he was forbidden to see. Thus Pausanias, himself an initiate in the mysteries of Eleusis, records a dream of his: "My dream forbade the description of the things within the wall of the sanctuary".[150] To see the invisible, or at least to approach it, to sense it, to make it perceptible, was certainly a deeply integral part of his enquiry, in fact of his pilgrimage.[151] It was in all these places where the sacred used to surface or still surfaced, either as an active principle, as at

Eleusis, or else simply in the form of a few traces, as in Phigalia, that the Greece that used to be could be "seen" and spoken of.

If Arcadia was a kind of "road to Damascus" for Pausanias, it certainly also was, at the end of the nineteenth century, for Victor Bérard. But whereas what Pausanias discovered there was the depth of the wisdom of the Greeks of the past who spoke in "riddles", Bérard, attentively reading Pausanias, found sure traces of the religion of the Phoenicians. Mount Lycaeum thus pointed him in the direction of Tyre! In his introduction to his thesis, published in 1897, he explains his position, one that was resolutely heretical in relation to the boundaries that the (German) science of antiquity had erected between Greece and the Semitic world. His travels and excavations in Arcadia had convinced him of, on the one hand, the scrupulous accuracy of Pausanias, who saw all that he described "with his own eyes", on the other the "difference that separated the Arcadian cults from the other, more strictly Hellenic, religions". Moreover, he got the feeling that Pausanias himself already had an "inkling" of this. "Zeus Lycaeus, with his child-sacrifices and his inviolable *temenos*, his tabernacle and his pillars, looked to me like a Semitic Baal. It seemed necessary to accept that his cult had come from a foreign land, probably Phoenicia".[152] The immediate objection was: how could this be? Phoenicians in the heart of the Peloponnese: surely not! Bérard's reply to this was to compare contemporary colonial ventures, in which plenty of Europeans were seen to go off "to the lands of Pelasgians no less distant or savage" and to throw themselves "into discovering African Arcadias". What Europeans were doing today, the Phoenicians of the past could equally well have done. But then another, graver, objection arose: but you are assimilating the ancient Pelasgians to the "modern Congolese"!

To this Bérard replied that we really should begin by shedding our "European chauvinism" and our "Hellenophile fanaticism". He then produced a spirited repudiation of the "Greek miracle". "We always trace Greek civilization back to the origins of history: it is as if this country one day suddenly emerged from the divine sea, complete with its towns, its temples, its helmeted hoplites, its robed orators, its Ionian women in their fine tunics, and, up there on the mountain-top, the assembly of its gods".[153] Yet, compared to "the Egyptians and the Semites", the Aryans were mere "savages": the material civilization of Greece "came from Phoenicia and from Egypt". As for the Pelasgians of Arcadia, they should be imagined as nice savages who had originally practised a "very simple" religion, which was subsequently

146

replaced by a Semitic one, organized around Zeus Lycaeus. Then, in the course of a third stage, the "workings of Greek rationalism" produced the anthropomorphic pantheon of the Arcadians.[154] There is every reason to believe that, before the Greek Mediterranean, there was a "Phoenician Mediterranean". That belief, initiated on the slopes of Mount Lycaeum, was by and large to determine the rest of Bérard's life and thought. Setting out to repeat Odysseus' voyages, he from then on continued to seek, behind Homer's text, for an earlier Phoenician *Odyssey*. Upstream from Odysseus there was a whole Phoenician wisdom, and the memory of Odysseus is also a Phoenician memory, the archaeologist of which Bérard passionately desired to be.

For Martin Bernal, an 1897 declaration of war upon the "Aryan model" such as this was both a god-sent surprise and a puzzle. How could Bérard's heresy be explained? By resorting to a rapid sociology of knowledge. A German Bérard would have been impossible and an English Bérard unlikely. But in France, in the aftermath of the 1870 war, in a republican and a native of the Jura to boot, who was not solely an academic, such an attitude became conceivable.[155] Without embarking upon a reconstruction of Bérard's multi-form career, it may also be supposed that it was this heretical choice of his that turned him into a somewhat marginal university professor. He certainly was opposed to Germany, but above all later on, when the 1914 war broke out. Meantime, he was content to cite, approvingly, F. Creuzer, who, in oppos-ition to "the exoticism of the Arcadian religion", was also of the opinion that "some colonist from Egypt or Phoenicia had introduced a more advanced culture into that rustic region".[156]

Making his way through Arcadia, Pausanias looked, listened and medi-tated. Faced with the enigmatic strangeness that many stories continued to breathe, he found a way through to the old wisdom of the Greeks, which said more than it seemed to be saying. By making sense of it, he preserved it. Its very strangeness became the mark of its authenticity. Plutarch had explained that the adventures of Isis and Osiris should not be taken at face value; and Pausanias discovered that no more should the cannibalistic meals of Cronos. Clasping his copy of Pausanias, Victor Bérard travelled and excavated in Arcadia. Struck by the "exoticism" of its religion, a vestige of pre-Hellenic times, he, for his part, was led to the East, that great manufacturer of reli-gions. "Asia relentlessly showers new religions upon Greece: like the waves of an incoming tide, century after century, we see them arriving, one after another, always gaining ground despite the resistance of the Hellenic mind".[157]

147

An enclave in the middle of the Peloponnese and completely surrounded by mountains though it was, Arcadia was also a place through which travellers passed. Odysseus was there. Once returned from Troy, he is supposed to have created a sanctuary on the frontier between Megalopolis and Tegea, in honour of Athena the Saviour and Poseidon. And in the region of Pheneus too, the people would draw attention to a statue of Poseidon, consecrated by Odysseus. Having set out to recover some horses that he had lost, he searched throughout Greece, and on the spot where he eventually found them he set up a sanctuary in honour of Artemis and also a statue consecrated to Poseidon Hippios.[158]

Even more importantly, Arcadia was also a point of departure, for, according to Dionysius of Halicarnassus, it was from the town of Pallantion that Arcadians, led by Evander, emigrated to Italy sixty years before the Trojan War. In this way, this ancient Arcadia came to establish a link between Rome and Greece and was even said to have provided the basis of Roman identity. The Arcadians settled on a hill not far from the Tiber, and called their settlement Pallantion, after their metropolis. They then "proceeded to adorn their town with all the buildings to which they had been accustomed at home and to erect temples", beginning with a temple to Pan Lycaeus (on the spot that the Romans later called Lupercal). With the passing of the years, Pallantion became Palatine.[159] When Pausanias visited the Arcadian Pallantion, he found there a temple consecrated to Evander and to Pallas (either a son or an ancestor of his). The emperor Antoninus, in memory of Evander, had conferred city status upon Pallantion and also freedom from taxation.[160] But that Evander, who was honoured by a cult, was more a Greek ancestor of the Romans than a Greek hero of ancient times. He may have returned to Arcadia from Rome. It was, at any rate, a way of showing that he really had left sixty years before the Trojan War.

Like all colonists, Evander took his cults with him, in particular the cult of Pan, the leaping god of the mountains of Arcadia. Ovid explains that that is why the Festival of the Lupercalia is still held, when Luperci are to be seen dashing naked around the Palatine. "The god himself loves to scamper, fleet of foot, about the high mountains . . . . He himself is nude and bids his ministers go nude". Ovid's explanation sheds some light upon this "exotic" ritual, in which the flamen of Jupiter played an important official part. It perpetuated the memory of those pre-lunar Arcadians who, not knowing how to cultivate the earth or how to weave, lived a life "similar to that of Beasts" in their huts made from leafy branches. On 15 February, every year, Roman piety thus as it were reactivated a slice of ancient Arcadian life.[161]

So it was that Arcadia, which was older than both Zeus and Jupiter and had been there, in the Peloponnese, for ever, a land of origins, nevertheless provided a link between Greece and Rome. But with Virgil, henceforth forever the poet of Arcadia, everything changed. In his *Eclogues*, composed in about 40 BC, he transformed it into somewhere that was nowhere. It may still have been "before", but it certainly was "elsewhere": distant from the present day and all its troubles, safely out of the way of civil wars and land confiscations, and far away from the City, which, as Livy put it, "has grown so much that today it is buckling beneath its greatness". To speak of Arcadia, to sing of it or, even more, to depict it, to name Lycoris, Corydon, Tityrus and Meliboea, would henceforth summon up a "spiritual landscape", a land of symbols.[162] Arcadia became utopia, offering distraction "from the deadly spectacles" with which the age had for so many years been presented.[163] With its peaceful shepherds, its taste for music, strongly emphasized by Polybius, and its *aura* of mystery, it provided Virgil with a plausible link. Arcadia was a convenient signifier that could be invaded by rêveries and amorous laments. Virgil's friend Gallus thus laments his love, which has been betrayed by Lycoris:

> Yet ye, O Arcadians, will sing this tale to your mountains; Arcadians only know how to sing. O how softly then would my bones repose, if in other days your pipes should tell of my love! And O that I had been one of you, the shepherd of a flock of yours, or the dresser of your ripened grapes! ... Here are cold springs, Lycoris, here soft meadows, here woodland; here, with thee, time alone would wear me away.[164]

A peasant or a shepherd: either will do. Arcadia is a refuge, but also a place in which to recall unhappy love affairs. Here, the lover's suffering can be transmuted into song, thanks to the Arcadian shepherds. In other words, thanks to the poet himself. In this way, Arcadia becomes another name for poetry.

Erwin Panofsky has retraced the avatars of the Arcadian theme from Virgil down to Watteau. The Renaissance endeavoured to reach or recreate the kingdom of Arcadia. The Medici villa in Fiesole was known as "Arcadia", and the members of its court were its kingdom's shepherds. According to Panofsky, this identification, by means of a real setting operating as a metaphor, was a way of "reducing the distance between the past and the present".[165] He then went on to show how the famous formula *Et in Arcadia ego* had changed its meaning between the time of Guercino and that of Poussin.

At first it was a *memento mori*, spoken by death itself: "Even in Arcadia, I (death) am [present]". Later, in a painting by Poussin, it came to mean: "The person in this tomb once dwelt in Arcadia". The shepherds seated around the funerary monument are "absorbed in calm discussion, and thoughtful contemplation". To be sure, death brings an end to everything, but first there is the happy time of life in Arcadia, which one should enjoy. It is possible to find the way to Arcadia. Later still, in the eighteenth century, the idea of death even fades away: at the beginning of his *Voyage in Italy*, Goethe wrote "Auch ich in Arkadien" which, according to Panofsky, simply meant "I too have been happy".[166]

For a poet from a northern land, to travel to Rome was thus to visit Arcadia. "*Eine Welt bist du, o Rom, doch ohne die Liebe / Wäre die Welt nicht die Welt; wäre denn Rom auch nicht Rom*", the *Roman Elegies* proclaim.[167] But Rome and Arcadia also mean the place of Beauty: only there can it be found, only there can one draw as near as possible to what Beauty once was on the earth that witnessed its birth: the earth of Greece. To discover Rome, with Winckelmann as one's guide, is also, is already, to make the voyage to Greece. Arcadia becomes "Greek" once more; and Greece becomes Arcadia.[168]

ALEXANDER BETWEEN ROME AND GREECE

Only the name links Virgil's Arcadia, that nowhere land seen from Rome, with Pausanias' Arcadia, the depository of a utopian Greek identity. Evander, the Arcadian who somehow "returned" from the Palatine to Pallantion in a Roman baggage train, constitutes a link between the earliest Rome and the most ancient Greece. He represents a good example of the interrelations and cultural quid pro quos between the Greek and the Roman frontiers of identity. Alexander the Great provides another example, a more important, more durable, more significant and also more conflictual one. Alexander, a dazzling symbol of both discord and unification, first for the Greeks themselves and later for the Romans, for several centuries constituted a disputed and symbolically charged figure for both Greeks and Romans. And continued to do so long after, for the moderns.

Whereas Anacharsis, the outsider-insider, was a fictitious being fashioned by the Greeks for their own purposes and through whose eyes they looked at themselves and doubted themselves while at the same time seeking reassurance, Alexander, conversely, seems to represent the eye through which they confidently viewed the outside world. By setting a high value on the frontier lands, Anacharsis seems to set in motion a centripetal movement, oscillating between a celebration of what he stood for and a questioning of it. Alexander, on the other hand, setting a high value on himself, seems to represent a centrifugal movement of expansion for *to Hellênikon* (and also for *Hellênismos*) that spread all the way to the edges of the earth. But he did so at the peril of losing his own "identity" and swinging over into Eastern barbarity. The present chapter, devoted to the Greeks' view of themselves, began with Anacharsis, and it ends with Alexander. But of course Alexander does not take over from Anacharsis any more than Anacharsis takes over from him. The avatars of their names and the interpretations and uses that have been made of them down the centuries leave the trails of two curves that sometimes diverge, sometimes draw closer together or even overlap.

Alexander the conqueror whom only death could halt, the civilizer of the East who wanted to forge a "mixed" civilization and who may even have been a visionary, dreaming of fraternity and the unity of all mankind: that is how he has been portrayed by some biographers, primarily modern ones, ranging from Johann Gustav Droysen, in 1833, to William Tarn, in 1933.[169] But they were preceded by an ancient intermediary, in the person of Plutarch. That vision of Alexander certainly corresponds neither to that of his Greek contemporaries nor to the findings of present-day research. How did it come to be constructed? "Alexander's objective never was to Hellenize the East. But he applied a Greek veneer to the practices and theory of Persian absolutism". That is the categorical conclusion of the Hellenist Paul Goukowsky's enquiry into the origins of the myth of Alexander.[170] He reminds us that in Greece itself Alexander was seen now as a tyrant, now as another Great King, in short as a man whose person re-emphasized the ancient proximity of those two figures as perceived by, for example, Herodotus.[171] Intellectuals criticized his *truphê* (luxurious softness), emphasized his insatiability and his mental instability, and condemned the cult of kingship. After his death, the Olynthian Ephippus circulated a bitter libel entitled *On the deaths of Alexander and Hephaistion*, in which he castigated his Persian lifestyle in his paradise (the traditional residence of the Great Kings), seated on his golden throne, clad in Persian robes and a crown, and then abandoning himself to drinking sessions and homicidal violence. He also reproved him for surrounding himself with incense-burners and, on certain occasions, dressing up as Ammon, Artemis or Heracles. This totally negative portrayal indicates an inability to think about Alexander and his achievements otherwise than in traditional terms: he is represented either as an Eastern despot or as a mad tyrant, an enemy of *to Hellênikon*, whose sudden death annihilated his pretentious claims to be a boundary-crosser, who overstepped all limits and ignored the established division of prerogatives.

Even in the mid-second century, when Polybius was reflecting upon the history of the world as recorded so far, he did not reckon that Alexander's conquests marked a deep caesura. In his view, the Macedonian empire, limited in both space and time, was simply the third in a line, preceded by the empires of Sparta and the Persians, which were likewise limited. Only the Roman conquest, which embraced practically the entire *oikoumenê*, marked a real break and the beginning of a new era of history. The fragmentation of partial and dispersed history had been replaced by a single, "oecumenical", truly universal history, resembling a huge living body, which a historian's account had to endeavour to reflect. Admittedly, Polybius, who looked at the world and its past from the vantage point of Rome, had consciously become the eye of Rome.[172]

If the Romans did try to minimize the scale of Alexander's conquests, the better to promote their own, that was, on the whole, a fair enough ploy. But Alexander's presence was too ubiquitous, and in the last century of the Republic and the early years of the empire became the focus of too many concentrated attacks, for there not to be more to it than that. A way of speaking of Roman matters through him was developed, a way of progressing from the moral condemnation of all despots to the mounting of a political opposition to the generals who, ever since Pompey, had presumptuously claimed to be his heirs. It was clearly in senatorial circles that his denigrators were the most persistent and unrelenting.[173] The struggle between Mark Antony and Octavius was a high point in this "Romanization", particularly because Mark Antony, for his part, assiduously imitated Alexander. The Macedonians who resisted the excesses of their absolute monarchs were seen as Romans defending their *libertas* against the tyranny (*dominatio*) of Antony, who was himself under the thumb of a Barbarian queen. Callisthenes, the champion of the Macedonians, is described by the historian Quintus Curtius as "the avenger of public liberty" (*vindex populi Romani libertatis*), an expression with no Greek equivalent that had been used by the Octavian party to justify the war against Antony.[174] More generally, the Senate, the defender of Italy's primacy within the empire, inevitably opposed Alexander, who symbolized a policy of fusion and integration. It was surely by no means fortuitous that Caracalla, who in 212 promulgated the Antonine constitution (which gave general access to Roman citizenship), was compared to a new Alexander.

In a famous digression, the exceptional nature of which the author is at pains to underline, Livy recapitulates with considerable virulence all the criticisms levelled at Alexander.[175] All the evidence suggested that had Alexander undertaken an expedition to the West, Rome would have remained invincible! Alexander was, admittedly, a good general, but plenty of Roman generals were his equal. Launching an attack on Italy would have been a quite different matter from hurling himself against Darius' chariots or advancing into India at the head of a drunken rabble. Besides, Alexander, carried along by *felicitas*, resembled not so much the earlier young conqueror of Darius, but rather Darius himself. He should be seen as the Eastern despot that he had, in truth, become, having "degenerated" under the influence of Persian customs. Finally, no comparison between the military fortunes of Rome and the achievements of Alexander could be justified by the argument that while Rome had lost more than a few battles (but never a war), Alexander had never lost a single one. Like should be compared only to like: the life of one general with the life of another, rather than the life of one man with a military history of four hundred years. If it came to a comparison of forces, with regard to both numbers and quality, the advantage would be massively in favour of Rome. Then comes Livy's extremely Augustan conclusion: "A thousand battle-arrays more formidable than those of Alexander and the Macedonians have the Romans beaten off – and shall do – if only our present love of domestic peace endure and our concern to maintain concord".

Plutarch's treatise on *The Fortune of the Romans* ends with a mention of the interrupted destiny of Alexander, who "was sweeping swiftly through the world like a shooting star from East to West, and was already allowing the lustre of his arms to gleam upon Italy", spurred on by his desire for glory and his determination to travel further afield than both Dionysus and Heracles.[176] That theme was to persist, as can be seen from the *Alexander Romance*, which without a qualm described his landing in Italy and his coronation as king of the Romans.[177] Plutarch, for his part, claims neither that Alexander would have been victorious nor that he would have been defeated, but he interprets the fact that he never did attack Rome as another mark of Fortune favouring Rome. He declares that the moment that Fortune arrived in Rome, having deserted the Persians and the Assyrians, and after crossing Macedonia and travelling across Egypt and Syria, she put aside her wings and sandals and decided that this was where she would remain. In this way he already adopted a very definite position in the *Roman* debate revolving around Alexander; and it was a position that was later to be clarified and confirmed by the treatise that he devoted to Alexander and entitled *On the Fortune or virtue of Alexander*. It would perhaps not be exaggerated to read this – not solely, but partly – as a riposte, for it produces the image of a *Greek* Alexander reconsidered in the light of the uses made of him by Rome:[178] a stronger, finer, unchallengeable image of Alexander, who is presented as a precursor. Given that we have already seen Plutarch criticizing Herodotus, celebrating Anacharsis, and interpreting Egypt and its religion in Greek terms, it comes as no great surprise to find Plutarch thus yet again engaged in a "defence and illustration of Greek identity".

This treatise, or rather both these treatises, declare forthrightly that Alexander, far from being simply a product of Fortune, was on the contrary forced to fight constantly against her. He made himself what he was, constructing his empire at the cost of his own blood. His wounds, which Plutarch enumerates, all testified to the hostility of Fortune, and the scars that they left upon his body were "images" engraved by his "virtue". Far from being an impulsive individual, he was the product of his own virtue, that is to say of his "magnanimity", "intelligence", "moderation" and "bravery". He carried with him the lessons that he had learned from Aristotle and he ought to be regarded as a true philosopher: not one of those confined to philosophical strolls around the Lyceum, but a philosopher out in the field. Whereas Socrates and Plato never had more than a handful of disciples, and those soon betrayed them, Alexander, for his part, taught the Hyrcanians the practice of marriage, the Persians not to marry their own mothers, and the Scythians to bury their dead instead of eating them. And "through Alexander, Bactria and the Caucasus learned to revere the gods of the Greeks". Not very many people read Plato's *Laws*, whereas entire populations live under the laws of Alexander. As an educator of the human race, who remedied the "savage nature" of countless peoples, he should by rights be regarded as "the greatest of the philosophers".[179]

Furthermore, he undertook to change the terms of the division between Greeks and Barbarians. Ignoring Aristotle's advice to treat the Greeks as a leader and Barbarians as a master, and to grant the former the solicitude that one shows to friends or kin, but to treat the latter as animals or plants, he dreamed of bringing them all together. Plutarch draws a contrast between on the one hand the perpetuation of ancient cleavages and, on the other, the image of mixture and fusion that is suggested by the famous banquet held at Opis on the Tigris. In the course of this banquet of reconciliation with the Macedonians, which, according to Arrian, had gathered nine thousand guests around Alexander, each participant was invited to pour a libation drawn from the same mixing-bowl, while the king prayed "for 'concord' between the Macedonians and the Persians and 'the exercise of hegemony in common'".[180]

Into this scene, the symbolism of which affected no more than the Persian and Macedonian aristocracies at the very most, Plutarch wanted, and believed it possible, to read an implementation of the cosmopolitanism of the Stoics – as if Alexander (in advance) realized the ideal of Zeno, the founder of Stoicism. This was that all men should consider themselves as fellow demesmen and citizens of one and the same city, his ultimate goal being to mix, as it were in a single mixing-bowl, people, ways of life and customs, and to turn the *oikoumenê* into "a single country" in which Alexander's "camp" would represent "the acropolis and the citadel". When this happened, Greeks and Barbarians would no longer be distinguished by their clothing or their weapons. Rather, "the distinguishing mark of the Greek should be seen in virtue (*aretê*), and that of the Barbarian in iniquity (*kakia*)".[181] As has been noted above, Eratosthenes had already had the same idea.

Plutarch puts the finishing touches to this picture with another scene: that of the weddings, "when [Alexander] brought together a hundred young Persian girls and a hundred Macedonian and Greek bridegrooms, united at a common hearth and board". He was the first to consecrate "the union of the two greatest and most mighty peoples, for he, of one maid the bridegroom and at the same time of all the brides the escort, as a father and sponsor united them in the bonds of wedlock". Plutarch, at this point quite carried away by his fervour, cannot resist evoking another scene from the historical repertory. Addressing the Barbarian Xerxes, he exclaims: "O dullard Xerxes, stupid fool that spent so much fruitless toil to bridge the Hellespont! This is the way that wise kings join Asia with Europe; it is not by beams nor by rafts, nor by lifeless and unfeeling bonds, but by the ties of lawful love and chaste nuptials and mutual joy in children that they join the nations together".[182]

By resorting, yet again, to the "fetishistic" image which, ever since Aeschylus, had permeated and oriented the whole of Greek history, Plutarch both set Alexander and Xerxes in opposition, and at the same time brought them together. Alexander or the Philosopher is the opposite of Xerxes, or a "good Xerxes", a "Greek" Xerxes. He sets up a true union. Then, recalling the encounter between Diogenes and Alexander, and the words "If I were not Alexander, I would be Diogenes", Plutarch drives his point home for the last time. Far from interpreting the statement as a confession of the king's inferiority to the philosopher, as Marcus Aurelius was to do,[183] it should be understood as a proud defence of his own destiny: "If I were not bent on fusing (*kerasai*) the Barbarian and the Greek worlds, on visiting all the continents in order to civilize them, on discovering the limits of the earth and the sea in order to roll the frontiers of Macedonia right back to the Ocean, on sowing and spreading the seeds of Greek justice and peace throughout all nations, I should not be content to sit enthroned amid the luxury of idle power: my ideal would be the simplicity of Diogenes". But I am Alexander! My historic mission is to explore the limits and push back frontiers. My kingdom is the world.

Such is Plutarch's portrait of the civilizing conqueror. Furthermore, the Alexander of these treatises possesses all the qualities of a good king, and very much resembles the *optimus princeps* soon to be presented to Trajan by the Sophist Dio of Prusa.[184] Working back from the present to the past, Plutarch also saw his Greek Alexander as a good emperor, concerned to defend a *Pax graeca* that had prefigured the *Pax romana*. This is a re-reading of Alexander in the light of the Roman empire, in a reaction that reallocates Augustus' attributes to Alexander. As the Baron de Sainte-Croix wrote at the beginning of the nineteenth century:

> One is bound to recognize that human civilization made great progress under the rule of Augustus. That prince united all nations from the Pillars of Hercules all the way to the banks of the Euphrates; and although a few peoples were autonomous, that is to say governed by their own particular laws, they were nevertheless subject to the general laws of the Empire and so, in a way, formed a single nation. The Greeks passed on to the Roman emperor the idea of such a fine system of government, and he then carried it even further.[185]

Unlike Plutarch, Arrian, who wrote a history of Alexander, borrowing the title *Anabasis* from Xenophon, did not at all promote this theme of a fusion of cultures.[186] He was a native of Nicomedia, and a member of the senatorial order who served under both Trajan and Hadrian. So he tended to portray the work of civilization and conquest initiated by Philip of Macedon on the model of Roman domination: he presents the Macedonians as conquering masters. Like the Romans, having started out with very little, they became the masters of the world. He also stresses how very much Alexander's conquest constituted a recapitulation of the whole of past Greek history ever since Troy, and also marked a new beginning. Herodotus' *Histories* ends with the revenge of Protesilaus at Sestus: the execution of the Persian Artaÿctes on the very spot where Xerxes' bridge had ended was a long-delayed riposte to the death of Protesilaus on the shores of Troy.[187] On his way to Asia, Alexander made sure he halted at Elaeous, to offer a sacrifice at the tomb of Protesilaus. Arrian adds, "The intention of the sacrifice was that the setting foot on Asian soil might be more propitious to Alexander than to Protesilaus". This was all the more important given that it was said that Alexander too, like a latter-day Protesilaus, was the first to leap from his ship on to the soil of Asia.[188] He was a pious Greek assuming his inheritance.

But at the very same time he also repeated a number of Xerxes' gestures: the very same, but without the hubris and giving them a different meaning, the *right* meaning. It was as if he believed that repeating them but performing them as they should be performed would open up the path to victory. When Xerxes crossed the Hellespont, he poured libations from a golden cup that he then threw into the sea. When Alexander was half-way across the straits, he offered up a sacrifice and made a libation, likewise using a golden cup.[189] Xerxes had insisted on seeing Priam's Pergamum, where he had sacrificed a thousand oxen to Athena Ilias. Alexander went up to Ilium and likewise sacrificed to Athena Ilias, but also to Priam (to assuage his anger), and placed a wreath on the tomb of Achilles.[190]

Arrian justifies his writing project with that evocation of the high walls of Troy. For it was up there that Alexander was said to have declared that Achilles was fortunate to have found "a Homer to be a herald to pass things on to posterity". The fact was that the exploits of Alexander had not been celebrated as they should have been, despite the fact that, as Arrian goes on to point out, in a somewhat Herodotean style, "no other single man performed such remarkable deeds, whether in number or magnitude".[191] He himself therefore proposed to be that "herald" whom posterity had so far lacked, but he would not recount the high deeds of both the Greeks and the Barbarians, only those of Alexander, who was without rival among Greeks and Barbarians alike. Contrary to the established practice of historians ever since Herodotus, if not Hecataeus, Arrian would not begin his work with his own signature in the manner of Herodotus ("Herodotus of Halicarnassus shows...") or Thucydides ("Thucydides of Athens writes..."). He would give neither his name nor his city, nor his titles. After all, Homer did not name himself at the beginning of the *Iliad*! As a latter-day Homer for a latter-day Achilles, he would do as Homer did, except – and this makes all the difference – he *says* that he will not say his name. He is most emphatic that he will not!

After Philip's victory at Chaeronea, the Younger Anacharsis returned to the Scythian wastelands, since Greek liberty was dead. Greece had given the world the very best of itself. In a different register, Barthold Georg Niebuhr reckoned that after Chaeronea the culture and talent of the Greeks were not dead, but the depth of spirit (*Geist*) that had been their national prerogative was gone.[192] The Alexander of Arrian and even more of Plutarch contradicted that view, but he was a retrospective Alexander: seen not from Rome, but in interaction with, if not in response to, Rome. It was Johann Gustav Droysen who plotted the new map of Hellenism, proposing to name the third period of Greek history (after the death of Alexander) *Hellenismus*.[193] As a result of that change of viewpoint and this shifting of frontiers, Demosthenes, the great Athenian orator, became one of the most "saddening" figures in history, because he "failed to realise" that a new era had begun and that it was about to "revolutionize the world".[194] In the first edition of his *History of Alexander*, Droysen points out that his book is neither a "monograph" nor a "biography". The great man's personality is simply the instrument of his actions, and his actions themselves are simply what provide the principal impulse of the age. So the important thing is to seize upon it "in its historical greatness".[195] The citation from Aristotle with which he introduces his book itself, in its own way, made that point: "Such a man is more like a god among men. For such men, there is no law; for they are themselves the law". There could be no better way of saying that he is above the limits and the shares apportioned in the city: he is a positive, not a negative *apolis*, a god, not a wild beast.

Following Arrian and Plutarch, Droysen redescribes the great scenes evoked above, beginning with the sea-crossing and the rites honouring Protesilaus and Achilles, and ending with the wedding ceremony in Susa. With the latter festivity, unprecedented in the annals of history, Alexander proclaimed and demonstrated that "the union of East and West had become a reality". What was Droysen's view of that union? "The elements that Alexander fused together were, in their supreme forms, the ardent vitality of Greece, which aspired to find a body, and the inert masses of Asia, which aspired to find a soul.... The peoples suddenly felt awakened into life: Alexander had achieved the task adumbrated by Dionysus". But that achievement was also the sign that he had reached his limit, as had the ancient world: with Alexander, "a man had become a god".[196] From that moment on the world lived in expectation, an expectation that was to lead to the reversal and completion of the story, with the appearance of "a God who became a

158

man". That was the task that fell to the Hellenistic period: to lead from the emergence of the expectation to its fulfilment.

All this smacks powerfully of Hegel, even if, as Benedetto Bravo has shown, it is a reinterpreted Hegel: using Hegelian terms, it establishes a period which, disregarded up until then, had not yet found its place in the schema of universal history. For Droysen, the Hellenistic period played the role that Rome played for Hegel, particularly in relation to Christianity.[197] However, I should like to draw attention to one particular point which use-fully links up with the discussions of Chapter 2, devoted to attitudes to Egypt. Egypt had been the starting point for Droysen's thinking, the subject of his earliest works, beginning with the Dissertation that he presented in Berlin in 1831. At that time, Egypt was attracting great interest: the Egyptian Expedition was not long ago, the deciphering of Egyptian hieroglyphics was just round the corner, and ever since the 1820s increasing numbers of papyri had been published. Egyptian antiquity was thus a domain that was develop-ing fast and that was bound to attract the young and ambitious discipline of philology. Droysen launched himself into a study of the Ptolemaic kingdom, paying particular attention to the reign of Ptolemy VI Philometor (who died in 146 BC). Why that choice? Partly for scholarly reasons no doubt, but there was more to it than that.

His preface begins by dividing Greek history into three parts. The first period is the shadowy time of fables; the second, the period of the flowering of Greek culture, had already attracted attention from all quarters; but the third had, on the contrary, been neglected, being considered sterile, scorned by the Roman historians, and misrepresented by the Christians.[198] To under-take to work on Hellenistic Egypt in itself suggested that this third period was to be looked at in a new way. And why that particular reign? The Ptolemaic kingdom had never been very healthy, but the reign of Ptolemy VI marked a definite turn for the worse, even the beginning of the end (*letale discrimen*). The various elements of which it was composed had just split apart and were now decomposing. At the beginning of its history, the Greek element had been predominant; but by the end the Egyptian element had gained the upper hand.[199] These pages of Droysen's thus unquestionably introduce a reassessment that leads to an overall interpretation of the "third period" of Greek history. Soon Droysen would be defining it, by analogy with modern Europe, as "the modern period of Antiquity".[200]

Above all, though, his Dissertation and his other works of the same period categorically affirm the superiority of the Greek world over the East. The

Egyptians are described as Barbarians, and Droysen is most disparaging on the subject of Egypt, the source of all human and divine knowledge.[201] In a lecture delivered in 1833, he briskly dismissed the very idea of Barbarian wisdoms.[202] The first chapter of *The History of Alexander* (omitted in later editions) starts off by recalling the struggle between the East and the West, Asia and Greece. The position that he adopts is thus similar to that of K. O. Müller, except that, in his work on *Orchomenus and the Minyans*, Müller had addressed the first period of Greek history, whereas Droysen sets out to devote himself to the third, until then neglected and misunderstood. Müller had found an ally in Pausanias; Droysen found one in Plutarch. But in the context of their respective times and to further their respective aims, for both those ancient and those modern authors the important thing was to defend the frontiers of a Greek *identity*. As is nearly always the case, the best defence was attack.

CHAPTER 5

Roman Voyages

For some time Rome has been present, either indirectly or directly, in the pages of this book. We have already made the journey to Rome with the Arcadians led by Evander, who left Greece even before the Trojan War. Then there was the journey, in the other direction, to an Arcadia that was Greek only in name, a nowhere land, transmuted by Virgil into the homeland of bucolic poetry. We have also made the journey with Alexander, an equivocal figure projected between Rome and Greece, whom Plutarch recast and recomposed. The "parallelism" that Plutarch, again, was to work upon in his *Parallel Lives* was to present readers with other itineraries between Greece and Rome.

Odysseus himself, whose figure as it were provides the framework for this book, may have set eyes on the shores of Italy, if – that is – we are to believe those who defend Homer as the father of geography. More importantly, Odysseus may even have got as far as Rome. Dionysius of Halicarnassus reports: "the author of the work on the priestesses of Argos says that Aeneas came into Italy from the land of the Molossians with Odysseus and became the founder of the city, which he named after Romê, one of the Trojan women".[1] What author was that? Hellanicus of Lesbos, a historian who was contemporary with Thucydides. But he was neither the first nor the only writer to record the arrival of Achaean and Trojan heroes in Latium. Records may even go back to the sixth century BC.[2] That presence of the two erstwhile enemies, as it were hand in hand, may at first sight seem somewhat surprising, but it may be understandable if regarded as an echo of the profuse literature devoted to *Returns*, which produced all sorts of combinations. As reworked, the episode fits in with a whole spate of endeavours to Hellenize the origins of the peoples of the world by conferring upon them genealogies

161

of "Greek" ancestors.[3] It is also worth noting that even if the Romans did not consider the pious Aeneas to be the official founder of Rome, he nevertheless remained closely associated with its foundation, whereas the memory of Odysseus lived on only in the margins of Latium. The piety of the vanquished hero won out over the cunning of the victor!

Now let us overstep a few centuries to reach 280 BC, on the banks of the River Siris, close to Tarentum, where for the very first time Greek phalanxes and Roman legions came face to face. Montaigne writes as follows:

> When King Pyrrhus crossed into Italy, after noting the excellent formation of the army which the Romans had sent ahead against him he said, "I do not know what kind of Barbarians these are" (for the Greeks called all foreigners Barbarians) "but there is nothing barbarous about the ordering of the army which I can see!"

Given that they were not Greeks, the Romans had, perforce, to be Barbarians. But what kind of Barbarians were these, who appeared to contradict one of the features that, since Herodotus at least, was considered to be distinctively Barbarian? That feature was that Barbarians knew nothing of the order of the hoplite phalanx, so did not know how to fight. The above remark provides Montaigne with an introduction to his famous essay "On cannibals", in which the perplexity of Pyrrhus, the king of Epirus, upon his first encounter with the Roman army under Laevinus serves him as a pretext to make his own observations on what is savage and what is civilized, taking in both the "ancient" Greek world and the "new" Roman one, and from there moving on to consider "this other world, which has been discovered in our own century".[4]

The first rule that he draws from all this is that before passing judgement, it is necessary to distance oneself from commonly held opinions, since clearly everyone starts off by labelling as "Barbarian" anything "that is not customary for himself". Then, having throughout the chapter demonstrated the instability of both terms, given that the most civilized person may sometimes prove to be the most Barbarian, Montaigne brings the discussion to a close with the impatient irony of his famous exclamation: "Ah! But they [Indians] wear no breeches!"

The example of the king of Epirus' astonishment, which serves Montaigne as his point of departure, is directly borrowed from his reading of Plutarch. "When [Pyrrhus] had observed [the Romans'] discipline, the appointment of their watches, their good order, and the general arrangement of their camp, he was amazed and said to the friend who was nearest him: 'The discipline of these Barbarians is not barbarous; but the result will show us what it amounts to'".[5] And the Greeks certainly did soon see what would happen! The remark is all the more noteworthy given that Pyrrhus, who claimed descent from Achilles, had reckoned that he was about to join battle with "Trojan colonists". Before responding to the pressing pleas of the Tarentines, he had "reflected upon the capture of Troy",[6] seeing himself as a new Achilles attacking a new Troy.

With the arrival of Rome upon the scene, that is to say with the victories of Rome and its legions, the great divide between the Greeks and the Barbarians definitively ceased to be a tenable way of summing up the human race. The wars against the Persians had encouraged its use in order to define a Greek identity. But in the wake of the Roman conquest, dissatisfaction with the formula was inevitable. Where were the Romans to be placed? Was it now necessary to distinguish Greeks, Barbarians and also a third group, the Romans? Or could the antonymous pair be retained, but with the Romans "passing over" to the Greek side? The latter solution was favoured by a number of Roman intellectuals – at least for a while – and, of course, also by the Greeks. Clearly, the Romans were not Barbarians, but nor could the Romans form a *third* group, since originally the future Romans were in truth Greeks. It was all a matter of genealogies. The thesis of Rome's Trojan origin, magnified by Virgil, was to break away from that view and set up Rome as a third group, from "the very start". This was all the more acceptable given that, as Thucydides had pointed out, the dichotomy between Greeks and Barbarians had, at that point, not been introduced. The Trojans may not have been Greeks, but they were certainly not Barbarians either.

THE VOYAGES OF POLYBIUS

The Greeks and the Romans had clashed and – more amazing still – Rome had soon conquered the Mediterranean. What had happened? How? Why? These were urgent questions to which one Greek visitor to Rome, initially a reluctant one, felt obliged to find answers. Polybius was sent to Rome as a hostage, along with one thousand other Greeks, after the defeat at Pydna. He was a Greek aristocrat, a native of Megalopolis in Arcadia, and he remained in Rome for seventeen years, from 167 to 150 BC, before he was allowed to return to Greece.[7] He was thirty-two years old when he arrived in Rome, with both political and military experience behind him, having served as a cavalry commander in the Achaean confederation. He was taken under the wing of the Roman aristocracy, got to know Cato, and became an intimate friend of the Scipios. He travelled, in the East but above all in the West, visiting the Alps, Southern Gaul, Spain and Africa. Thanks to Scipio Aemilianus, whose mentor he had been, he was present at the capture of Carthage, and cruised along the Atlantic coasts of Morocco and Portugal. Eventually he returned to Megalopolis, where he ended his days, having carried out a number of missions for Rome. In Arcadia, honorific inscriptions and statues commemorated him as an ally of the Romans who had managed to calm their anger against Greece (*to Hellênikon*) and who, with the Romans' permission, had even acted as a veritable "legislator" for the cities of Arcadia.

The inscription attached to his statue, which stood in the agora of Megalopolis, described him primarily as a traveller, a man who, like Odysseus, had seen the world. Pausanias writes that he had "wandered over the whole earth and sea" before, again like Odysseus, being able to return to his homeland almost twenty years later.[8] Polybius, a new Odysseus? Was that reference to Odysseus just municipal eloquence of a purely sycophantic nature? Up to a point, yes. However, it is worth noting that Polybius himself staunchly defended his Odyssean view of a historian's way of life. In opposition to Timaeus, the carpet-slippered historian safely ensconced in his library, he was in favour of men who saw with their own eyes and endured with their own bodies all that they recounted. "Nature has given us two instruments, as it were, by the aid of which we inform ourselves and inquire about everything. These are hearing and sight, and of the two sight is much more veracious according to Heracleitus. 'The eyes are more accurate witnesses than the ears', he says".[9] And who was Timaeus? A native of Tauromenium in Sicily, who was exiled by the tyrant Agathocles at the end of the fourth century. He then settled in Athens, where he worked for half a century, writing the history of the Greeks in the West with passionate determination and "doing for the West what Herodotus had done for the East".[10] He was the first to recount the war and defeat of Pyrrhus in Italy and to see Rome as reflected in the astonished eyes of the king of Epirus, the first to encounter Rome as a historical actor.

As opposed to the soft pillow afforded by voyages through books, Polybius argued that a historian needed the asceticism of autopsy. Like Odysseus – and Polybius at this point cites the first lines of the *Odyssey* – a historian needs to have been drenched by the sea-spray and been present on the fields of battle.[11] Above all, Odysseus represents the very best of historians because, in the eyes of Polybius, he is the very model of a political man. Polybius' ideal historian is not the ancestor of the great war correspondents. History and politics must go hand in hand.

Polybius was rediscovered at the beginning of the fifteenth century and soon after was translated into Latin. At first he was regarded as a historian, but then Machiavelli enrolled him into the ranks of political thinkers, and his account of the Roman regime came to be regarded as authoritative on constitutional matters, and continued to be right down to Montesquieu and beyond. At the end of the sixteenth century, Justus Lipsius (=Joost Lips) set him up as a military expert.[12] But in the modern period his aristocratic convictions and his choice of conqueror damaged his reputation. Some came to regard him as a *realpolitiker*, if not a downright collaborator. In his list of the successive empires that preceded the Roman domination, he had named Persia, Sparta and Macedon, but completely ignored democratic Athens. When, in 1858, the young Fustel de Coulanges devoted his French thesis to Polybius, entitling it *Polybe ou la Grèce conquise par les Romains*, the author of one review deplored what he regarded as an excessive rehabilitation of the historian: Polybius may have been a "crafty" citizen, but he was certainly a "bad" one.[13]

Evidence for his "stay" in Rome is plentiful. Cicero, praising his skills as a historian, calls him "our Polybius",[14] including him in the intimacy of the Roman "we". Polybius himself, it must be said, had certainly not discouraged such a development. A perceptive study has shown that his grasp of the Latin language and the Romanization of his thought went hand in hand.[15] He is even to be found taking over the famous Roman expression *mare nostrum* on his own account (albeit translating it into Greek), to designate the Mediterranean sea, as if he already included himself in that "we" and spoke for it. It therefore comes as no surprise to find that he never refers to the Romans as "Barbarians". He, better than anyone, knows that a representation of the world founded upon the Greek–Barbarian dichotomy is no more than a *flatus vocis*, which has no grip upon reality. Since history is being made in Rome, it is in Rome that he decides to write history.

A new world deserved a new history. First he diagnoses the situation: "Previously the doings of the world had been, so to say, dispersed, as they were held together by no unity of initiative, results or locality". Persia, Sparta and the conquests of Alexander were all still limited empires. For that reason single histories, themselves dispersed, that is to say monographic histories, were all that seemed necessary, but those days were now gone. Time itself was no longer external to history. From about 220 BC on, with the advent of the

Second Punic War, history, which now resembled a great "organic whole", became universalized, and "the affairs of Italy and Libya have been inter-linked with those of Greece and Asia, all leading up to one end".[16]

Intellectually speaking, this new space, this new temporality and this new kind of historicity were the factors that constituted the *raisons d'être* for Polybius' endeavour. They were what he set out to convey. The interlacing (*sumplokê*) of events called for the weaving of a history capable of taking what was general (*katholou*) as its framework. The right response to this change which, as Polybius saw it, was due to the action of Fortune, had to be history that was universal. Within his own particular register, that of the writing of history, a self-respecting historian had to find an analogue to the change of scene produced by Fortune. Such was the task or mission that Polybius, the hostage and exile, set himself. His journey to Rome, which, for a Greek, involved a decentring or conversion of his point of view, or even "treachery", established the conditions that made this possible.[17] The intelligibility of all that had happened over the last fifty years, beginning with the recent history of Greece, was at stake here:

> For what gives my work its peculiar quality, and what is most remarkable in the present age, is this. Fortune has guided all the affairs of the world in one direc-tion and has forced them to incline towards one and the same end; a historian should likewise bring before his readers, under one synoptical view, the oper-ations by which she has accomplished her general purpose.[18]

Clearly, everything hinged upon that "likewise". What form of exegesis should he adopt in order to represent that "general purpose"? How could he conjure up this "synoptic" view of history before the eyes of his readers? These were questions to which Polybius was to find a solution, setting him-self in opposition to Aristotle. But before that, exiled in Rome, he understood that history would from now on have to be written from a different point of view, which identified Fortune with Rome, at the risk of writing a history solely of "the conquerors", and of confusing seeing things *from* Rome and seeing things *from the point of view of* Rome with the temptation of regarding himself as the eye of Fortune itself, and becoming merely the spokesman of the Roman aristocracy.

Yet Polybius' work ends with the funereal vision of Carthage in flames, and its conqueror Scipio Aemilianus tearfully evoking the fate of Troy, in the words of Homer: "A day will come when sacred Troy will perish / And Priam and his people shall be slain". The Carthaginian conflagration thus recalls not only the destruction of Troy and the fall of all the empires that succeeded it, those of the Assyrians, the Medes, the Persians and the Macedonians, but also prefigures the end of Rome, as Polybius expressly makes Scipio say.[19] The day would come when, like all things human, the new Troy too would perish.

Having resolved one question of a general nature, Polybius then addresses another, which is more specific. Why Rome? Why did virtually the whole of the inhabited world pass under the authority of Rome, in fifty-three years? It was thanks to the superiority of its political regime (*politeia*). According to Polybius, the main cause of the success of any city lies in "the form of the state's constitution".[20] This explanation based on *politeia*, which has continued right down to the present day to cause much ink to flow (particularly as Book VI, in which it is developed, has partly disappeared), reflects a high point in the relations between Greece and Rome. How could the Romans possibly still be regarded as Barbarians when their success stemmed precisely from what the Greeks had always considered the very foundation of civilized life: namely city life and its framework of *politeia*? Rome belongs to the same *political* space as Greece; possibly it had done so ever since Aristotle's enquiries into a wide range of constitutions which, we know, included those of both Rome and Carthage.

If that point is conceded – and Polybius takes it for granted – in order to understand Rome, one has only to observe it through the grid constructed by classical Greek political philosophy. But does that really make things clear or is its effect, on the contrary, one of mystification? Does Polybius describe what he sees or does he conveniently see whatever he is determined to describe? Here, scholars disagree. Mommsen thought that to explain Rome and its successes by its theoretically "mixed" constitution was "stupid". Frank Walbank, the leading modern commentator on Polybius, adopts a more qualified and balanced position: there is certainly something "too formal" and "too abstract" about the theory but, as an analytical instrument, it does reveal certain things – the Romans' genius for compromise, for example. On the other hand, it conceals other aspects – for instance, all that made it possible for the *nobiles* to ensure and promote their own domination.[21]

Claude Nicolet takes a quite different view. The "only way to understand Rome is through Polybius, Dionysius, and Cicero" since, fundamentally, Aristotle's definition of the city as "a structure of participation" accounts for the Roman achievement.[22] So not only is Polybius' exegesis legitimate in its aims, but it furthermore becomes an investigation which "over and above the principles of law and appearances" emphasizes "the practical implementation and the reality" of the Roman regime. Far from it being the case that Polybius saw only what he wanted to see, he "explains what he does see". So efficiently does he do so that "theory soon fades in the face of a strictly practical analysis of the mutual *powers* and the *brakes* set upon them that are at work in the functioning of the Roman regime". Nicolet even arrives at the following apparently paradoxical conclusion: what is so striking in the philosophical "parenthesis" constituted by Book VI of Polybius' work "is not so much the presence of philosophy as its absence".[23]

Taking a totally opposite view, Philippe Gauthier defends the specificity of the Greek *polis* or, at least, declines to subscribe to this "Hellenized" view of Rome that is promoted by both Roman and Greek intellectuals and also by many of their modern successors. He challenges Polybius, whom he calls "a great mystifier", because he does "not believe that his analysis of Greek politics, as elaborated in particular by Aristotle, is applicable to Rome", or at least to the Rome of the fourth to the first centuries BC.[24] Clearly, there is no such thing as *the* ancient city of Fustel de Coulanges, only a *variety* of ancient cities. Rome was one of many, quite different from the Greek cities, which were themselves extremely diverse.[25]

Polybius, for his part, never for a moment doubted that he had hit upon the truest explanation for the power of Rome. Was there any way in which he could have harboured "doubts"? I do not think so. Although certainly not the first to draw a parallel between Rome and Greece, this historian who wrote in Greek and primarily for Greeks, but did so *from* Rome, did disseminate the idea of that parallel more widely and conferred upon it greater and, above all, more lasting authority. His starting point was the then current idea that *politeia*, as Isocrates put it, constituted the "soul" of the city: "For the soul of a state is nothing else than its polity, having as much power over it as does the mind over the body".[26] That constitution, understood in the widest sense of the term, provided the basis and expression for the "community" (*koinônia*).[27] For Polybius, it was the "spirit" of the city and the "principal cause of its success or failure".[28] That idea was then complemented by the principle, equally widely accepted since Aristotle, according to which a "mixture" was better than a simple form. The best constitution would thus be the one that managed to combine as many forms as possible.[29]

Now, the example *par excellence* of a mixture was Sparta, the model to which Greek political thinkers indefatigably and repeatedly returned.

Polybius was no exception. He used it to construct his parallel, but introduced a number of modifications. His constitutional vocabulary avoids the "mixed" image which, ever since Plato, if not Thucydides, had been currently used to describe the excellence of a constitution. Polybius argues purely in terms of a balance of antagonistic forces: a constitution is a system of weights and counterweights. Such was the Spartan *politeia* conceived by Lycurgus: no part of it could acquire excessive importance as each part was counterbalanced by the rest, "kingship being guarded from arrogance by the fear of the commons, who were given a sufficient share in the government, and the commons on the other hand not venturing to treat the kings with contempt from fear of the elders who, being selected from the best citizens, would be sure, all of them, to be always on the side of justice".[30] Such too, was the Roman constitution. But whereas the constitution of Sparta had, so to speak, emerged, ready armed, from Lycurgus' head, that of Rome had developed gradually in the course of many "struggles and trials". The former had known nothing of the vicissitudes of history; the latter was their product. Polybius has not the slightest doubt that that ability to learn and improve "by imitating good examples" in order eventually to create "the finest political system of our time" redounds to the credit of Rome. In all probability Polybius was here identifying with the view of Rome's development taken by Cato, who had already contrasted the main Greek constitutions, produced by a handful of legislators working on their own, to the centuries-long construction of the Roman *res publica*.[31] Rome had a long-term process going for it. Its history had proceeded gradually within a long space of time that greatly exceeded the brief span of individual lives.

How should the success of a city be judged? If the *telos* of a constitution is its ability to safeguard its citizens' possessions and ensure their security, there can be no doubt that Sparta had always excelled. However, Polybius goes on:

> But if anyone is ambitious of greater things, and esteems it finer and more glorious than that to be the leader of many men and to rule and lord it over many and have the eyes of all the world turned to him, it must be admitted that from this point of view the Laconian constitution is defective, while that of Rome is superior and better framed for the attainment of power.[32]

When the Spartans took it upon themselves to assume external command, they soon threatened the equilibrium of their regime, whereas Rome achieved its full potential through conquest. According to Polybius, this proves the superiority of the Roman constitution. Rome is a *polis* in the fullest sense, and is furthermore a city better "armed" and more perfect than the model Greek city, Sparta. Any comparison between the two is to the advantage of the Romans. Dionysius of Halicarnassus was to develop this theme further, but with different arguments.

To give an account of the new world, Polybius thus proposed the general form of a "universal" (*katholou*) history, which seemed to him to be historically analogous to the new "plan" of Fortune. Therein lay his task as a historian. Once he had conceived of this new space of intelligibility, within this interpretative framework, he evolved his "constitutional" explanation, that is to say accounted for the existing situation by the superiority of the Roman regime. Those two solutions make sense within a system of Greek intellectual coordinates: historical reflection and political philosophy. But to those two responses to the present situation, Polybius added another, albeit of rather more limited impact. Why, one may wonder, was Polybius, a positive thinker if not a positivist historian, so keen to defend Homer as a geographer and to localize Odysseus' voyages to Sicily and Italy?

In opposition to Aristarchus and Eratosthenes, who maintained that Homeric geography was fictitious, Polybius, like his contemporaries Hipparchus the astronomer and Crates of Mallus, the Pergamum librarian, argued that it was true. The point of departure existed in reality, whether it was the Trojan War or the wanderings of Odysseus. Then came the mythopoetic treatment that transformed and embellished it, with the aim of producing "pleasure and terror", but that did not do away with the initial kernel of *historia*, true information. This theory of *muthos*, certainly not invented by Polybius, made it possible to preserve the fundamental value of the Homeric epics as sources of knowledge. Homer knew, and then he created a poetic work so as to reach out to a huge audience. Contrary to Eratosthenes, who reckoned that "the scenes of Odysseus' wanderings would be located on the day of the discovery of the identity of the cobbler who sewed together the goatskin that held the winds", Polybius believed that Aeolus was really a man who provided information for travellers approaching the straits of Messina. On the strength of this he became known as the organizer of the winds and was credited with royal or even immortal status. Polybius complemented this Euhemeristic general information with a number of his own observations. He compared Homer's description of the monster Scylla to a description of swordfish-hunting as still practised in his own day out at sea off Cape Scylleon (in Calabria).[33]

Thanks to such comparisons, it became increasingly credible that Odysseus' wanderings really did take place in this part of the world.

At the same stroke, and over and above the arguments between geographers, he suggested that geography had always been a Greek science anyway. Homer had already been well informed about the *oikoumenê* and its limits, including the lands to the West. Or, to be more precise, Greeks had always known how to describe the world and spell out its place names and singularities: all they had to do was understand Homer. Admittedly, this was a Greek area of knowledge that required corrections and additional details where possible, but here too the principal "coordinates" were Greek and had long been available. The Romans may have conquered the world, but the Greeks already knew it and had known it long before the Romans even thought of conquering it. Perhaps this was what a realist interpretation of Homer and the voyages of Odysseus really set out to establish, particularly when produced by a conquered Greek confined within the shores of Italy.

THE VOYAGES OF DIONYSIUS OF HALICARNASSUS

Who were the Romans? Authentic Greeks; and Rome had always, ever since its first day, been a Greek city. Even before Rome was established in Rome, it was already Greek. That is the simple and remarkable thesis advanced, repeated and demonstrated with heavy doses of genealogy and etymology, citations and other evidence, by the most famous work of Dionysius of Halicarnassus. It was also the *raison d'être* for the long enquiry that engaged this first-century BC man of letters, who travelled from Halicarnassus to Rome and settled there to exercise his profession of *rhetor* and to pursue his researches. A century and a half earlier Polybius had been forced to go there as a hostage; but Dionysius, for his part, went there of his own free will soon after Augustus brought the civil wars to an end. It was in Rome that he *wanted* to work.

Twenty-two years later he was to present his work to Rome as a "return gift" for all the advantages, in particular the *paideia* (culture), that it had showered upon him.[34] The word *paideia* is clearly not a neutral one, for it was well known, ever since Isocrates' definition of Greekness, that the difference between a Greek and a Barbarian was above all a matter not of nature but of culture.[35] So if Rome, like fourth-century Athens, was regarded by Dionysius as a place where a Greek could learn and become cultured, it was only too clear that the Romans were not, or were no longer, or, better still, had not ever been Barbarians. Furthermore, in the prologue to his essay on *Ancient orators*, Dionysius declares himself absolutely delighted by the return of the old rhetoric (*philosophos rhêtorikê*), which had been virtually ousted by the arrival, but yesterday or the day before, of a rhetoric from some "Asiatic hell".[36] He reckons that this fortunate change is thanks to the power of Rome, "who has ... made every city focus its entire attention upon her", and the valour of its leaders, who are men of high quality both in their judgement and in their culture. They are, in fact, *eupaideutoi*.[37] Unlike the towns in Hellas, which are so neglectful of their heritage, it is they, the Romans, who have proved themselves the true depositories of classicism (or of Atticism), the true men of culture: in short, true *Greeks*. Dionysius, a literary critic settled in Rome, intends to boost that success further by his decision to study the most famous ancient (that is Greek) orators:[38] he will promote the taste of the Roman leaders, render them ever more "Greek", and help them to gain a better understanding of "their" intellectual heritage. Greece is already and must increasingly be in Rome.

It is reasonable to suppose that another, or at least a symmetrical, purpose may also have been behind his *Antiquities*: reminding the Romans (but in Greek) of their Greek origins was in fact a way to impress upon the Greeks – hitherto ill- or insufficiently informed – the fact that they are the "ancestors" of the Romans. For the first time he, Dionysius, will provide all the details necessary to prove that the Romans are no hearthless, wandering vagabonds but, on the contrary, the most authentic of all the descendants of the Greeks.

That is how his preface justifies his choice of subject. The beginnings of the City may have seemed mediocre and hardly worthy of an "archaeology", but in reality they deserve their rightful place in world history (*koinê historia*), for Rome, through the unprecedented extent of its dominion both in space and in time, has arrived to occupy the last (which is also the first) place in the schema of a succession of empires. Archaeology can thus justifiably be claimed to be history, and – indeed – general history, and its author from the outset presents himself not as an antiquarian but as a historian: he is *ho suntaxas*, the one who assembles facts and sets them in order, a historian producing works of history.[39]

"I begin my history ... with the most ancient legends ... and I bring the narrative down to the beginning of the First Punic War". That is an orthodox enough declaration for a historian who begins by chronologically delimiting his subject.[40] Except that most historians begin by, in one way or another, drawing attention to a dividing line (Herodotus marks the difference between on the one hand the time that he personally can know about and, on the other, the time that is beyond such knowledge; and Thucydides, in his *Archaeology*, explains that it is impossible to write the true history of the past). In contrast, Dionysius claims that there is a continuity: one passes from *muthoi* to *historia* and from *historia* to *muthoi*. At the end of his work, his *terminus ad quem* reveals a curious use of the practice of legitimation according to which, in the chain of historians, one tends to begin where the last left off. Historians pass away and are replaced, the story goes on, history continues to be written in the present. However Dionysius, for his part, chooses to stop at the very point where his already distant predecessor, Polybius, began. His is a back-to-front legitimation and his is a history not of the present but of the past.

The *Antiquities* claim to be not just Archaeology and History, but moreover a "total" history of Rome: external wars are recorded, but likewise internal ones; constitutions and laws, but likewise customs, making it a "cultural" history, a *Bios*. In the past Dicaearchus had written a *Life of Greece* (*Bios Hellados*), and now Dionysius offered his readers an *Archaios Bios* of Rome, in which it was proved that Rome had always had a "Greek life" (*Bios hellên*). That shift from the noun (*Hellas*) to the adjective (*hellên*) reflects the shift in Dionysius' project.[41]

Right from the start the project is placed under the sign of "mixture". Dionysius above all does not want to write history in the style of Polybius, who sticks to one genre and limits himself to a single form: "pragmatic" history, the austerity of which guarantees its utility for the only kind of reader at whom it is aimed, the man of politics.[42] He prefers to emulate the "polychromy" (*poikiliê*) of Herodotus or the "polymorphism" of Theopompus.[43] The way to prevent his readers' attention from flagging is to mix genres and vary styles, thereby compounding pleasure with utility (in the form of *exempla*) for the delectation of men proficient in political eloquence or interested in philosophy, and likewise of ordinary readers who are simply after entertainment.[44]

The Romans may not be Barbarians, but does that mean they are truly Greeks? Yes, says Dionysius, at the same time taking care to point out that this was not his discovery. For in the final analysis the more Roman the discovery is, or is said to be, the greater his own authority. He explains that the first to put that discovery into words were those of the Roman historians who were of "the greatest learning" (starting with Cato).[45] The Aborigines, the first true inhabitants of Italy, were not autochthonous but Greek. To find authentic autochthonous people, born from the soil, you have to turn to the

Etruscans, Dionysius explains. That is a by no means anodyne remark, for it enables him to imply a difference in nature between the Etruscans and the Romans. The Roman identity therefore owes nothing to Etruria.[46]

As for the hypotheses and other suggestions put forward by Greek authors (and since the fifth century there had been quite a few),[47] they are simply swept aside as not worth considering. Neither Timaeus nor even Polybius fares any better. The earliest Roman historians are likewise dismissed, and for the same reasons. Neither Fabius Pictor nor the first annalists researched the beginnings of their town with *acribeia* (precision). Only those historians "of the greatest learning", mentioned above, are thus left in the field. They are dominated by the lofty and austere figure of Cato, an incontestable authority in such matters since he wrote the *Origins* or book of *Foundations* (of the principal cities of Italy). He was hardly to be suspected of being excessively pro-Greek (although he did know Greek),[48] but was, along with Cicero, Varro and a handful of others, among the great Roman intellectuals who really did "think through" the origins of Rome. The Roman Aborigines were of Greek origin, for they had arrived many generations before the Trojan War and before Aeneas' landing close to the mouth of the Tiber. By sleight of hand, Dionysius thus makes the thesis his own (which now becomes: the Romans are Greeks). His contribution and energies were to be devoted, not to discussing it by comparing it to others (all of which were discredited from the outset), but to strengthening it by providing extra details and complementary evidence, bringing into play all the Greek techniques of literary criticism and the whole apparatus of Greek antiquarian erudition.

The elucidation of the identity of the Aborigines provides a good example of his methods.[49] Who were these people who, with two changes of name, became first Latins, then Romans? Clearly, this was an important question. Dionysius takes etymology as his point of departure: his whole demonstration consists in moving from a defective etymology to a "correct" one. Some people maintained that Aborigines meant "autochthonous" people. But, Dionysius points out, in Greek "autochthonous" would be *genarchai* or *prôtogonoi*. Others, taking the opposite view of that first explanation, emend Aborigines to Aberrigenes (*aberrare*) and, in conformity with a whole tradition, thus turn Aborigines into "wanderers": this etymology thus corresponds to their way of life. On this basis they suggest a link with the Leleges, wandering tribes well known to tradition and still available.

Without even bothering to refute these explanations (which, being contradictory, demolish each other?), Dionysius immediately introduces the argument based on authority: the Romans "of the greatest erudition" say that … the Aborigines were Greeks who had come from Achaea many generations before the Trojan War.[50] The essential thesis, thereafter never to be called into question, was thus established. This was where the world of the archaeologist began, for that was as far as the knowledge of the Roman historians went. A migration had taken place, but from where, with whom, and why? Dionysius takes over with the words: "If their thesis is sound (*hugiês*)", then the Aborigines "cannot have been colonizers from any people other than that now called Arcadian". In support of that declaration, he starts by producing an Arcadian genealogy that goes right back to the son of Lycaon, Oenotrus, who, precisely, emigrated to Italy. Then he cites three weighty witnesses, all of whom confirm the presence of Oenotrus in Italy: Sophocles, the tragedian, Antiochus of Syracuse, "a historian of considerable antiquity" (second half of the fifth century), and Pherecydes of Athens, "who is second to none as a genealogist". In conclusion he declares that he is convinced (*peithomai*) that the Aborigines were descended from the people of Oenotrus. This is the point at which to introduce the "sound" etymology of their name: sound because it provides an accurate description of their history and their way of life. Why Aborigines? Because they were mountain people: *ab-oros*, according to a mixed etymology, half-Latin, half-Greek. They lived in and came from the mountains. And, precisely, "a particular characteristic of the Arcadians is their love of a mountain life".[51] That is how Dionysius handles his proof.

Not content to mobilize genealogy, etymology and appeals to "witnesses", the enquirer, to convince both himself and others, then resorts to all the "marks", "traces", "vestiges" and "objects" still to be seen.[52] To these he adds the evidence provided by festivals, rituals and sacrifices. On one level, the Great Games confirm the kinship (*suggeneia*) of the Romans and the Greeks.[53] Appealing to the twofold authority of Fabius Pictor and Homer, Dionysius (who once again rubbishes the entire Etruscan side of the story)[54] discovers dazzlingly clear confirmation of the Greek character of Roman rituals in sacrificial methods in particular. From his study of both Greek and Roman rituals, it even emerges that the Romans retained certain customs that the post-Homeric Greeks abandoned. The Romans apparently remained more faithful to Homeric times than the Greeks themselves.[55]

Why did Dionysius make this choice? Was this simply the work of a sycophant, a scribbler paying his dues (his "return gift") to the powers of the day? Or was it perhaps just a scholarly game, an amusement with very little to do with reality, in which a skilful manipulation of genealogies and an ability to play off one tradition against another were all that was needed to amuse a cultivated readership and to exhaust the subject? In short, was this a project that had more in common with Ronsard's *Franciade* and all the ancient variations on the Trojan origins of the Franks than with the *Recherches de la France* by Etienne Pasquier (a lawyer who published the first volume of this work in Paris, in 1560), who was careful to include the Gauls in the picture? In truth, does it not make more sense to recognize that there was more at stake in the choice that Dionysius made and in his answer to the question of the identity of the Romans? What was really the purpose of this man who, at a time when Roman domination had long since become clear to everyone, set about explaining to his ill-informed or hostile compatriots how Rome had originated? Was he simply repeating, in Greek and rather late in the day, what the Romans had long been writing in Latin? Was Dionysius behind the times? Had he stood alone it might be possible to make that claim. But at the very same moment Varro, Livy and above all Virgil were all concerned with the same subject. Far from its being old-fashioned, it seems to have been very much in vogue.

Furthermore, does that declaration (that the Aborigines were of Greek origin) have the same meaning when Cato puts it forward and when Dionysius, citing it, takes it over? In Cato, who was the first to choose to write history in Latin, it may have served as a symbolic instrument of emancipation, which made it possible to escape from the Greeks–Barbarians dichotomy, or rather to subvert it. "You Greeks, you classify us among the Barbarians, but we are certainly not Barbarians as our ancestors were Greek". Repeated in Greek, for a Greek readership, that statement transmits a piece of information which, it must be admitted, had already certainly lost its novelty almost two centuries earlier. By the beginning of the Augustan period, no Greek can still have believed that the Romans were purely and simply to be classified as Barbarians. After all, at this very moment Strabo was recognizing the Romans' historic mission to take over from the Greeks in the task of civilizing the *oikoumenê*. The meaning of "The Romans are Greeks" now surely became "We Greeks are also, in a way, Romans. We are their parents, or rather their grandparents, so their empire is, in a way, also ours". In short, genealogy is used to legitimate not only the indisputable existence of this Graeco-Roman empire, which, with the advent of Augustus, established itself ever more firmly, but also the place that Greek figures of note claimed within it: "their" place, fully acknowledged.

The intellectual framework within which Dionysius' Roman archaeology was produced was a Greek area of knowledge long since recognized to have been organized initially by Homer. The five successive waves of migrations that it recorded enfolded Italy in the closely woven net of a Greek genealogy that could establish an unbroken continuity of generations and "races".

Dionysius and Strabo adopted identical strategies. The former produced a genealogy, the latter explored a particular space, but both suggested or proved that the initial points of reference were Greek. Why did Strabo devote so many pages and so much care to establishing Homer as the *archêgêtês* of geography, if not to prove that, thanks to Homer's travellers and the Argonauts, the Greeks already knew and therefore "controlled" the *oikoumenê* and its frontiers. Menelaus had established its Eastern frontiers, Odysseus the Western world, and Jason its Northern reaches. True, Homer was a poet, but all the same he spoke the truth. His starting point was *historia* (real knowledge about the world); and on to that it was justifiable to graft a measure of *muthos*.[56] Besides, it was perfectly possible to draw a distinction between what was clearly locatable (the Cyclopes, the Laestrygonians, Aeolus) and what not (Circe, Calypso, the Phaeacians), which, accordingly, had to be consigned to the Ocean. *Exoceanism* was a process that involved tipping back into the Ocean anything that *historia* could not encompass. Strabo, who in his own way was careful about boundaries (between myth and history, and between Ocean and such space as was nameable and controllable), was bound to defend a realistic reading of the voyages of Odysseus, which, after all, were set within the framework of Sicily and Italy and of which many traces (*ichnê*) remained. As we have seen, Polybius, cited approvingly by Strabo, had already reckoned it necessary to refute the hypercriticism of Eratosthenes and Aristarchus. And it was, besides, extraordinary that the very Alexandrians who had done so much to monumentalize Homer should at the same time defend a non-realistic reading of Homeric geography. To maintain that, on the contrary, geography was Greek in the first place was to declare that Odysseus was certainly the first to see and above all to tell of these places, and that Homer was the first to have put space, the whole of space, into (Greek) words.[57]

For us today, Dionysius, whom we regard as testifying to the relations between Greece and Rome, also played a major part in the construction of a new representation of those relations. It was still the view of one of the conquered, but by now he belonged to the seventh generation of them! Like Polybius, Posidonius, Panaetius, Strabo, and (in the near future) Plutarch and Aelius Aristides, he belonged to the lineage of Greek intellectuals who not only turned to Rome but also adopted a Roman viewpoint. What, in his day, did it mean to make that voyage to Rome? It meant adopting the view of the conqueror, but also "translating" it into Greek (for themselves in the first place, and for their Greek readers, but also for the Romans, who, for their part, could also speak and read Greek). And this meant mobilizing, reactivating or constructing the Greek coordinates of knowledge so as to give it form and intelligibility and, primarily, to indicate wherein the superiority of Roman power lay. But that operation could also lead to the elaboration of Greek counter-views, such as that put forward by Plutarch, in response to Roman interpretations of Alexander.

Dionysius of Halicarnassus' reputation has encountered a number of posthumous vicissitudes: first the spotlight of renown, then the dust of oblivion, followed by a more recent revival of interest.[58] The period of oblivion is signalled by the following judgement passed by Daunou in his history course at the Collège de France: "Dionysius is one of those unknown gods of literature whose cult is guaranteed by the respect with which people steer clear of their altars. They are willingly offered the homage due them, except for the only mark of respect that would have some value and utility, namely the reading of their works".[59] However, between the time of his rediscovery (the first Latin translation of the *Antiquities* appeared in 1480, and the great edition produced by R. Estienne followed in 1546) and the eighteenth century, he enjoyed great authority. He was considered to be superior to all the other Latin historians, and also to the Greeks, by reason of the way in which he presented the earliest days of Rome. He was also praised for speaking more honourably of the Romans than the Romans ever had of the Greeks. Scaliger congratulated him on his meticulous chronology and Bodin praised his serious commitment. He was unquestionably judged to be superior to Livy.

A similar opinion was expressed in the prefaces of the two French translations that appeared, in rapid succession, in 1722 and 1723.[60] Bellanger, the translator of the latter, praised him in particular for having set out to break down "the most odious classification of peoples into either Greeks or Barbarians", with the clear assumption that "Greek vanity" had relegated the Romans to the latter category. Dionysius had opted for Rome in order to counterbalance such indefensible Greek arrogance.

But those were Dionysius' last moments of a posthumous existence in which compliments and marks of deference abounded. The curve of destiny was about to swing in the opposite direction for many years to come. As the archaeologist of Rome's earliest times, he was inevitably totally caught up in the huge and lengthy debate on "the uncertainty of the first centuries of Rome". His public rejection came in the polemic that raged in the Académie des Inscriptions et Belles-Lettres from 1722 to 1725, in which Lévesque de Pouilly stood in opposition to Abbé Sallier.[61] Pouilly, a mathematician and the man who introduced Newton to France, sought to demonstrate the uncertainty. Sallier, professor of Hebrew at the Collège Royal, defended the certainty. In this debate, which was doubly overdetermined by the quarrel between the Ancients and the Moderns and also by the question of Pyrrhonism in history, what was at stake went far beyond the *Antiquities* and even Rome itself. But Dionysius was nevertheless questioned as to his sources and challenged as to his proofs: where had he learnt what he knew? Pouilly, echoing Cicero, declared: "If it was claimed in Athens that there one walked solely on monuments celebrated by History, it could be said of Rome that there all that could be seen were monuments illustrated by Fables". Sallier's only recourse was to maintain (appealing to the authority of Cicero) the exist-ence of "a continuous chain of confident and uninterrupted tradition" that stretched from the very origins of Rome all the way to the author of the *Antiquities*. Although that reduced Pouilly, who was accused of being a "philosophe", to silence, questions continued to be asked.

They resumed in force a few years later when Louis de Beaufort produced his *Dissertation sur l'incertitude des cinq premiers siècles de l'histoire romaine*,[62] which set the seal on the disgrace of Dionysius. Beaufort, who was a Protestant scholar living in the Low Countries, directed his criticism at the evidence produced by all the most generally respected ancient historians and aimed, somehow, to turn it against them so as to undermine the bases upon which the history of those first centuries rested. He had no difficulty in showing that not one of them claimed to have seen the famous *Annals* of the Pontiffs or "Chief Priests" with his own eyes, not even Dionysius, to whom he devoted an entire chapter, meaningfully entitled "On the character of Dionysius of Halicarnassus and the credibility of his history".

This was the first time that both the choice made by Dionysius and his very personality were challenged. His character undermined his work, the authority of which was denounced as false. It was above all "ostentation". Dionysius did not (and could not possibly) possess proof for his theses, but he acted as though he did, affecting precision and sincerity. "As he makes a great show of criticism and erudition in much of his research work and many of his discussions, one is easily dazzled by an appearance of precision and good faith which, however, turns out to be totally spurious as soon as it is placed under a spotlight".[63] What was his purpose? "To get the Greeks to bear with greater patience the yoke that a nation that they considered to be Barbarian had imposed upon them". His opting for Rome, a decision hitherto judged lucid and courageous, was charged with negative connotations: Dionysius was nothing but a flatterer, making up to the Romans (and a traitor to Greece). At this point Beaufort introduces an extremely interesting comparison with Flavius Josephus, who was "far more concerned to pay court to the pagans than to stick to the exact truth":[64] Dionysius, in his own way, was also a "court Jew". And furthermore he was a failure, since the Romans, whose vanity he flattered so much, continued to tell their own story of their origins, without paying much attention to his demonstrations.

Livy, in contrast, was rehabilitated: not that he knew any more than Dionysius about the origins of Rome, but precisely because he admitted that he knew virtually nothing. He was saved by his "sincerity", and this made him preferable to Dionysius, who was condemned both as a man and as a historian.[65]

The author of the *Antiquities* had entered a long period of purgatory! German historiography of the nineteenth century, which by and large fell into line with the criticisms of the Protestant Beaufort, held him in low esteem. He was just a *Graeculus*, a little Greek. He was both too much of a literary dabbler to respond deeply to the human drama of the Greeks' conquest by Rome and also too limited, too ignorant, to apprehend the formidable reality of Rome (both the state and its law). So intent was he upon singing the praises of Rome as the true representative of Hellenism that he was incapable of grasping what the study of their origins really meant to men such as Cato and Varro. Eduard Schwartz's conclusion was that he truly was just "a little Greek pedant".[66]

One last mode of attack used Dionysius the literary critic to discredit Dionysius the historian. Even his rhetorical work (the importance of which was recognized) devalued his historical endeavours. That was the verdict of Max Egger at the beginning of the twentieth century. At a moment when history was declaring its horror of literature and proclaiming itself a positivist science, ensconcing itself as a discipline securely in the bastion of the new Sorbonne, where Thucydides tended to be regarded as the father of that history, Dionysius, the incorrigible *rhetor*, was severely denounced and admonished in the name of the necessary separation (of which he had no inkling) between history and the rhetoric which, as Egger pointed out, Michelet regarded as a foretaste of Byzantine imbecility. The most telling proof of his presumptuous ignorance was provided by the criticisms that he had seen fit to address to Thucydides in person. He had even gone so far as to correct or even rewrite whole passages of the historian's work. Egger, pacific but lucid, wound up by declaring "We must forgive him for not having understood the genius of Thucydides".[67] Once again, as compared to his great ancestor, Dionysius was judged to be just a minor Greek professor, a *rhetor* playing at being a historian but incapable of seeing beyond his own rhetoric. The *Antiquities* remained a model, but were now an altogether negative one, "a perfect model of what can result from the intrusion of rhetoric into history".[68] Meanwhile a historian, as trained by the new Sorbonne, was expected not to indulge in fine writing, but to efface himself before the facts, leaving history to speak for itself.

So what was left of Dionysius? He was inferior to Livy, inferior to his subject as a historian, and inferior to himself as a man. In fact, was anything at all left of Dionysius? Yet the curve of his destiny was about to alter course once again and to experience both a reversal and a boost. That has been proved over the past twenty-five or so years by the work of G. W. Bowersock in the United States and E. Gabba in Italy.[69] It is not that Dionysius overnight became or became again an authority on the origins of Rome. Simply, he was a witness at whom different questions began to be directed. Views shifted and the questions posed took a different form. This was a Dionysius who prompted a real revival of interest.

As soon as one reads the *Antiquities* as not just a history *of* origins, but also and perhaps primarily a history *on* origins, one's attitude changes. As one leafs through the text, one becomes attentive to his way of speaking of the past in the present tense, of looking at the past from a standpoint in the present, and also in Rome, yet writing in Greek and still deploying Greek knowledge and Greek know-how along with Roman understanding and a Roman agenda. At any rate, the *history* of the beginnings of Rome, itself prompted by different circumstances and responding to purposes that did not always remain the same – history as it was written in Rome itself – drew upon multiple strata and pooled materials of different kinds and from a variety of provenances and ages.

In the service of Rome and subscribing to the values of the Roman aristocracy (which explains both his staunch loyalty to the Roman order and also the presence of the theme of the decadence of a Rome which, precisely, has "forgotten" the values of its origins), Dionysius, along with others and already in

the wake of others, aims to re-elaborate a past, revisit a culture, in short rein-
vent a tradition. Or at least to attempt to do so with the means and likewise
the limits peculiar to a *rhetor* of the first century, whose discourse sets out to
"state whatever is 'credible' or 'the most credible'". His archaeological endeavour consists in removing the "mythical" element so as to increase the element
of verisimilitude as much as possible, and so become an account that "resembles the truth" as much as possible.

Rome is a Greek city. The Romans have always lived a "Greek life". Given
that they first came from the Greece that was Arcadia, Dionysius concludes
that there can be no Greeks who are more "purely" and "anciently" Greek
than the Romans.[70] But by introducing a third term, did he really blow apart
the Greek–Barbarian dichotomy, as Bellanger congratulates him for doing?
One might think so when he declares, for example, that he will prove to his
readers that Rome, right from its earliest times, provided more proofs of
excellence (*aretê*) than any other city, whether "Greek or Barbarian".[71] But
the expression had been current for so long that it had simply become a fixed
way of saying "in the whole world" or "anywhere". Could the words even be
understood without regard to whoever pronounced them or heard them?
And anyway, what was a Barbarian city? Was this not simply a way to designate the emergence of a new and exceptional entity which, even though it was
certainly not on the side of the Barbarians, could nevertheless not be confused with the other term in the dichotomy?

At other times, in particular when successive immigrants have to fight
against "Barbarians", Dionysius seems simply to be extending the use of
"Greek", being content to include future Romans *ipso facto* within the general concept of Greeks.[72] Yet, when writing of sacrificial rituals (in which
Dionysius takes a keen interest, as he considers they testify to a cultural
identity), he lets slip the expression "we Greeks" (use barley), whereas "the
Romans" (resort to spelt, i.e. wheat). That contrast between "us" and "them"
seems to be a fleeting lapse.

According to the logic of this view, the history of Rome becomes that of a
"barbarization" resulting from an "admixture", a barbarization of what had
originally been pure Greekness. That is another version of the theme of decadence. One might even "be surprised that Rome has not been completely
barbarized as a result of having taken in Opici, Marsi, Samnites, Tyrrhenians,
Bruttians, and thousands of Umbrians, Ligurians, Iberians, and Celts, etc.".
The example of other colonial cities established in Barbarian surroundings

certainly shows that Rome, even if it has "unlearnt" some of its early customs, has resisted astonishingly well:

> Many others by living among barbarians have in a short time forgotten all their Greek heritage, so that they neither speak the Greek language nor observe the customs of the Greeks nor acknowledge the same gods nor have the same equitable laws (by which the nature [*phusis*] of the Greeks differs most from that of the barbarians) nor agree with them in anything else that relates to the ordinary intercourse of life.[73]

The Achaeans of the Black Sea, in contrast, have totally "forgotten" their original Greekness and have become "the most savage of Barbarians". Through his remarks on acculturation, Dionysius suddenly tells us that, for him, there is not only a Greek culture (*to Hellênikon*) but also a Greek nature (*phusis*), which is distinct from the nature of the Barbarians. How do the two interact? We do not really know. At any rate, the Romans have both.

That mixture is clear, in particular, from the Latin language, which is neither completely Greek nor really Barbarian, but a compound of the two (a compound dominated by the Aeolian dialect):[74] which is why the Romans are unable "to pronounce all their sounds properly"![75]

But Dionysius cannot claim that the mixing began only when the city took in Opici and other Barbarians, for the entire tradition insists that right from the start Rome was characterized by mixture. Mixture yes, but only between Greeks, he might have retorted. However, he does not risk it, and leaves the matter somewhat vague. The Aborigines mix with the Pelasgians, the Latins mix with the Trojan arrivals;[76] Albans are said to result from a mixture of Greeks of various origins, but also with a Barbarian element.[77] As for the group of colonists who one fine day left Alba to found Rome, all we are told is that Romulus and Remus mixed it with "those who were there", a local population that was somehow already present.[78]

As used by Dionysius, the metaphor of mixture, which is at once expressive yet vague and which, depending on the circumstances, is sometimes given a positive slant (producing growth), sometimes a negative one (resulting in barbarization), shows that in his attempt to conceptualize the foundation of Rome, he oscillates between two Greek models: *apoikia* and *synoecism*.[79]

Let us consider the colonial model first: the expedition and settlement of colonists. Rome is, strictly speaking, a colony (*apoikia*). The gradual evolution of Rome can even be regarded as a slow colonization that begins with the first Arcadian migration and is completed only with the final departure from Alba, which Dionysius describes with a great wealth of detail. The two young leaders are not only entrusted by their grandfather with a group of colonists (itself composed of a number of different categories). He also provides them with "money, arms, wheat, slaves, draught animals, and everything indispensable for the construction of a city". The future colony certainly lacked for nothing! Dionysius not only uses this model, he also milks it for all it is worth, for the more Rome results from an *apoikia*, the better its chances of being Greek.

At this point in the story, Dionysius has yet to get rid of Remus. As a rule, after all, a colony did not have two *archêgêtai* (founders). His way of proceeding is interesting, for it appeals to Greek notions and references that enable him both to respect the tradition (the inevitable death of Remus) and to produce a believable account leading up to that act of violence. When the group of colonists leaves Alba, it is composite, but united. And it remains so, even after "mixing" with the remains of the local population living on the Palatine and around the hill of Saturn.

But then comes the split. Romulus and Remus decide to divide the group into two in order, they think, to foster a spirit of competition (*philotimia*) and thereby hasten the completion of the work connected with the foundation of the colony. But, alas, the *philotimia* (positive behaviour) immediately turns into *stasis* (discord), which is entirely negative. Even before the foundation of the city the reader is thus plunged, through this spirit of competition that turns into its opposite, into a familiar world of struggles for power, as within a Greek city. Rome is not yet Rome, but already it resembles the city that would be described by, for example, Plutarch, in his *Precepts of Statecraft*. The same political vocabulary is already used to evoke the rivalries, ambitions and bids for power that set the nobles and their factions at loggerheads and eventually lead to civil war and murder.[80] The root of it all, in short, was the ambivalence of that *philotimia*, from which "emerged" an account that conferred intelligibility and verisimilitude upon events which otherwise would have been seriously lacking in those qualities. In the end it was not surprising that things turned out as they did!

This totally political register is overlaid by another, which might be termed pre-political. Here, the sphere of reference is not the Hellenistic city with all its power-struggles, but rather Hesiod's *Works and Days*, with its famous introductory passage devoted to *Eris*, Strife, that Hesiod addresses to his brother Perses, with whom he is, precisely, in dispute. Strife is itself double: one facet of it prompts people to enter into competition and is "far kinder to men", while the other "fosters evil war and battle".[81] In Dionysius' account, too, *Eris* establishes itself openly between the two brothers, Romulus and Remus, as soon as they divide the colonists into two groups. It immediately turns into "evil strife".[82] Movement between the two registers is easy: one can pass either from *philotimia* to *eris* or from *stasis* to *eris*. By specifically choosing the word *eris*, Dionysius adds a new dimension to his text, almost a new plot, from which he can draw out the thread of his own story. The desire to command, by which both the brothers are consumed, is described as *akoinônêtos*. The word is revealing, for it operates on both registers simultaneously. In the first place, their desire for power can tolerate no sharing: each of them wants everything for himself. This is the domain of "pre-political" strife. But that desire for domination also expresses a total negation of any form of community (*koinônia*): it thwarts or destroys all social links.[83] So this *eris/stasis* is bound to lead to slaughter, and this too intermingles the two registers: brother kills brother, citizen kills "fellow-citizen".[84] Romulus, who emerges victorious but saddened by this criminal victory, is now the sole founder and can proceed to bring Rome into existence.[85]

But, just as Dionysius was unable totally to dismiss the mixed origins of Rome, so too he cannot altogether defend the model of a colonial foundation right up to the hilt, particularly as he finds himself quite isolated and, on this score too, in all too obvious opposition to the tradition. Neither Cicero, nor Livy, nor Virgil, nor even Plutarch lines up with him. According to Plutarch, Rome's was quite the opposite of a foundation by immigrant colonists, since it was the citizens of Alba who, refusing to accept among them this band of marginals recruited by the two brothers, left them no choice but to go off and settle elsewhere, on their own.[86]

The second possible model was that of a synoecism: the city did not result from the arrival of colonists from a metropolis, but from the amalgamation of populations already present on the site. Dionysius allusively makes use of this model too, implying that Rome did result from a synoecism or at least that synoecism had something to do with the story. But he never questions the compatibility of the two models or how they intermesh. Is Rome an *apoikia* or a synoecism? Or is it a mixture of the two? The implication of a synoecism does of course offer an added advantage to the extent that where synoecism was concerned the expert *par excellence* was Theseus.

Admittedly, Dionysius does not draw a direct parallel between the creation of Athens as a city and the foundation of Rome, but, for a Greek, his Romulus was bound to seem a kind of Theseus (and it would not be long before Plutarch drew a direct comparison between the two). The extremely long speech delivered by Romulus at the beginning of Book II, his surprising uncertainty as to the best regime to establish, more or less an offer to abdicate power, find a precedent in (and are illuminated by), for example, the behaviour of the Theseus of Isocrates. The figure of Theseus, which provides a model of behaviour (that is both plausible and well known), helps Dionysius to construct an account of the foundation of Rome and to elaborate his own line on the matter, once – that is – Remus is out of the way and the demands of the tradition have been satisfied. It made his questioning of the constitution almost plausible. Like Theseus in his own day, Romulus put before an assembly of the people the question of what regime should be established.[87] But, needless to say, in the aftermath of Polybius, who had made this the crux of his reflections on Roman power, nobody could set out to speak of Rome without laying the emphasis upon its constitution. That was the price that had to be paid for the credibility of a Greek historian of Rome. Dionysius' "constitution of Rome" was his way of satisfying that demand and expectation. However, it involved a certain amount of self-contradiction. First, following Polybius and Cicero, he explains that the Roman constitution could not have emerged, ready armed, from the head of some legislator, however divine, but must have been a continuous creation that evolved from numerous experiments. He then abruptly introduces the idea that the complete constitution was produced as the climax of the process of foundation, in fact in itself almost represented a new foundation. Romulus divided things up, established procedures, laid down ground-rules, etc.[88]

The implication of this untraceable Romulean constitution is that Rome is definitely a city. Polybius had already provided ample proof of that. His Book VI corresponds to Dionysius' Book II; but whereas Polybius developed a structural type of reflection on regimes in general, Dionysius tells a story (Romulus did this, undertook that, resolved the other ...) and historicizes (this institution, or that mechanism, was borrowed from Greece ...). Furthermore, now that times had changed, politically speaking "mixture" was no longer in fashion: the senate no longer played the key role in the machinery of power; it was more reminiscent of the council of Elders that advised a Homeric king. All those kings "had a council composed of the best men, as both Homer and the most ancient of the poets testify; and the authority of the ancient kings was not arbitrary and absolute as it is in our days".[89] So much for senatorial nostalgia.

According to Dionysius, Rome, a city right from the start, was moreover more successful than even the most famous of the Greek cities, Sparta, Athens and Thebes. Not content simply with borrowing this or that institution, the Romans, right from the time of Romulus, were intent upon perfecting the model. For instance, they changed patronage, an ancient Greek practice (but in those days in fact closer to servitude), into an institution of central importance: a whole gamut of reciprocal obligations, which in the long run functioned as veritable links of kinship, was established between a patron (a patrician) and his client (a plebeian).[90] Patronage, which created concord (*homonoia*), turned Rome into a city capable of controlling its internal conflicts, its *stasis*, the struggle for power that the Greek cities, for their part, never managed to quash for long. Rome, despite having started out under the sign of fratricidal warfare, the worst possible kind, subsequently, for 630 years (up until the advent of Caius Gracchus, to be precise, says Dionysius), managed to substitute persuasion for murder.[91] That was a considerable achievement, and one that incontestably testified to Rome's superiority. Modern historiography, particularly German, was to echo that favourable judgement.

Not only was Rome for a long time free of *stasis*, it was also an "open" city. Unlike the ancient Greek cities, always so concerned to preserve the "nobility of their blood" and so closed upon themselves that they seldom granted new rights of citizenship, Rome had always been generous in this area. This is where Dionysius introduces a theme destined for a fine future in comparisons between the Greeks and the Romans: namely, the theme of Roman "generosity" as compared to Greek "avarice".[92] For Dionysius, this constitutes the second element in Rome's manifest superiority, for, having adopted that attitude, Rome managed to turn it into a positive policy and, all in all, a powerful basis of its empire. It would not be hard to show that any such project would have made no sense at all in a Greek city, since it was defined, by Aristotle, as a "fully perfected and self-sufficient" community: right from its foundation it was thus complete. But at this point all that is relevant is what Dionysius, and many historians after him, believed and said: namely, that Rome had found a path that the Greeks had missed. Yet again, Rome turns out to be a better city; the same *polis* as in Greece, but perfected. Dionysius describes it as "the most hospitable and friendly of all cities", the one which learned how to be the truest, most profound and most enduring community (*koinotatê*).[93]

With the *Roman Antiquities*, the shift and subsequent reversal of perspective was complete. Rome, as a city, was no longer judged from a Greek point of view; now it was the Greek cities that were assessed from the point of view of Rome, which was considered to be a fully perfected city. The Greek city did not die at Chaeronea, for Rome was its future. The younger Anacharsis, returning to his Scythian deserts, had no way of knowing that! Not only was there Hellenism in Rome, but it was necessary to make the journey to Rome in order to grasp what it was that the classical Greek city had lacked. Dionysius, by showing that the Romans were Greeks, did not only Hellenize Rome; reciprocally, when he "restored" Romulus' constitution, he "Romanized" the Greek city. Pursuing the thrust of the Polybian argument to the limit, he reached the point where, in effect, he was insisting that Rome was a city, a city whose success testified to the excellence of its constitution, a perfected city, but still the very model of a *polis*.

That was his thesis, and those were his aims. The subject seemed to be of crucial relevance. At a time when Rome had "grown to the point of buckling beneath its own greatness", the masters of the world seem to have been bothered about their identity. In the manoeuvres of the game of origins, in answer to those who, like Virgil, declared that the Romans were neither Greeks nor Etruscans, but Trojans, Dionysius insisted: clearly you are not Etruscans as you are Greeks and the sons of Greeks; and even if you are Trojans, you are still or were initially Greeks. That is the starting point for everything.

THE VOYAGES OF STRABO AND AELIUS ARISTIDES

Dionysius of Halicarnassus and Strabo proceed in similar fashion. The former is in quest of a genealogy, the latter is inventorying a space. But both, like Polybius before them, are intent upon persuading their readers and, possibly even more, themselves that, when it comes to knowledge, all the first points of reference are Greek.

Strabo, who was born in Amaseia, on the Black Sea, in about 65 BC, travelled to Alexandria and to Rome and lived in both places. He started out as a historian and wrote a work entitled *Histories*, now lost, which took over where Polybius left off and covered a period that extended down to the death of Cicero. Then, as a geographer, he composed a universal geography in seventeen books, which has been preserved. This *Geographical Tableau* of the inhabited world, written by "a Greek from Asia, highly considered in Rome, sets out openly to be a *political geography*, above all for the use of governments, and designed to account for a particular *state of the world* (around the early years of the reign of Tiberius) which, at the time, was considered to be satisfactory: a world that was both open (thanks to the recent establishment of direct trading links with India) and also closed, thanks to the *pax romana*".[94]

Like Polybius before him, he called the Mediterranean "our sea", a clear indication that he viewed the world with the eyes of Rome.[95] At the same time, however, he, just as staunchly as Polybius, defended the veracity of Homer, whom he wished to establish as the *archêgêtês* of geography.[96] Why? How? Setting himself up, in his turn, against Eratosthenes, he began by anchoring that defence in the concept of poetry, regarded as the first vehicle for philosophy, and in the theory that *muthos* was a conveyor of truth, not just a fiction aimed solely at captivating an audience. The Stoics even went so far as to declare that "only a sage is a poet".[97] Homer not only knew, but knew for "certain" (*akribeia*), both that which was close at hand and that which was distant.[98] So it must be concluded that, already with Homer, the Greeks knew the world and were in control of its limits. Homer, whom Strabo regarded as a man with a taste for travelling and an enquiring mind, knew how to describe the world, or rather how to sing of it, reaching the widest possible audience by drawing upon the power of fable and the reserves of allegory.[99]

Nestor, Menelaus and above all Odysseus testify to the connection between travelling and practical wisdom (*phronêsis*). And the knowledge of the world that they manifested (and that, in consequence, Homer must also have possessed) was the very same knowledge that was now dispensed by geography: it laid the foundations for "practical wisdom". Polybius used to say: all will be well – for the writing of history, at any rate – when statesmen become historians and when historians think as statesmen, and he would invoke Odysseus, both as a historian and as a statesman, in fact as a historian because he was the model of a statesman. Strabo followed a similar line of reasoning: Odysseus remained his reference, but geography now took the place of history. Basically, geography was a political science.[100] Its function was to assist government. But it was pointless for those governing to become geographers themselves: all that was needed was for geographers to place themselves at the service of the statesmen. To each his own task! Furthermore, Odysseus was not simply a geographer, but also a philosopher. This Odysseus, credited with every talent and taken over from the Stoic tradition, was bound to be of great help to Strabo in his geographical "operation", the aim of which was to legitimate geography as philosophy if, as the opening words of his work maintained, it was true that "the science of geography ... is, quite as much as any other science, a concern of the philosopher".[101]

For Polybius, the historian's task was to produce a "universal history", that is to say to interweave the particular (*kata hekaston*) with the general (*katholou*). But as he was working in Rome, he ran the risk of, so to speak, identifying Rome with what was "general", or even consciously opted to do so. Strabo, in his "universal" geography, a geographical analogue of Polybius' work, similarly set out to combine the particular and the general. But this time, his avowed objective was to adopt the point of view of the Roman masters as the measure of what was "general". A geographer had to work like a sculptor carving a colossal statue in which, in the last analysis, it was the over-all, general effect that mattered most, not the precision of every last detail.[102] Just as, in the world unified by the Roman conquest, fragmented or monographic history was obsolete, similarly in the world of Augustus the space of the *oikoumenê* had to be seen as a whole which only a general point of view could apprehend, construct and represent correctly. That was the only way to master it.

To carve up space and classify different peoples, the Greeks had deployed a whole set of climato-political concepts, organized around the representation of centrality, mixtures and balances. In Herodotus and Hippocrates those concepts had held good for Ionia. Later, they had been transferred to the whole of Greece or, to be more precise, to the *genos* of the Greeks.[103] Strabo, in his turn, adopted that same grid, but extended it to include Europe, which was no longer limited to the boundaries of Greece alone. In this way, the superiority of Europe over the rest of the world was given a "scientific" basis and a "scientific" explanation. He writes as follows:

I must begin with Europe because it is both varied in form and admirably adapted by nature for the development of excellence in men and governments, and also because it has contributed most of its own store of good things to other continents; for the whole of it is habitable with the exception of a small region that is uninhabited on account of the cold. Of the habitable part of Europe, the cold mountainous regions furnish by nature only a wretched existence to their inhabitants, yet even the regions of poverty and piracy become *civilized* (*hêmerountai*) as soon as they get good administrators. Take the case of the Greeks: though occupying mountains and rocks, they used to live happily (*kalôs*), because they took forethought for *good government*, for the arts, and in general for the science of living. The Romans too took over many nations that were naturally savage owing to the regions that they inhabited, because those regions were either rocky or without harbours or cold or for some other reason ill-suited to habitation by many, and thus not only brought into communication

190

with each other peoples who had been isolated, but also taught the more savage how to live *under forms of government*. But all of Europe that is level and has a temperate climate (*eukratos*) has nature to cooperate with her towards these results; for while in a country that is blessed by nature everything tends to peace, in a disagreeable country everything tends to make men warlike and courageous; and so both kinds of country receive benefits from each other, for the latter helps with arms, the former with products of the soil, with arts, and with character-building. But the harm that they receive from each other, if they are not mutually helpful, is also apparent; and the might of those who are accustomed to carry arms will have some advantage unless it be controlled by the majority. However, this continent has a natural advantage to meet this condition also; for the whole of it is diversified with plains and mountains, so that throughout its entire extent the agricultural and civilized element dwells side by side with the warlike element; but of the two elements the one that is peace-loving is more numerous and therefore keeps control over the whole body; and the leading nations too – formerly the Greeks and later the Macedonians and the Romans – have taken hold and helped. And for this reason Europe is the most self-sufficient (*autarkestatê*) of all countries as regards both peace and war; for the warlike population that she possesses is abundant and also that which tills her soils and holds her cities secure. She excels also in this respect, that she produces the fruits that are best and that are necessary for life, and all the useful metals, while she imports from abroad spices and precious stones – things that make the life of persons who have only a scarcity of them fully as happy as that of persons who have them in abundance. So also, Europe offers an abundance of various kinds of cattle, but a scarcity of wild animals: such, in a general way, is the nature of this continent.[104]

The above long quotation is remarkable for a number of reasons. The whole European space, embraced in one sweeping look, is seen as the territory of a single city, defined as self-sufficient to the highest degree. It is true that Strabo does not declare that Europe actually constitutes a single city, but his return to the concept of self-sufficiency, the pivot of Aristotle's definition of the Classical city, at least implies the possibility.[105] Although the vocabulary has an Aristotelian ring, there is a profound difference since, in Aristotle's view, not even the Peloponnese, surrounded by a single rampart, could have been considered as forming a *polis*.[106] Let alone Europe! But anyway, within this space, in which variety can be combined with complementarity and peace can prevail over war, the constraints or defects of nature can be corrected by learning how to follow a "political" way of life. Ensconced in their mountainous land, the Greeks managed to accomplish that "political" work for their own benefit, achieving a combination of civilization, civility and citizenship. But in the historical picture sketched in by Strabo, the Greeks are simply the inhabitants of one small province and represent but a fleeting moment. They were succeeded by the Macedonians, then the Romans, and it is the latter who are now the strong-armed institutors of civilization. Links are in this way established between Europe and the name of Rome. And when all is said and done, is it not Rome, that unique city, that is present just below the surface of the universal image that Strabo creates of the European space? It is as if Europe is a *polis* the name of which is Rome. Rome's centrality is thus established in accordance with a Greek mode of logic. But this way of translating the Roman vision of that centrality *into Greek* is, at the same time, a kind of betrayal of the Greek definition of what a city is.

Furthermore, the idea of Europe is itself more Greek than Roman. Europe, which was at first only a way of designating part of the Greek mainland, was then extended and acquired greater weight as the antonym of Asia.[107] That was the time of a polemical and political Europe, in a world divided into two parts. And even when the world was generally accepted to be divided into three continents, the Europe–Asia division long remained the principal dichotomy. For Rome, in contrast, there was from very early on no horizon other than that of the world.[108] From 76–75 BC on, the coins of the Republic displayed the image of a globe. Pompey already, on the occasion of his triumph in 61 BC, announced that he "had rolled back the boundaries of the Roman Empire to the very limits of the earth", and Augustus, in his *Res gestae*, proclaimed that he had "subjected the world to the empire of Rome".[109] Pompey, furthermore, had congratulated himself on having received Asia as a "frontier province" and then turned it into the centre of an empire: a clear indication that the power of Rome did not recognize the old divisions. In short, Asia, initially a frontier province, had been digested by the empire. Only Rome's enemies, the Parthians, and later the Sassanids, envisaged confining the Romans "to Europe" and demanding a return to the frontiers of Darius.[110] Roman space truly was the space of Rome. Geographically speaking, Europe did not represent a limit of any significance, and the relation between the *Urbs* and Europe could not be classed as metonymic. On the other hand, there were many variations on the City–World (*Urbs–Orbis*) theme. That was a genuine metonymy. First there was the City and the World, then the City that became the mistress of the World, and finally the City with no limits but those of the World itself. The territory of the former was coextensive with the space of the latter: "*Romanae spatium est urbis et orbis idem*", as Ovid, addressing the god Terminus ("Boundary"), put it.[111]

That was a *topos* that was central to eulogistic literature and very much to the fore in the *Speech to Rome* delivered by Aelius Aristides in Rome, in the presence of the emperor, in 143 or 155 AD.[112] This famous sophist, the scion of an influential family from the neighbourhood of Pergamum, having completed his training in Athens under Herodes Atticus, felt it imperative to go to Rome. It was no longer just a matter of making the voyage to Rome but also of making *the Roman voyage*. Only by doing so could renown and prestige be won: higher fees could then be charged by a professor or a lecturer, and a greater social and political role could be exercised, in particular as an (effective) intercessor on behalf of one's native city. In all these matters the dialectic between the City and the Empire was clearly important.[113]

The speech opens with a passage on the immensity of the City, impossible to take in all at once (and therefore superior to anything that could be said of it) but, in the last analysis, an appropriate image for the immense empire of which it was the centre. Already, in itself, it *was* the empire. A little further on, the empire is described as the territory of a single city, of which Rome represents now the agora, now the acropolis.[114] According to Plutarch, Alexander had wanted his camp to be, as it were, the acropolis of the universe. What is implied by these variations on the theme of the City and the World, variations expressed using Greek political vocabulary? Were they just word games or pure political cant, in the aftermath of the conceptual trend initiated by Polybius, "the great mystifier"? After all, to suggest that the empire was a city was to drain the very notion of the *polis* of all meaningfulness. Was this a way of masking the reality of the imperial regime: of avoiding having to look too closely into its nature, perhaps because the means (particularly the conceptual means) to do so were lacking? Was it a way of pretending that this was still the same world, with the same reference points and an unimpaired continuity? Did such claims express the impossibility (felt by both the Greeks and the Romans) of conceiving of a world that would no longer take the *polis* as its horizon, just as it was impossible to conceive of a world without slaves or, to be more precise, a world in which the city no longer stood for the "good life", the civilized life? In these circumstances, how could Rome, the mistress of the world, possibly be presented as anything but a city *par excellence*: the finest, greatest, most perfect of all cities?

According to Aelius Aristides, just as the Great King was not truly "great", so Alexander was no longer to be seen as a challenger or precursor of the power of Rome. He was simply a king who, so to speak, never reigned. His destiny was like that of a victor in the Olympic Games who, upon crossing the finishing line, collapses even before he can be properly crowned.[115] Homer, on the other hand, remains more than ever a major reference, but of rather a different kind: not so much as the *archêgêtês* of (Greek) knowledge, as he was for Polybius and Strabo, but as the repository of a wealth of comparisons and a text which can conveniently be interpreted as predicting the future power of Rome. Take, for instance, the allusion to the coming reign of Aeneas and his descendants over the Trojan race, or the observation that Rome has, in truth, made "the earth common to all".[116] Rome is seen as fulfilling the Homeric text. But here again, Aelius Aristides' tactic should not be taken literally; it is a game in which the reader does not really believe, but which makes the transition from Greece to Rome even more acceptable, at the same time reinforcing the status of Homer as a classic or rather as the Bible common to the whole ancient world.[117]

What is the basis for this vision of Rome as the fulfilment or crowning achievement of history?[118] A line in Virgil, which recognizes that it is Rome's destiny to exercise dominion: *tu regere imperio populos, Romane, memento / hae tibi erunt artes.*[119] This art of *kratos*, which hitherto had eluded mankind, was a discovery that they were destined to make. The Romans *are* sovereignty, neither more nor less: this is the reign of Zeus (Jupiter). And that means, first and foremost, the imposition of order. The Romans have rejected the old times, with all those wars, which were real enough both in the past and in the domain of myth: those are now just stories to be listened to,[120] in the same way as the Phaeacians listened, purely for pleasure, to their bard singing of the Trojan War and the death of so many heroes. The Romans have dominated the entire space of the *oikoumenê*, surveying it, linking it together with roads and bridges, in short setting it in order and controlling it, just as if it really was a single estate (*oikos*). So efficiently have they accomplished this that there is no longer any call for travellers to tell of the exoticism of the world or for geographers to map it.

Odysseus' voyage is well and truly completed, with all limits explored and all frontiers firmly fixed. The masters of the world have no further need of travellers and geographers, for they themselves have become the universal geographers or, to borrow Aristides' expression, "travellers for all" (*koinoi*)[121] – in deed, not just in word. Finally then, we come to the answer proposed by

Aristides to the question: "Where should the Romans be placed?" The old division, long since obsolete, between the Greeks and the Barbarians must now be replaced by a new one that is all-encompassing and more relevant: between Romans and non-Romans. For the Romans are not simply one "race" (*genos*) among others, but the one that counterbalances all the rest.

Their name, overspilling the boundaries of a city, designates a "common race": the *genos* of Roman citizens.[122] Even a man who has never set eyes on Rome may call himself "Roman". Such a horizontal division, which picks out a small elite but is not bounded by the frontiers and territories of particular cities, signals a new concept of the city and new relations with "others". Rather than acknowledge this or because they were at a loss as to how to account for it, Greek intellectuals (and Romans too) opted to represent Rome as a *polis* more perfect than the best of Greek cities. Polybius was the first to devote himself to the task, as a historian steeped in political philosophy; he was followed by Dionysius of Halicarnassus as an "archaeologist", by Strabo as a geographer, and by Aelius Aristides as a *rhetor*. Each, in his way, played his part in this invention of Rome. And the moderns followed in their footsteps, praising Roman "generosity" in the matter of the rights of citizenship and contrasting this to the "avarice" of the Greeks.

Plutarch had recalled attention to the upsurge of the "Roman question" among the Greeks, by crystallizing it in the powerful image of the encounter of Pyrrhus, the Greek ruler, with the Roman legions. How should the Romans be classified? That was a question that was also – if not initially – posed and pondered by the Romans themselves, for they were extremely concerned and anxious about their origins. Montaigne, an attentive and inventive reader of Plutarch, took over the image but transferred it to the scene of the New World, to help him to come to grips with the idea of the Savage. He started by attacking the forces of prejudice. Plutarch's response to the problem, for its part, was twofold: a staunch defence of the Greek identity coupled with a systematic use of comparison. In the present work, we have already come across the man of Chaeronea and priest of Delphi often enough to be in no doubt as to the decisive role that he played in this construction or invention of a tradition. But comparison, as used in the *Parallel Lives*, operates in a different register: that of the *exemplum* and self-improvement. It operates somewhere between the private and the public levels, or is used for a private appropriation of the great men of the past. But the very use of comparison indicates that the "question" of the Greeks and the Romans is by now considered settled. For by systematically matching the biography of a famous Greek to the biography of a famous Roman, two comparable men, who shared the same values and the same nature and obeyed the same laws, Plutarch placed the Greeks of the past and the men responsible for the greatness of Rome on the same side and on the same level. It was a matter no longer of Greeks, Barbarians, and Romans as a third party, but rather of Greeks and Romans, equally men and equally citizens, who presented the men of the present time, who were all citizens of the same empire, with models of behaviour to emulate and great (Graeco-Roman) memories to share.[123]

Aelius Aristides had made the long journey to Rome to celebrate the City's anniversary on 21 April 143 (according to our own method of dating). Montaigne, also a traveller keen to visit Rome, stayed there from November 1580 until April 1581, to celebrate Christmas and Easter. It was the ultimate goal of the long voyage upon which he had set out six months earlier. While in Rome, he saw the pope and received his blessing, visited the churches, relished the Lent sermons, and also took an interest in ancient Rome. While visiting the Vatican Library, he paused before the statue of "the good Aristides", Aelius Aristides, his distant predecessor, and was impressed by his "fine, bald head", his "thick beard", his "lofty brow" and his "gaze full of gentleness and majesty".[124] But his comment on the ancient Rome that he was "amusing himself studying" was that "there was nothing to be seen of it except the sky beneath which it had lain and the plan of its foundations ...; those who said that one could at least see the ruins of Rome were exaggerating, for the ruins of such a redoubtable machine would inspire more honour and reverence for its memory; this was nothing but its sepulchre".[125]

He wandered through the existing city and reckoned that Rome was "the most communal city in the world, where foreignness and national differences are of the least account, for in its very nature it is a city pieced together with foreigners; and each of them seems to be at home". Detectable in his words is an echo, albeit reformulated in accordance with a different, Catholic, logic, of all those ancient variations on the theme of the City and the World. The "most communal" city, "pieced together with foreigners", means that, because Rome constitutes a summary of the world, it is the most cosmopolitan of all cities. The world is in Rome, and a Roman is, as it were, a citizen of the world. Montaigne immediately goes on to say that he went to great trouble to acquire the title of Roman citizen, "if only for the ancient honour and the religious memory of its authority". That says it all: he was surrounded by the memory of what no longer existed. Aristides, praising the authority of Rome, had proclaimed: "You have divided humanity into Romans and non-Romans". And Montaigne, who obtained the coveted title before leaving the town, concluded: "It is a vain title; but it gave me great pleasure to receive it".[126] He expressed reverence for the memory of a Rome that was no more: Roman citizenship was by now just a fine souvenir of a voyage.

Almost two centuries later, Johann Joachim Winckelmann, from Dresden, finally arrived in Rome on 19 November 1755. His attitude and expectations were very different. What mattered for him was not a title of Roman citizenship, but the very meaning of life. The name of Rome signified antiquity. Rome was the resting place of the Beauty of the art of the ancients. In order to approach it and study it, Winckelmann had even been prepared to abandon Lutheranism and convert to Catholicism. "Come and see", he had recently written, borrowing the words of the Gospel of Saint John, in his *Description of the Dresden Art Gallery*.[127] For the man who was to open up again the path to Greece for his fellow-Germans, antiquity was well worth the price of a mass and probably much more besides!

The journey to Rome seemed to promise a new birth. "It was when I came to know Rome that I, so to speak, entered the world as a newborn child".[128] Thirty years later, Goethe, clasping his copy of Winckelmann and feeling equally moved, was likewise to discover Rome and was to write that he "reckoned the day of [his] arrival to be that of a second birth, a veritable renaissance".[129] Winckelmann was to declare repeatedly in his letters and to print in the preface to his *History of Art among the Ancients* that it was impossible to write anything of serious interest on antiquity "outside Rome". And in 1804, Wilhelm von Humboldt was to write, from Rome, in similar vein, to his friend Goethe, declaring that "Rome is the place where, as we see it, the whole of antiquity is gathered together and presented to our view".[130]

But there is a paradox here: for Winckelmann, Rome was the home of the history of art, yet art was not Roman but Greek. Beautiful nature was Greek. The Romans merely imitated the Greeks.[131] Winckelmann takes over and elaborates upon the division between Greece and Rome as it had originally been formulated by Greek and Roman intellectuals. So why Rome and not Athens? As we know, Winckelmann never set foot in Athens despite having several times planned a voyage to Greece. The answer to the above question is: because, in his view, Athens was not a *place* that could ever now be reached. Greece was an ideal. The voyage to Greece had to be mediated by Rome, in fact *was* a voyage to Rome. For Rome combined presence with absence: what it offered to the eyes of anyone who had learnt how to see was also a trace of what could no longer be seen.

It was, as the last extraordinary lines of the *History of Art* tell us, "as if a loving mistress, her eyes following the vessel that is carrying her lover away, thinks that she can make out the image of her loved one upon its receding sail". Like her, "we possess, so to speak, only the shadow of the object of our desires; but its loss fuels our desire, and we contemplate copies of it with more attention than we would have the originals, had they been in our possession".[132] Relics presuppose absence. In the same letter to Goethe, Humboldt went on to say: "But it would be an illusion to wish ourselves citizens of Athens or Rome. It is only in the distance, separated from ordinary life, only as a past gone forever that Antiquity can appear before us".[133] For Winckelmann, the loss was irremediable and his unrequited desire was unremittingly painful. Humboldt, more "reasonable", accepted the distance and refused to be deluded. But for both, Rome was the only place where the irremediable absence of Greece could be appreciated.

When, on his way back to Germany – on what would be his last journey, tragically ended in Trieste – Winckelmann finally accepted the impossibility of continuing on his way and also his separation from the vestiges of Greek beauty, his one thought, as he feverishly muttered "*Torniamo a Roma*", was indeed to return to Rome, the Rome that he would never see again.

Conclusion: Memories of Apollonius and the name of Pythagoras

"I have spoken with the Samanians of the Ganges, the astrologers of Chaldea, the magi of Babylon, the druids of Gaul, and the priests of the negroes! I have climbed the fourteen Olympuses, fathomed the lakes of Scythia, measured the greatness of the desert!" Those are the proud words of Apollonius of Tyana, when he appears before the unfortunate Saint Antony, agonizing in doubt. Gustave Flaubert describes him as "tall, with a gentle expression and a grave demeanour. His blond hair, parted in the middle, like Christ's, fell tidily to his shoulders". He is accompanied by his faithful disciple, Damis, who, for his part, is "short, fat, pug-nosed, thick-necked, with frizzy hair and a naive expression". "Both are bare-foot, bare-headed, and covered in dust, like men who have been travelling".[1] Apollonius travelled right into the imagination of the "hermit" of Croisset, who then "sang" of him.

Like Odysseus, our guiding thread through these pages, all the way from Troy to the shores of Ithaca and to Rome itself, Apollonius was a man on the move. He too had seen cities and experienced the feel of them. He had travelled, in fact had been travelling ever since his father took him to Tarsus to embark on his education. But he was a voyager in search of wisdom, travelling the world from city to city, and sanctuary to sanctuary, visiting, one after the other, all the great traditional centres of (pagan) spirituality. And, unlike for Odysseus, for him a life on the move was a deliberate choice. As he declared before setting out for India, travelling befitted a young man. He thus placed himself squarely in the line of the *theôroi*, inaugurated by Pythagoras and Solon, for whom "to see" and to philosophize went hand in hand.[2] But Apollonius was motivated by a far more marked "care for himself" than his predecessors. To be sure, one travelled in order to learn, but also, if not above all, to dispense one's own knowledge, in accordance with the model provided by the Seven Sages. And Apollonius, who set out to assess the various wisdoms of the world and assess himself in relation to them, was, all in all, to dispense far more lessons than he received.

Also unlike Odysseus, he was never bothered by any desire to return. After the death of his father, he distributed his possessions among the other members of his family and left his city, Tyana, forever. Later, he told his disciple that "for a sage, Greece is everywhere".[3] But at the end of the day there was no tomb for his remains either at Tyana or anywhere else. Did he ever really die? A number of opinions circulated. Some said that he died in Ephesus; others that he disappeared in Lindos or in Crete, adding that he rose into the sky.[4] At any rate he passed through there, this earthly pilgrim who worshipped the sun. Centuries later, an Alexandrian Greek who had been reading Philostratus asked "Where did he go, where is the sage hiding?" This "insignificant man", one of the few remaining pagans, cravenly converted to Christianity but, he said, nevertheless continued to hope that Apollonius "would re-establish the cult of our gods/and the sophistication of our Greek ceremonial".[5] But that is a purely poetical testimony borrowed, once again, from Constantine Cavafy, who was born and died in Alexandria.

Like Odysseus, Apollonius remembered, but for him remembering was the chosen way of life, a philosophy represented by the name of Pythagoras and which resulted from an ascetic regimen. "He used to chant a hymn addressed to memory, in which it is said that everything is worn and withered away by time, whereas time itself never ages, but remains immortal because of memory".[6] His memory became the sign that indicated that he was elect and that, as a "divine man", he was a superior being who had liberated himself from time, whereas in the case of Odysseus the determination not to forget about the day of his return simply marked his finite state, his acceptance of the human condition, and the painful discovery that historicity did not coincide with the story of a single individual. Through his exercise of memory, Apollonius eluded "becoming" and death, whereas Odysseus, by never forgetting, accepted his own death and faced up to the process of becoming.

Like Plutarch, who set Alexander on a pedestal, like Pausanias, who recorded the marvels of Greece and heeded the murmured messages of the old Greek wisdom, and, later on, like Diogenes Laertius, Apollonius was a zealot of Hellenism and a defender of Greek identity.[7] Diogenes was to proclaim the intrinsically Greek nature of philosophy, while Apollonius, claiming allegiance to Pythagoras, turned his own "life" into a "defence and illustration" of Greek *sophia*.

Was there another Apollonius, other than the one that was authenticated and deified by Philostratus, whose first concern was clearly to establish and repeat that Apollonius was neither a magician nor a charlatan? Not a charlatan such as the Alexander represented by Lucian. Apollonius, neither a *magos* nor a *goês*, did not seek to exploit the gifts ascribed to him but was a true sage, a philosopher, a divine man.[8] Only a few, much later sources tell us, for example, that Caracalla consecrated a sanctuary (*heróon*) to him and that Alexander Severus placed his portrait alongside those of Abraham, Orpheus and Christ in his private chapel. We also know that, under Diocletian, one high imperial official, Hierocles, dared to draw a parallel between the miracles of Apollonius and those of Christ. His pamphlet, directed against the Christians, provoked the ire and refutations of Eusebius and Lactantius. The fourth century AD saw the minting of an honorific coin (Contorniate) representing the effigy of a bearded man called Apollonius.[9] Tradition attributes to him a number of works, in particular on sacrifices and oracles, as well as a life of Pythagoras and a number of letters. However, these trails do not, on the whole, lead very far: all that they show is that this "divine man", born in Cappadocia in the first century AD, reached the peak of his fame in the third century AD. And that was thanks to his "biographer". We cannot escape Philostratus.[10]

"A wise man finds Hellas everywhere" or "For a sage, Greece is everywhere" means, primarily, that, wherever he is, a sage attracts all eyes and himself lives under the eye of virtue.[11] It is a matter of not so much cosmopolitanism as panoptism. A sage has constantly to live as though competing in the Olympic Games. He comes to see, or rather to be seen. And he is just as visible in Babylon or some remote spot of the universe as in Olympia. So wherever he is, he must behave as though he is in Greece.

But in this text, which is presented as the palimpsest of a whole culture, "Greece is everywhere" also means that Apollonius always finds or rediscovers traces and signs which show that, at one time or another, the Greeks have "passed through". The space–time coordinates of the world in which Philostratus sets his hero are resolutely Homeric, and his history naturally starts with the Trojan War. That is the space and the history within which he moves. He certainly devotes much of his time to enquiring into the Trojan War and even allows himself the luxury of a long nocturnal conversation with Achilles.[12] Quite simply, without making any sacrifices and without shedding any blood, he does better than Odysseus. The world may be Roman, but the "map" that he uses is (still) Homeric.[13] Or rather, in the *Life*, the Homeric poems are present as a subtext. In another of his works, Philostratus did not hesitate to bring back to life a Homeric figure whom we have already encountered at the end of Herodotus' *Histories* and also with Alexander: Protesilaus. And once resuscitated, he confidently puts Homer right![14] This unfortunate hero, assaulted by the Persians, avenged by the Greeks, and honoured by Alexander, is admitted by literature to the elite club of those who have been brought back to life.

The precursors of Apollonius' travels in the East were, of course, Dionysus, Heracles and – above all – Alexander, who is himself presented as a latter-day Dionysus.[15] Near the town of Taxila, Apollonius sees a very old elephant that Alexander had consecrated to the sun! On the banks of the Hyphasis river, a stele proclaims "Alexander stopped here".[16] But Apollonius' own conquest is entirely spiritual. He repeats Alexander's voyage and finds traces of his passing, but in the last analysis outstrips him. He goes even further, all the way to the hill of the Sages, following a route never before taken by any Greek.[17]

This literary adventure is an opportunity to recall many fine stories of distant lands, many well-known episodes and many famous names, introducing them all with an "it is said that", which leaves the narrator free to recount whatever he wishes and the reader free to "go along" with him (or not). In this way Apollonius gains entry to the (ideal) "Library" of great Greek travellers, to join his predecessors, whom he salutes and whose journeys he recapitulates. Alexander and Apollonius so to speak authenticate each other. The fact that Apollonius reports having found traces of Alexander's presence confirms that Alexander did indeed pass that way and, at the same time, that Apollonius did too. Any moderately cultivated reader must have felt that familiarity outweighed the impact of the foreignness of these lands, and his pleasure at encountering such new scenes was enhanced by his sense of "déjà-vu". Apollonius corrects, invalidates, confirms or completes previous information, but hardly ever finds himself confronted with something totally unprecedented or, if he does, never seems taken by surprise. From Dionysus right down to Apollonius, and taking in Alexander and all the other Greek accounts of India written since Herodotus' *Histories*, one and the same bubble of knowledge encloses all those Eastern places. The continuity is unbroken, or – to be more precise – time stands still, acquiring no depth. What is remembered by Apollonius, who has "more memories" than if he were "a thousand years old" (as Charles Baudelaire was to put it in "Spleen",

Les Fleurs du Mal), itself testifies to that suppression of time: Greece has always been there, and has always been the same.

Similarly, when Apollonius, keen to see the tides of the Ocean, sets off for the extreme western limit of the *oikoumenê*, what do his eyes alight upon in the neighbourhood of Gades? An altar in honour of Heracles – which is all that is needed to prompt the appearance of Geryon and his oxen.[18] Here too, the world has been discovered, mapped and named by the Greeks. The geography of the South, for its part, is manifestly Homeric: Ethiopia is presented as the Western horn of the earth, India as the Eastern horn: a reworking of the theme of the *Odyssey*'s double Ethiopia, one part turned towards the West, the other towards the East.[19] Such is the heterogeneous space within which Apollonius is presented as moving! It is composed of perfectly real names, towns and regions and at the same time of areas of space from different ages, visited or traversed by figures whose own statuses and ages vary widely (mythical heroes, historical figures, contemporaries). Only by dint of the progress of Apollonius can all these eclectic fragments or sequences be held together, for logically they could never overlap in this way. It was in similar fashion that Odysseus unified all the different spaces through which he alone passed.

Although Apollonius understands all languages without ever having learnt them, Greek is the one that has the greatest affinity with wisdom. All his more superior interlocutors understand and speak Greek, starting with Iarchas, the wisest of the Indian brahmins: he welcomes Apollonius in Greek and goes on to reveal to him the truth about Palamedes and to rehabilitate Tantalus, who tried to give human beings immortality. "We know everything", he says, "because we begin by knowing ourselves": the Delphic maxim makes sense among the Indians too. But for these champions it is a starting point rather than a goal. We are even told that, of all the young people who come to them, these sages prefer to teach those who know Greek, "as if they are already disposed to the right way of living".[20] That is another way of saying that Greek is the language of philosophy. Damis, the Assyrian, hopes that remaining assiduously in the company of Apollonius will turn him into a Greek who will at last "be worthy of mixing with Greeks".[21] As for Apollonius (of Tyana), needless to say he speaks the purest Attic Greek with no hint of a provincial accent![22]

This athenocentrism also finds expression in the comparison suggested by Philostratus between the hill of the Indian sages, the navel of India, and the Acropolis of Athens: they are of comparable height. And on this Indian hill,

Apollonius (the man who is never surprised) *is* amazed to find "extremely ancient statues" of Athena Polias, Delian Apollo and Dionysus, all honoured in accordance with the Greek rites.[23] So at the heart of the heart of the most ancient and lofty wisdom, Greece has been present virtually from time immemorial.

One narrative detail tellingly conveys Apollonius' self-confident attitude in his relations with the world. It is true that he sets out in quest of the wisdoms that the world has to offer, but when the customs officer at the border of Mesopotamia asks what he has to declare, he replies: "I export Wisdom, Justice, Virtue, Self-control, Valour, and Discipline".[24] Almost the same answer as that given by Plutarch's philosopher – Alexander. He is an exporter of wisdom, not an importer. The days of Barbarian wisdoms, that is to say of doubt or of a show of doubt in one's own *sophia*, are over. The distant lands on the edges of the world are not necessarily superior. A Greek no longer has any doubts, or is at least careful to give that impression.

Having made its mark in space and time, and ever-present, as it is, in world culture, Greece is truly everywhere, including in the heads of non-Greeks. In his voyages, Apollonius would like to be seen as the herald and ambassador of this renovated form of pan-Hellenism, founded upon the memory of Greece: a Greece that is forever embalmed, forever patrimonial, the Greece of Épinal, the Greece of the Second Sophistic, of the treatises of Plutarch, and of Pausanias' *Description of Greece*. He speaks with Achilles and is on intimate terms with the whole crowd of past sages, Pythagoras, Empedocles, Democritus, Anaxagoras and Socrates. The gymnosophists of Egypt and Apollonius even had a discussion about old Aristides, nicknamed "the Just". To denounce Domitian and his tyranny, Apollonius tells the story of the famous tyrannicides of Athens, Harmodius and Aristogiton, as if it happened only yesterday. He, who rejects all forms of idolatry, almost goes so far as to embrace the statue of Leonidas. When he visits and reforms Sparta, he is honoured there as a new Lycurgus. Reading the edition of the *Life* produced by the Second Sophistic is like leafing through a *Who's Who* of Greece.

Apollonius is a renouncer: he leaves his city, abandons his possessions, takes the vow of chastity, and practises silence for five whole years. But his very "eccentricity", which makes him a stranger wherever he goes, at the same time confers upon him the authority of a new lawgiver. He does not retire far from the world, to an Eastern temple, to devote himself to contemplation. In similar fashion, the purifiers and lawgivers of the old days often arrived from elsewhere, then moved on again once their task was accomplished. In his incessant tours of Greece, Apollonius never tires of correcting, or rather restoring, old forgotten laws and re-establishing rites that have become deformed. As one who respects the old ways, he undergoes initiation at Eleusis and visits the oracle of Trophonius at Lebadea or "Lebadeia".[25] Far from leading him to lose interest in the affairs of men and gods, his quality of divine man reintroduces him at the very heart of the city, as a doctor for both bodies and souls, who brings to an end epidemics, ousts demons, and is eager to re-establish concord between citizens.[26] When asked how it befits a sage to speak, he replies "like a lawgiver", meaning that, like a lawgiver, a sage should "deliver to the many the instructions of whose truth he has persuaded himself".[27] And he does indeed act like a lawgiver when, upon arriving in a city or receiving an embassy, he diagnoses what is wrong and prescribes a remedy. Quite simply though, in this universe of *mimêsis*, to be a lawgiver or an *archêgêtês* means to restore or rediscover the tradition and re-establish it, with all the retrospective illusions and present-day fabrication that such a policy dependent on memories implies.

This role, which by and large is reminiscent of that famous and distant figure from the past, the Lawgiver, is complemented by a second one, that of the Sage who acts as a counsellor to the Prince. The philosopher and the sovereign? In Taxila, King Phrastos, a lover of wisdom, is perfectly prepared to acknowledge the pre-eminence of wisdom over royalty.[28] But that is in far-away India! What about kings who bear the oppressively real names of Roman emperors, and who have never been regarded as great lovers of philosophy? Apollonius clashes with Nero and opposes Domitian, who claps him in prison and seeks to condemn him to death. Vespasian, on the other hand, goes to Alexandria expressly to ask for his advice: "Turn me into a king", he is supposed to have begged him.[29] Whatever the circumstances, Apollonius reaffirms his opposition to tyranny. He has no hesitation in sketching in the portrait of a good ruler. Above all, he proclaims his own inalienable freedom: Nobody can force him, nobody can shut him away, he depends upon nobody at all and, to a satrap who enquires who has sent him, he replies "I have sent myself... All the earth is mine and I have a right to go all over it and through it".[30] That is, of course, the corollary to "Greece is everywhere". And what about Rome? Of course he goes there, but in order to defend philosophy. He goes there under Nero, "who could not tolerate that anyone should be a philosopher", and manages, as is his wont, to find lodging in temples. Under Domitian he returns there, as the champion of wisdom. Having ventured into the jaws of the wolf, he is imprisoned, cast into chains, and brought before the emperor's court; but at that point he decides that the game has gone on long enough, and miraculously vanishes. Rome is portrayed merely as the centre of tyranny. His voyage to Rome is an act of resistance.

If Apollonius is supremely free, that is because he recognizes a master, one whom he chose at a very early date: Pythagoras. In some respects, the biography of Apollonius mirrors that of Pythagoras: Pythagoras is his master, and the whole of his own life testifies to the fact that he is a new Pythagoras. Moreover, a number of commentators suggest that when Philostratus wrote the biography of Apollonius he was following, if not producing a pastiche of, a *Life* of the master which Apollonius, the disciple, had himself written.[31] It is at any rate clear that literature for which the watchword was imitation was bound to delight in such duplications.

"My own system of wisdom is that of Pythagoras, a man of Samos", Apollonius proudly declares in Babylon, in the course of his conversations with the king.[32] Similarly, among the Egyptian gymnosophists, he insists that his way of life is Pythagorean and that it has served him as a touchstone when trying out other philosophies:

> For I discerned a certain sublimity in the discipline of Pythagoras, and how a certain secret wisdom enabled him to know not only who he was himself but also who he had been; and I saw that he approached the altars in purity, and suffered not his belly to be polluted by partaking of the flesh of animals; and that he kept his body pure of all garments woven of dead animal refuse; and that he was the first of mankind to restrain his tongue ... I also saw that his philosophical system was in other respects oracular and true. So I ran to embrace his teachings.[33]

In Greece itself, Pythagoras is justified and his doctrine is supported by the authority of Trophonius, who, when questioned by Apollonius, declares that Pythagoras' is the most complete and the most pure of all philosophies.[34]

Furthermore, the reference to Pythagoras lends a new dimension to the Homeric subtext. Like Pythagoras himself, and like Abaris perched on his arrow, Apollonius can move in the blink of an eye from one place to another. After mysteriously disappearing from Domitian's court, he reappears in a spot that has very rich allegorical connotations: close to Dicearchia (Pozzuoli), where the island of Calypso used to lie or, to be more precise, in the cave of the nymphs.[35] Naturally Damis, whom Apollonius has sent there to await him, thought he was dead, as did the philosopher Demetrius. This Pythagorean-style resurrection scene plays on the two themes worked and reworked by the allegory constituted by Calypso and the cave of the nymphs. "The allegory, as later summarized by Eustathius, makes Calypso stand for the human body which, like a shell, conceals and encloses the pearl that is the soul: this nymph detained the wise Odysseus, like a man who was the prisoner of his flesh".[36] By escaping from Domitian's prisons, Apollonius showed that there was no prison, be it material or corporeal, that could hold him. Philostratus certainly does not use such themes in a "systematic" way, but he does evoke a whole context of possible interpretations which greatly increase the impact of the Homeric reference.

It is thus Pythagoras who stands as the guarantor of Apollonius' authority and who, both in Greece and beyond it, enables him to proceed with a steady step and speak with assurance wherever he is. He is the guarantor of Apollonius' unshockability and the figure who legitimates this operation confirming the superiority of Greek wisdom over Barbarian wisdoms, although – as it goes without saying – all true wisdoms are fundamentally recognizable from their endorsement of maxims and ways of life that are similar, if not identical. The way in which Philostratus constructs his account of the Egyptian episode, which relies heavily on the technique of reversal, testifies in amusing fashion to his intentions here. As we have seen, Pythagoras was reported to have longed passionately to go and learn from the Egyptian priests and, as Apollonius himself points out, he was the first of the Greeks to adopt their principle of abstention from the exploitation of living creatures.[37] But in the case of Apollonius, the situation is reversed. It is Egypt that longs for Apollonius and hopes that he will visit: "As the people of Upper Egypt are intensely religious they ... prayed him to visit their several societies".[38] Apollonius does not go to seek advice from the Egyptian sages; rather, it is he who can teach them a thing or two when it comes to wisdom.[39] He knows more about them than they know themselves, for they have forgotten the Indian origins of their wisdom. Whereas in the past Pythagoras had come to Egypt as a seeker, Apollonius, for his part, is an "exporter" of *sophia*. But his legitimacy is entirely underpinned by the authority of Pythagoras, who, as we have seen, was, by around the third/fourth century, generally accepted as a sage who could rival the very greatest representatives of Barbarian wisdoms. We should not forget that both Pythagoras and Plato sought for and received the sanction of Egypt.

For Philostratus, Pythagoras is a fiction which, quite literally, makes Apollonius "go". He provides the reference and starting point for Apollonius' wisdom. But is that basis really so firm? Who was Pythagoras? A Greek from Samos? A Syrian, or even a Tyrian? An incarnation of the Hyperborean

Apollo? A radical critic of the *polis* or merely a reformer of its sacrificial practices? We cannot at this point go into the "question" of Pythagoras. However, by simply raising those few questions, we can return, one last time, to the question of identity and otherness.[40]

Is not Pythagoras himself essentially one of those shifting, multivocal, travelling signifiers, the name of a voyager who visited Phoenicia, Egypt, Babylon, and travelled the world from east to west and who, in the last analysis, cannot be placed? Yet at the same time he is, without a doubt, a master-signifier for Greek culture, which he illuminates with his obscure brilliance, reaching both backward and forward in time. Ever since the Trojan War or even before, he has been there, even before the syllables of his name were heard, already himself yet also other, remembering (as does Apollonius) all his earlier existences. That was his way of being immortal even before, as the centuries passed, his name, that travelling signifier, came to be transmitted, repeated, glossed and reinterpreted, finally to reappear in this *Life of Apollonius* (possibly modelled on the *Life* of the master himself), which declines it yet again. Pythagoras shines in the sky of Greek *sophia*, but as soon as you try to pin him down, he disperses into a shower of stellar bodies that are themselves all of different ages. He is assuredly a point of reference, but perhaps only because there is something about him that is always elusive. We cannot say of him, as we can of Odysseus, that his whole journey is simply a "return" to "his native island". Such a formula does not exhaust his "personality" and does not do justice to his name, which is really that of a traveller for whom there is no return, an itinerant purveyor of wisdom.

Pythagoras is both human and divine, a Greek and not a Greek, a man of both science and mysticism, a student of Barbarian wisdoms and a purely Greek philosopher. He is a multivocal, sometimes contradictory sign that indicates how the Greeks combined otherness with identity, by selecting certain figures who, they were sure, could do this for them. That was his destiny, his *raison d'être* and his means of survival, in fact his identity: to be both the same, yet other. He is one of the figures through whom Greek culture manifested the place that it had made for otherness. In other words, he represented a device for both opening outward and checking from within, expressing both unease and confidence, recognition and incomprehension, translation and treachery, which in the first instance depended upon the filter and the authority of the Greek language.

Among the figures of travellers entrusted with that "mission", which was of course constantly reformulated, Dionysus must certainly be included, for

208

virtually right down to the present time, he has been considered one of the most impressive of them. Arriving from elsewhere, he erupted noisily into the city and established otherness there, "at the centre of the social mechanism", as Jean-Pierre Vernant has put it.[41] Odysseus, to whom it fell to experience the human condition so thoroughly, also became one of those emblematic figures brought to us, in his case, by the sea-swell rolling from the shores of Troy. Anacharsis, the Scythian "Persian", the outsider inside, is another, albeit one of second rank since he was from the start a creation of the Greeks. But at any rate he can be regarded as symptomatic of the situation.

All that remains to the Pythagoras who became Apollonius, that Pythagoras *redivivus*, is the function of reassurance (laying the emphasis upon sameness rather than otherness). Pythagoras is a magic name that fully merits the Greek *appellation controlée* label. Whereas the whole point of Anacharsis was to arouse alarm, the purpose of Apollonius is to inspire reassurance. The coordinates of the world are Greek, "Greece is everywhere": everywhere, and always has been. But such a formula can quite easily be reversed into its contrary, If Greece is everywhere, then it is also "nowhere", and consequently that famous Pythagoro-Apollonian *sophia*, the instrument used for the "rehellenization" of the world, is in the last analysis neither purely Greek nor forthrightly Barbarian, or "no longer" truly Greek. But had such wisdom ever really existed? Philostratus, intent upon justifying his hero, is in no doubt at all about that: "Empedocles and Pythagoras himself, and Democritus consorted with magi ...; and Plato went to Egypt and mingled with his own discourses much of what he heard from the prophets and priests there".[42] And, according to an oracle of Apollo mentioned earlier, Apollonius was the only man, apart from Moses and Hermes, to have a direct vision of god in his own lifetime. "Everywhere", "nowhere": without wishing to continue to spin those two words around and embark on a dissertation on syncretism, it is not hard to see that the *Life of Apollonius*, a deliberate attempt to "rehellenize" the world, at the same time cannot help revealing the inanity of such a project. Its wisdom that is at once everywhere and nowhere is simply for the edification, or possibly amusement, of some Syrian princess.

Let us now leave Apollonius, the last in our list of travellers, and allow the last word to Flaubert. Saint Antony, who is both impressed and terrified by Apollonius, refuses to go off with him. "Master, it is time!", exclaims Damis, "The wind is getting up, the swallows are awakening, and the myrtle leaves have blown away!". Saint Antony takes refuge at the foot of the cross and in prayer.[43] The future did not belong to Apollonius.

Notes

TRANSLATOR'S NOTE

I have used the following translations of ancient texts:

Penguin Classics, Harmondsworth

Herodotus, *The Histories*, trans. Aubrey de Sélincourt, 1971, rev. repr. 1996.
Homer, *Iliad*, trans. Martin Hammond, 1987.
Thucydides, trans. Rex Warner, 1954 and repr.

The Complete Greek Tragedies, University of Chicago Press, Chicago and London

Aeschylus, *The Persians*, trans. David Grene, 1956.

Loeb Classical Library, London and Cambridge MA

Aristotle, *Metaphysics*, trans. Hugh Tredennick, 1968; *Politics*, trans. H. Rackam, 1969 (repr.).
Arrian, *Anabasis*, 2 vols, trans. E. Iliff Robson, 1954, and P. A. Brunt, 1976–83.
Dio Chrysostom, trans. J. W. Cohoon, 1961.
Diogenes Laertius, *Lives*, trans. R. D. Hicks, 1980 (repr.).
Dionysius of Halicarnassus, *Roman Antiquities*, trans. Ernest Cary, 1968 (repr.); *Critical Essays*, trans. Stephen Usher, 1974.
Hesiod, *Works and Days*, trans. Hugh Evelyn White, 1982 (repr.) (also in this volume, *Homeric Hymn to Poseidon*).
Hippocrates, *Airs, Waters, Places*, trans. W. H. S. Jones, 1972 (repr.).
Isocrates, *Areopagiticus*, trans. George Norlin, 1968 (repr.); *Busiris*, trans. Larue van Hook, 1986 (repr.); *Helen*, trans. Larue van Hook, 1986 (repr.); *Nicocles*, trans. George Norlin, 1966; *Panegyricus*, trans. George Norlin, 1966.
Josephus, Flavius, *Against Apion*, trans. H. St. J. Thackeray, 1966.
Livy, trans. E. O. Foster, 1963.

Lucian, *A True Story, How to Write History*, trans. K. Kilburn, 1968 (repr.).

Ovid, *Fasti*, trans. Sir James George Frazer, 1933.

Pausanias, trans. W. H. S. Jones, 1965 (repr.), 1968 (repr.), 1969 (repr.).

Pindar, *Olympians*, trans. William H. Race, 1997.

Plato, *Epinomis*, trans. W. R. M. Lamb, 1979 (repr.); *Laws*, trans. R. G. Bury, 1967 (repr.); *Phaedrus*, trans. Harold North Fowler, 1923; *Timaeus*, trans. R. G. Bury, 1929.

Philostratus, *Life of Apollonius*, trans. F. C. Conybeare, 1960.

Pliny the Elder, *Natural History*, trans. H. Rackham, 1992 (repr.).

Plotinus, *Enneads*, trans. A. H. Armstrong, 1984.

Plutarch, *Moralia, Isis and Osiris*, trans. Frank Cole Babbit, 1969 (repr.); *The Dinner of the Seven Sages*, trans. Frank Cole Babbit, 1962 (repr.); *On the Eating of Flesh*, trans. William C. Helmbold, 1968 (repr.); *On the Fortune of Alexander*, trans. Frank Cole Babbit, 1972 (repr.); *On the Fortune of the Romans*, trans. Frank Cole Babbit, 1972 (repr.); *Parallel Lives: Pyrrhus, Romulus*, trans. Bernadotte Perrin, 1967–9.

Polybius, *The Histories*, trans. W. Paton, 1967, 1968 (repr.).

Strabo, *The Geography*, trans. Horace Leonard Jones, 1968 (repr.), 1969.

Virgil, *Aeneid*, trans. W. F. Jackson Knight, 1971; *Eclogues*, trans. H. Rushton Fairclough, 1999 (repr.).

FOREWORD

1. See, e.g., F. Hartog, *Le miroir d'Hérodote: essai sur la représentation de l'autre*. Paris, 1980, 1991, Eng. trans. 1988; "Premières figures de l'historien en Grèce: historicité et histoire", in *Figures de l'intellectuel en Grèce ancienne*, eds N. Loraux and C. Miralles, Paris, 1998, pp. 123–42; "Le témoin et l'historien", *Gradhiva*, 27, 2000, pp. 1–14. See also N. Z. Davis and R. Starn, "Introduction", in *Memory and Counter-Memory, Representations*, 26, 1989; J. R. Gillis, ed., *Commemorations: The Politics of National Identity*, Princeton, 1994; J. Le Goff, *Histoire et mémoire*, Paris, 1988, Eng. trans. 1992; G. S. Shrimpton, *History and Memory in Ancient Greece*, Montreal, 1997.

2. M. I. Finley, *Mythe, Mémoire, Histoire*, ed. F. Hartog, Paris, 1981.

3. See, e.g., S. Friedländer, ed., *Probing the Limits of Representation: Nazism and the "Final Solution"*, Cambridge MA, 1992; G. Hartman, ed., *Holocaust Remembrance: The Shapes of Memory*, Oxford, 1999; R. Hilberg, *The Politics of Memory: The Journey of a Holocaust Survivor*, Chicago, 1996; D. LaCapra, *History and Memory After Auschwitz*, Ithaca NY, 1998; J. E. Young, *The Texture of Memory: Holocaust Memorials and Meaning*, Princeton, 1993; also *History and Memory*, 9.1/2, 1997 (special issue celebrating the work of S. Friedländer).

4. For the distinction and yet connection between "witness" and "historian", see Hartog, "Le témoin et l'historien", *op. cit.* (above, n. 1).

5. W. B. Stanford, *The Ulysses Theme*, rev. edn, Oxford, Blackwell, 1968. See also P. Boitani, *L'ombra di Ulisse*, Bologna, Il Mulino, 1991; *Sulle Orme di Ulisse*, Bologna, 1999; P. Boitani and R. Ambrosini, eds, *Archeologia dell'uomo moderno*, Rome, 1999.

6. L. Hardwick, *Translating Words, Translating Cultures*, Classical Inter/Faces series, eds P. Cartledge and S. Morton Braund, London, 2000, Ch. 6.

7. See A. Horton, *The Films of Theo Angelopoulos: A Cinema of Contemplation*, Princeton, 1997, Ch. 9.

8. B. Cohen, ed., *The Distaff Side: Representing the Female in Homer's Odyssey*, New York, 1995; W. G. Thalmann, *The Swineherd and the Bow: Representations of Class in the Odyssey*, Ithaca NY and London, 1998; I. Malkin, *The Returns of Odysseus: Colonization and Ethnicity*, Berkeley, Los Angeles and London, 1998.

9. See generally F. Hartog and M. Casevitz, *L'histoire d'Homère à Augustin: préfaces des historiens et textes sur l'histoire*, Paris, 1999. On the premium value of autopsy in historiography, see also J. Marincola, *Authority and Tradition in Ancient Historiography*, Cambridge, 1997 (App. IV § 1 "Appeal to Eyewitnesses/ Contemporaries/Oldest Historians"), pp. 281–2.

10. See, e.g., R. Browning, "Greeks and Others", in *History, Language and Literacy in the Byzantine World*, Northampton, 1989, pp. 8–11; P. A. Cartledge, *The Greeks: A Portrait of Self and Others*, rev. edn, Oxford, 1997; "Historiography and ancient Greek self-definition", in *The Routledge Companion to Historiography*, ed. M. Bentley, London and New York, 1997, pp. 23–42; J. M. Hall, *Ethnic Identity in Greek Antiquity*, Cambridge, 1997; Malkin, *op. cit.*; S. Saïd, ed., *Hellenismos: quelques jalons pour une histoire de l'identité grecque*, Paris, 1991.

11. J. Clifford, *Routes: Travel and Translation in the Late Twentieth Century*, Cambridge MA, 1997.

12. See, esp., P. Ceccarelli, "Figures du voyage, figures de la frontière", *Dialogues d'Histoire Ancienne*, 23/1, 1997, pp. 313–21; G. Lenclud, "Les grecs, les autres (et nous)", *Annales, HSS*, May–June 1998, pp. 695–713.

INTRODUCTION

1. The publicity brochure of Alitalia, the Italian Airways company, is entitled "Ulysses 2000".

2. J. Lacarrière, *L'été grec: une Grèce quotidienne de 4000 ans*, Paris, Plon, 1976, p. 378.

3. *Odyssey*, I, 2–3, trans. E. V. Rieu, rev. D. H. C. Rieu, Harmondsworth, Penguin, 1991; P. Pucci, *Odysseus Polutropos: Intertextual Readings in the Iliad and the Odyssey*, Ithaca NY and London, Cornell University Press, 1987 (French trans. 1995). *Polutropos*, in the first line of the *Odyssey*, can mean "who travelled extensively", "gifted with many cunning tricks", and possibly also "endowed with many figures of speech".

4. J.-P. Vernant (ed.), *The Greeks*, trans. Charles Lambert and Teresa Lavender, Chicago and London, University of Chicago Press, 1995; P. Brague, *Aristote et la question du monde*, Paris, PUF, 1988, pp. 9–13. On to see, to know, *idein* and *eidenai*, P. Chantraine, *Dictionnaire étymologique de la langue grecque*, Paris, Klincksieck, 1968–80. On autopsy, F. Hartog, *The Mirror of Herodotus: The Representation of the Other in the Writing of History*, trans. Janet Lloyd, Berkeley, Los Angeles and London, 1988, pp. 260–73.

5. Aristotle, *Metaphysics*, 980a25.

6. M. de Certeau, *L'invention du quotidien*, Paris, Gallimard, new edn 1990, pp. 170–91, in particular his definition of space as "used space" (*lieu pratiqué*) and his comments on frontiers and bridges, "boundary-imposing operations" and the limit that "circumscribes only in an ambivalent fashion, making space for the foreigner whom it appears to be ejecting".

7. On Pythagoras, see F. Wehrli, *Dikaiarchos*, Basel and Stuttgart, 1967, frag. 33; Porphyry, *Life of Pythagoras*, 18–19; on Hecataeus, *F.Gr.Hist.* (Jacoby), 1 *T* 12a.

8. Herodotus, I, 30.

9. C. Lévi-Strauss, *L'identité*, Paris, Grasset, 1977, p. 332: "Identity is a kind of virtual foyer to which we have, perforce, to refer to explain a number of things, but which has never had any real existence".

10. Here are two examples. (1) A quite recently published Greek magazine, written in English, entitled *Odyssey: The World of Greece*, which is addressed to the Greek diaspora (mainly in America) and the aim of which is to defend and promote Hellenism abroad. (2) Since 1989, a periodical entitled *Ulysses*, which takes the form of a review of ideas, and which has been appearing in Moscow. The initiators of this project (A. Gourevitch, Y. Bessmertny, L. Batkine) write as follows: "Why this title? Our *Ulysses* stands for a voyage through many lands and periods in world culture. Everywhere Ulysses is a guest and outsider... According to Bakhtin, a culture is only recognizable at the frontier where it encounters other intellectual worlds. Ulysses is our own cultural consciousness meeting other cultures and remaining capable of listening and amazement. It is through such an interminable voyage that contemporary culture has struck out in search of itself. For there is nothing harder to understand than oneself: it is surely no mere chance that Ulysses was not recognized on his native island. Ulysses is a thread that links different cultures to one another... He seems to be the first ethnologist or cultural anthropologist, a man through whom cultures so to speak come into existence... Ulysses is a symbol of uncertainty but also of culture's aspiration to survive despite the unprecedented trials to which the twentieth century has subjected it". I am grateful to my colleague Nikolai Kopossov, who drew my attention to this editorial and intellectual project.

11. G. Flaubert, *Correspondance*, Paris, Gallimard, 1973, vol. I, p. 751: "I saw the cave of Trophonius into which that worthy Apollonius of Tyana, whose praises I once sung, descended" (Letter to L. Bouilhet). Flaubert is here alluding to his *Temptation of Saint Antony*, the first version of which he completed in 1849, just before his departure for the East.

12. M. Bernal, *Black Athena: The Afroasiatic Roots of Classical Civilization*, London, Free Association Books, 1987–91.

13. *Xenos* designates both a Greek abroad, someone who is foreign to the community, and a guest, a man who, once he is taken in charge by a member of the community, benefits from a special status and is linked to him by reciprocal obligations. See E. Benveniste, *Le vocabulaire des institutions indo-européennes*, Paris, 1969, vol. I, pp. 87–101, completed by P. Gauthier, "Notes sur l'étranger et l'hospitalité en Grèce et à Rome", *Ancient Society*, 4, 1973, pp. 1–21.

14. Thucydides, II, 39, 1.

15. M. I. Finley, *Economy and Society in Ancient Greece*, London, Chatto & Windus, 1981, pp. 133–67.

16. Herodotus, IX, 11.

17. Job, 28.20–7.

18. Extending the line of investigation followed in *The Mirror of Herodotus*, which tried to reflect upon one particular work and one particular moment.

19. J.-M. André and M.-F. Baslez, *Voyager dans l'antiquité*, Paris, Fayard, 1993.

20. E. Levinas, *L'humanisme de l'autre homme*, Paris, Fata Morgana, 1972, p. 43. Contra Pucci, *op. cit.* (above, n. 3).

21. Plutarch, *Life of Lycurgus*, IV, 1–7.

22. See for example M. Vegetti, "L'homme et les dieux", in Vernant, *op. cit.* (above, n. 4), pp. 319–54.

23. Clement of Alexandria, *Les Stromates* (*Stromateis*) V, Paris, Éditions du Cerf, 1981, pp. 89–141, together with the introduction and commentaries of A. Le Boulluec; by the same author, "Clément d'Alexandrie et la conversion du parler grec", in *Hellenismos: quelques jalons pour une histoire de l'identité grec*, ed. S. Saïd, Leiden, Brill, 1991, p. 233.

24. Clement, *Stromateis*, I, 15, 69–70.

25. Diogenes Laertius, *Lives of the Ancient Philosophers*, I, 1, in which he sets out to refute Aristotle and the Peripatetic school.

26. Diogenes Laertius, *op. cit.* (see above, n. 25), I, 4.

27. Le Boulluec, *op. cit.*, p. 245; Clement, *Stromateis*, VI, 8, 67, 1. This proposition seems to contradict the theory of a theft, but does not really belong in the same context.

28. A. Momigliano, *Alien Wisdom: The Limits of Hellenization*, Cambridge, Cambridge University Press, 1975.

29. Plato, *Timaeus*, 22 b; see below, Ch. II, pp. 41–73.

30. Flavius Josephus, *Against Apion*, I, 9–10.

31. Numenius, *Fragments*, 8. Festugière points out that the expression is also to be found in Clement of Alexandria and Eusebius, who cites it from Clement.

32. Diogenes Laertius, *Lives*, VI, 73; M.-O. Goulet-Cazé, *L'ascèse cynique*, Paris, Vrin, 1986.

33. G. W. Bowersock, *Augustus and the Greek World*, Oxford, Oxford University Press, 1965.

34. *The Invention of Tradition*, eds E. Hobsbawm and T. Ranger, Cambridge, Cambridge University Press, 1983, pp. 1–14; G. Lenclud, "Qu'est-ce que la tradition?", in *Transcrire la mythologie*, ed. M. Detienne, Paris, Albin Michel, 1994, pp. 25–44.

35. J. Redfield, "Herodotus the tourist", *Classical Philology*, 80, 1985, p. 102: "They had a culture and relied on it; this does not mean that they were unobservant travelers or without anxieties, or that their principles of observation were trivial".

36. A. Momigliano, "The fault of the Greeks", in *Sesto contributo alla storia degli studi classici e del mondo antico*, Rome, Edizione di Storia e Letteratura 1980, vol. II, p. 513. Momigliano also notes (*The Classical Foundations of Modern Historiography*, Berkeley and Oxford, University of California Press, 1990) that, even if there were Egyptians and Babylonians who learnt Greek and wrote in it, this did not result in an equivalent to Hellenistic Judaism, which "well and truly constituted a particular branch of Hellenism".

37. C. Castoriadis, *Les carrefours du labyrinthe* II, Paris, Éditions du Seuil, 1986, p. 262.

38. This book grew out of a number of articles published earlier. Some are reproduced here, with significant modifications: "Des lieux et des hommes", postface to *Odyssée*, trans. Philippe Jaccottet, Paris, La Découverte, 1982 (above. n. 3); "Le passé revisité: trois regards sur la civilisation", *Le temps de la réflexion*, IV, 1983, pp. 161–79; "Les grecs égyptologues", *Annales ESC*, 5, 1986, pp. 953–67; "Bêtises grecques", *Le temps de la réflexion*, IX, 1988, pp. 53–71; "Rome et la Grèce: le choix de Denys d'Halicarnasse", in *Hellenismos, op. cit.* (above, n. 23), pp. 149–67; "Conoscenza di se/conoscenza dell'altro", *Storia d'Europa*, II, Turin, Einaudi, 1994, pp. 891–923.

1 THE RETURN OF ODYSSEUS

1. C. Cavafy, *Oeuvres poétiques*, Paris, Imprimerie nationale, 1992, p. 31.

2. *Odyssey*, IX, 229; XII, 192.

3. *Odyssey*, X, 472.

4. J.-P. Vernant, "Mythical aspects of memory", *Myth and Thought among the Greeks*, London, Routledge & Kegan Paul, 1983, pp. 75–105.

5. *Odyssey*, XI, 119–137; P. Scarpi, *La fuga e il ritorno*, Venice, Marsilio, 1992, pp. 194–7.

6. *Odyssey*, XIII, 187–96.

7. I. Malkin, *Religion and Colonization*, Leiden, Brill, 1987, pp. 2, 134; M. Detienne, "Apollon archégète: un modèle politique de la territorialisation", *Tracés de fondation*, ed. M. Detienne, Louvain and Paris, Peeters, 1990, p. 310.

8. *Odyssey*, XI, 10; I. Malkin, *The Returns of Odysseus: Colonization and Ethnicity*, Los Angeles and London, California University Press, 1998, which tackles the question of the role played by the whole literature of returns (*nostoi*) in Greek colonization; D. Frame, *The Myth of the Return in Early Greek Epic*, New Haven and London, Yale University Press, 1978.

9. J.-P. Vernant, *L'individu, la mort, l'amour: soi-même et l'autre en Grèce ancienne*, Paris, Gallimard, 1989, p. 151.

10. *Odyssey*, IV, 105–7.

11. F. Hartog, "Premières figures de l'historien en Grèce: historicité et histoire", in *Figures de l'intellectuel en Grèce ancienne*, eds N. Loraux and C. Miralles, Paris, Berlin, 1998, pp. 123–41.

12. G. Nagy, *The Best of the Achaeans: Concepts of the Hero in Archaic Greek Poetry*, Baltimore and London, Johns Hopkins University Press, 1979.

13. *Aeneid*, III, 11.

14. *Aeneid*, II, 780.

15. *Aeneid*, III, 94–6.

16. *Aeneid*, III, 132–71.

17. That is only part of the story. It is also necessary to make room for Evander's Latins (themselves by origin from Arcadia). At the express request of Juno, Jupiter (XII, 837) makes it clear that all of them (Latins and Trojans alike) must unanimously (*uno ore*) acknowledge themselves to be Latins.

18. *Aeneid*, VIII, 36–7, the god Tiber's words to Aeneas: "Thou who from foemen's hands bringest back to us our Trojan city, and preservest her towers for ever".

19. Y. Thomas, "L'institution de l'origine: *sacra principiorum populi romani*", in *Tracés de fondation, op. cit.* (above, n. 7), pp. 143–70.

20. Exodus, 13.3.

21. On the Exodus, see *La Bible d'Alexandrie. II: L'Exode*, trans. A. Le Boulluec and P. Sandevoir, Paris, Éditions du Cerf, 1989, p. 26. Opinions vary about these passages from Genesis: some authors consider them to be late, from the period of the Exile, when indeed possession of the land was in question; others, on the contrary, regard the Covenant as an extremely ancient element that goes right back to pre-Canaanite times, and that was made by the god of a nomadic tribe; yet others believe that Abraham had already entered the land of Canaan when the Covenant was made and that it concerned the territory close to

Hebron. See W. D. Davies, *The Territorial Dimension of Judaism*, Berkeley, University of California Press, 1982, pp. 6–28. The vocabulary of the Septuagint suggests to me that the third interpretation is the correct one. If that is so, the Covenant should be understood as the legitimation of the patriarchs' establishment in the land of Canaan.

22. Exodus, 6.2–4.
23. Genesis, 17.8. We know that Yahweh's first words to Abraham were "Get thee out": "Get thee out of thy country, and from thy kindred, and from thy father's house, unto a land that I will shew thee" (Genesis, 12.1).
24. See the remarks of M. Harl, *La Bible d'Alexandrie. I: La Genèse*, Paris, Éditions du Cerf, 1986, p. 66, notes p. 221.
25. Genesis, 15.13: "Know of a surety that thy seed shall be a stranger in a land that is not theirs, and shall serve them; and they shall afflict them four hundred years". On his deathbed Jacob asks Joseph to swear not to leave his remains in Egypt, but to take them away to be buried with his forefathers (Genesis, 47.30).
26. The Septuagint uses the word *kataskhesis*, "possession", which corresponds to the expression *katekheingên*: see Harl, *op. cit.* (above, n. 24), notes p. 170.
27. On the Exodus and its later meanings, see M. Walzer, *Exodus and Revolution*, New York, Basic Books, 1985.
28. Exodus, 32.1.
29. J.-P. Vernant, "A la table des hommes: mythe de fondation du sacrifice chez Hésiode", in M. Detienne and J.-P. Vernant, *La cuisine du sacrifice*, Paris, Gallimard, 1979, pp. 37–132 (= *The Cuisine of Sacrifice among the Greeks*, trans. Paula Wissing, Chicago and London, University of Chicago Press, 1989).
30. P. Vidal-Naquet, *The Black Hunter*, trans. Andrew Szegedy-Maszak, Baltimore and London, Johns Hopkins University Press, 1986, pp. 15–30.
31. *Odyssey*, V, 215–20.
32. *Odyssey*, IX, 94; X, 230–6; XII, 340–51.
33. P. Chantraine, *Dictionnaire étymologique de la langue grecque*, Paris, Klincksieck, 1968–80. The two words are sometimes put together to form a kind of syntagma designating total savagery. See below, Ch. 4, pp. 107–50.
34. Diogenes Laertius, *Lives of the Philosophers*, I, 33. Odysseus himself (*Theogony*, 1013) is said to be the father of a son called Agrios.
35. E. Lévy, "*Astu* et *polis* dans l'*Iliade*", *Ktèma*, 8, 1983, pp. 55–73.
36. M. I. Finley, *The World of Odysseus*, London, Chatto & Windus, 1956, 2nd edn 1978; E. Scheid-Tissinier, *Les usages du don chez Homère: vocabulaire et pratiques*, Nancy, Presses Universitaires de Nancy, 1994.
37. A. Ballabriga, *Le soleil et le Tartare: l'image mythique du monde en Grèce ancienne*, Paris, Éditions de l'École des hautes études en sciences sociales, 1986.

38. *Odyssey*, III, 319–22.

39. P. Gauthier, "Notes sur l'étranger et l'hospitalité en Grèce et à Rome", *Ancient Society*, 4, 1973, pp. 1–21.

40. *Odyssey*, XII, 340–425. The episode of the monstrous "sacrifice" of the cattle of the Sun, to be followed by the disappearance of Odysseus' last surviving companions, is very clear in this respect.

41. On the use of wine in a banquet, F. Lissarrague, *The Aesthetics of the Greek Banquet* (English trans. 1990 Princeton).

42. *Odyssey*, VII, 112–31.

43. Aristotle, *Politics*, I, 2, 1252 b 23.

44. E. Scheid-Tissinier, "Remarques sur la représentation de l'étranger dans le monde homérique", *Civiltà classica et cristiana*, XI, 1, 1990, pp. 7–31.

45. *Odyssey*, IX, 364–70.

46. Strabo, I, 1, 2, even if the expression has a particular meaning for Strabo; see below, Ch. 3, pp. 79–103.

47. See the *Homeric Hymn to Poseidon*. On the domains of Poseidon, M. Detienne and J.-P. Vernant, *Cunning Intelligence in Greek Culture and Society*, trans. Janet Lloyd, Hassocks, Harvester Press, 1978, in particular pp. 238–48.

48. *Iliad*, XXIII, 316–17.

49. J. Cuillandre, *La droite et la gauche dans les poèmes homériques*, Rennes, Imprimeries Réunies, 1943, pp. 185–208.

50. *Odyssey*, III, 319–22.

51. *Odyssey*, XIV, 199–359.

52. *Odyssey*, X, 194–7.

53. *Odyssey*, XII, 340–425.

54. F. Frontisi-Ducroux, "Homère et le temps retrouvé", *Critique*, May 1976, pp. 543–4.

55. Hartog, "Premières figures de l'historien en Grèce", *op. cit.* (above, n. 11).

56. J.-P. Vernant, *L'individu, la mort, l'amour, op. cit.* (above, n. 9), pp. 144–6.

57. *Odyssey*, IX, 142–5.

58. *Odyssey*, IX, 104–6, for example.

59. *Odyssey*, IX, 275–6.

60. *Odyssey*, XI, 518–40.

61. *Odyssey*, XI, 632–5. See J.-P. Vernant, *L'individu, la mort, l'amour, op. cit.* (above, n. 9), pp. 88–9. There is another dwelling place for the dead, the Elysian Fields, which is at once Olympian and Oceanian, situated at the very edge of the earth, where the climate is always mild. Rhadamanthys is to be found there, and Menelaus is to go there when he dies (IV, 563–9).

62. *Odyssey*, VII, 32–3 points out, however, that foreigners are barely tolerated.

63. *Odyssey*, VII, 19–20.

64. *Odyssey*, VIII, 561–3.

65. *Iliad*, XXIII, 74.

66. *Odyssey*, XI, 72–5.

67. *Odyssey*, I, 161–2.

68. *Sêma* is anything that constitutes a sign, a mark of recognition.

69. *Odyssey*, IV, 710. On the name Telemachus, see the remarks of J. Svenbro, *Phrasikleia*, trans. Janet Lloyd, Ithaca NY and London, Cornell University Press, 1993, pp. 68–9.

70. *Odyssey*, IX, 502–5; IX, 19–20.

71. *Odyssey*, I, 215–16.

72. P. Pucci, "The songs of the Sirens", *Arethusa*, XII, 2, 1979, pp. 121–32.

73. *Odyssey*, XXIII, 248, 267–8; A. Ballabriga, "La prophétie de Tirésias", *Metis*, IV, 2, 1989, pp. 291–304. Pucci, *Ulysse*, pp. 210–11 (= *Odysseus Polutropos: Intertextual Readings in the Iliad and the Odyssey*, Ithaca NY and London, Cornell University Press, 1987 (French trans. 1995)).

74. *Odyssey*, XI, 121–37.

75. Philostratus, *Life of Apollonius of Tyana*, VI, 32; Philostratus adds that Titus had to beware of the sting of the ray, by which, according to tradition, Odysseus was wounded.

76. Porphyry, *Cave of the Nymphs*, 34, 35; F. Buffière, *Les mythes d'Homère et la pensée grecque*, Paris, Les Belles Lettres, 1973, p. 415; R. Lamberton, *Homer the Theologian*, Berkeley, University of California Press, 1986.

77. Plutarch, *On exile*.

78. Buffière, *op. cit.* (above, n. 76), pp. 372–86; J. Pépin, *Mythe et allégorie: les origines grecques et les contestations judéo-chrétiennes*, Paris, Études augustiniennes, 1976, p. 107.

79. Maximus of Tyre, *Dissertations*, ed. M. B. Trapp, Leipzig, Teubner, 1994, 16, 6. Maximus was a second-century philosopher, of Platonic inspiration.

80. N. Kazantzakis, *The Odyssey: A Modern Sequel*, New York, Simon and Schuster, 1958, Book 2.

81. *Odyssey*, I, 13.

82. Hartog, "Premières figures de l'historien en Grèce", *op. cit.* (above, n. 11).

83. See below, Ch. 5, pp. 161–98.

84. Diodorus Siculus, *Historical Library*, I, 1, 2.

85. B. Andreae, *Odysseus: Archäologie des europaïschen Menschenbildes*, Frankfurt, Societäts Verl., 1984.

86. F. Hartog, *The Mirror of Herodotus: The Representation of the Other in the Writing of History*, trans. Janet Lloyd, Berkeley, Los Angeles and London, 1988, pp. 306–9; S. Greenblatt, *Marvelous Possessions: The Wonder of the New World*, Chicago, University of Chicago Press, 1991.

87. J. F. Lafitau, *Moeurs des sauvages américains comparées aux moeurs des premiers temps*, Paris, Sagrain l'ainé, 1724, p. 4.

220

88. W. B. Stanford, *The Ulysses Theme*, Oxford, Clarendon Press, 1963; P. Boitani, *L'ombra di Ulisse*, Bologna, Il Mulino, 1992.

89. Lucian, *True History*, II, 28; M. Fusillo, "Le miroir de la Lune: l'*Histoire vraie* de Lucien de la satire à l'utopie", *Poétique*, 73, 1988, pp. 109–35; D. van Mal-Maeder, "Le détournement homérique dans l'*Histoire vraie* de Lucien: le repatriement d'une tradition littéraire", *Études de Lettres: Revue de la faculté de lettres, Université de Lausanne*, April–June 1992, pp. 123–46.

90. Lucian, *True History*, I, 5.

91. *The Divine Comedy: Inferno*, trans. John D. Sinclair, London, John Lane and Bodley Head, 1948, p. 327.

92. G. Séféris, *Essais, hellénisme et création*, Paris, Mercure de France, 1987, p. 264. It is worth adding that this was the canto that came into Primo Levi's mind when he was in Auschwitz, and in particular these very lines, which he quoted to one of his companions doing forced labour (who knew no Italian): "'Take thought of the seed from which you spring. You were not born to live as brutes, but to follow virtue and knowledge'. And there is that terrible 'as One willed' which he feels it is so 'necessary and urgent' for his companion to 'hear and understand before it is too late'" (*If This is a Man*, trans. Stuart Woolf, London, Abacus, 1987). It was precisely the memory of Odysseus, the man who never ceased to remember that he was a man, that rose into the mind of this Jewish writer deported to Auschwitz.

2   EGYPTIAN VOYAGES

1. *Description de l'Égypte ou recueil des observations et des recherches qui ont été faites pendant l'expédition de l'armée française*, historical preface by Fourier, Paris, 1809–22; see B. Lepetit, "In presenza del luogo stesso ... Pratiche dotte e identificazione degli spazi alla fine del XVIII secolo", *Quaderni storici*, 90, 1995, pp. 657–78.

2. Vivant Denon, *Voyage dans la basse et la haute Égypte*, Paris, Didot l'ainé, 1802, pp. 1, 234, 112, 220.

3. Charles-François Dupuis, *Origine de tous les cultes*, Paris, H. Agasse, 1794, 4 vols, 1795; H. Coulet, "Quelques aspects du mythe de l'Égypte pharaonique en France au XVIIIe siècle", in *Le miroir égyptien*, eds R. Ilbert and P. Joutard, Marseilles, J. Lafitte, 1984, pp. 21–8.

4. *Encyclopédie*, vol. V (1755); in his articles "Apis" and "Initiation" in the *Dictionnaire philosophique*, Voltaire was to try to demolish Bossuet's Egypt.

5. J. B. Bossuet, *Discours sur l'histoire universelle*, Paris, 1692 edn, pp. 459, 443, 453, 449, 16.

6. M. Badolle, *L'Abbé Jean-Jacques Barthélemy et l'hellénisme en France dans la seconde moitié du XVIIIe siècle*, Paris, PUF, 1926; P. Vidal-Naquet, "Athenian

democracy in 1788", in *Politics Ancient and Modern*, trans. Janet Lloyd, Cambridge, Polity, 1995.

7. See below, Ch. 4, pp. 107–60.

8. M. Bernal, *Black Athena: The Afroasiatic Roots of Classical Civilization*, London, Free Association Books, 1987–91. Whether as a model or a paradigm, the author refers to T. Kuhn, whom he cites at the beginning of his book. Proposing a revision of the ancient model – which means first returning to it – he presents himself to the reader as the inventor of a new paradigm. Nothing more, nothing less. There have been many discussions and reviews of Bernal, mostly in the United States, where the book has given rise to wide controversy: *Arethusa*, special number, autumn 1989; M. Lefkowitz, "The origins of Greece and the illusions of Afrocentrists", *New Republic*, 10 February 1992, pp. 29–36; C. Ampolo, "Atene nera Atene bianca: storia antica et razzismi moderni", *Quaderni storici*, XXVIII, 1, 1993, p. 267f.

9. K. O. Müller, *Geschichte hellenischer Stämme und Städte*, 3 vols, Breslau, J. Max, 1820–4; I, *Orchomenos und die Minyer*; II and III, *Die Dorier*. For a recent appreciation of Müller, see C. Ampolo, "Per una storia delle storie greche", in *I Greci, I: Noi e i Greci*, ed. S. Settis, Turin, Einaudi, 1996, p. 1088.

10. Pausanias, IX, 36, 5.

11. Bernal, *op. cit.* (above, n. 8), p. 329. Grote's *History of Greece* appeared between 1846 and 1856; on Grote, see A. Momigliano, "George Grote and the study of Greek history", in *Essays in Ancient and Modern Historiography*, Oxford, Blackwell, 1977.

12. Ampolo, *op. cit.* (above, n. 9), p. 263. On the foreign policy of Egypt and Egyptian attitudes to foreigners, D. Valbelle, *Les neuf arcs: l'égyptien et les étrangers de la préhistoire à la conquête d'Alexandre*, Paris, Armand Colin, 1990.

13. A. Kleingünther, *Prôtôs Heuretês: Untersuchungen zur Geschichte einer Fragestellung*, *Philologus*, suppl. 26, Leipzig, 1933.

14. C. Froidefond, *Le mirage égyptien dans la littérature grecque d'Homère à Aristote*, Aix-en-Provence, Ophrys, 1971; A. Bernand, *Leçon de civilisation*, Paris, Fayard, 1993; see hereafter the works of J. Assmann.

15. *Odyssey*, IV, 483.

16. *Odyssey*, XIV, 244–6.

17. Herodotus, II, 84.

18. Herodotus, II, 152.

19. J.-M. Bertrand, *Inscriptions historiques grecques*, Paris, Les Belles Lettres, 1992, pp. 30–1.

20. Herodotus, II, 158. On the inscription and his commentary, see Bertrand, *op. cit.* (above, n. 19), pp. 35–6.

21. Herodotus, IV, 46.

22. Aeschylus, *Supplices*, 561.

23. Herodotus, II, 19f.

24. Herodotus, II, 17.

25. F. Hartog, *The Mirror of Herodotus: The Representation of the Other in the Writing of History*, trans. Janet Lloyd, Berkeley, Los Angeles and London, 1988; *Hérodote: Histoires*, Paris, La Découverte, 1980, pp. 5–21.

26. Herodotus, II, 33; see below.

27. Herodotus, II, 142–3; see below, pp. 56–7.

28. Herodotus, II, 45, 82.

29. According to P. Chantraine, *Dictionnaire étymologique de la langue grecque*, Paris, Klincksieck, 1968–80, s.v. *theos*, the etymology is not known.

30. It is worth noting that Herodotus does not for a moment consider the question of translation (or even that translation raises a question). Nor does it occur to him to make the distinction (drawn by Plutarch in his treatise *On Isis and Osiris*) between the name (*onoma*) and the power (*dunamis*) of a deity: the two are inseparable.

31. Herodotus, II, 53.

32. Herodotus, II, 39; M. Detienne and J.-P. Vernant, *La cuisine du sacrifice*, Paris, Gallimard, 1979, pp. 37–132 (= *The Cuisine of Sacrifice among the Greeks*, trans. Paula Wissing, Chicago and London, University of Chicago Press, 1989).

33. Herodotus, II, 41.

34. Herodotus, II, 45, where, however, Busiris is not mentioned; see Pherecydes, *F.Gr.Hist.* (Jacoby), 1 I 12a, F. 17, Apollodorus, II, 5, 11. One of Euripides' satyr plays bore this title. Above all, there is considerable iconographical documentation: J.-L. Durand and F. Lissarrague, "Héros cru ou hôte cuit", *Image et céramique grecques*, Actes du colloque de Rouen, 1983, pp. 153–67.

35. *La mort, les morts dans les sociétés anciennes*, eds G. Gnoli and J.-P. Vernant, Cambridge and Paris, Cambridge University Press and Editions de la Maison des Sciences de l'Homme 1982.

36. Herodotus, II, 85.

37. Herodotus, II, 49. On Dionysus, as an embodiment of the Other, see J.-P. Vernant, "Le Dionysos masqué des Bacchantes d'Euripide", *L'Homme*, 93, XXV, 1, 1985, p. 38.

38. E. Havelock, *Preface to Plato*, Cambridge MA, Harvard University Press, 1963. On writing, *Les savoirs de l'écriture*, ed. M. Detienne, Lille, Presses universitaires de Lille, 1988.

39. Herodotus, II, 123.

40. Herodotus, II, 50, 52.

41. Herodotus, II, 147.

42. Herodotus, II, 139.

43. Aeschylus, *Supplices*, 234–6; but these "foreign women" claim Argive, therefore Greek, descent.

44. Cicero, *Republic*, I, 10, 16; Diodorus, I, 96, 2; A. S. Riginos, *Platonica*, Leiden, Brill, 1976, pp. 64–5.

45. L. Brisson, "L'Égypte de Platon", *Les Études philosophiques*, 2–3, 1987, pp. 153–67; H. Joly, "Platon égyptologue", *Revue philosophique de la France et de l'étranger*, 2, 1982, pp. 255–66.

46. P. Vidal-Naquet, *The Black Hunter*, trans. Andrew Szegedy-Maszak, Baltimore and London, Johns Hopkins University Press, 1986, "Athens and Atlantis", pp. 263–84.

47. Plato, *Phaedrus*, 274c–275d, *Timaeus*, 21e–24c. J. Gwyn Griffiths, "Atlantis and Egypt", *Historia*, XXIV, 1985, pp. 3–28, tries to show that Plato's Egypt is based on Egyptian etymologies and an Egyptian background.

48. J.-P. Vernant, *Myth and Thought among the Greeks*, London, Routledge & Kegan Paul, 1983, pp. 64–5.

49. On the whole of this text and in particular on the essential ambiguity of the word that translations such as "remedy" and "poison" fail to convey, see J. Derrida, *La dissémination*, Paris, Éditions du Seuil, 1972, pp. 108–20.

50. Plato, *Philebus*, 18b–d.

51. Plato, *Timaeus*, 21e–24c: "a goddess whose name in Egyptian (*aiguptisti*) is Neith, and in Greek (*hellênisti*), as they assert, Athena". The story was transmitted from the priests of Saïs to Critias the Younger, via Solon and Critias the Elder.

52. So what the Greeks recount about Phaethon, the Sun's son, is a *myth*, "but the truth is that the alternation of the things that move around the earth in the sky takes place only at long intervals and, as a result, things on the earth are destroyed by fire" (Engl. trans. from the French trans. by L. Brisson, *Platon, les mots et les mythes*, Paris, Maspéro, 1982, p. 138); see also M. Detienne, *L'invention de la mythologie*, Paris, Gallimard, 1981, pp. 163–6 (= *The Creation of Mythology*, trans. Margaret Cook, Chicago, University of Chicago Press, 1986).

53. The expression echoes the famous words used in Herodotus' opening sentence in the *Histories*.

54. Joly, *op. cit.* (above, n. 45), p. 261.

55. This is a theme that recurs frequently in the fourth century. Herodotus already spoke of a division into classes, but counted seven of them: II, 164.

56. Plato, *Timaeus*, 24c–d.

57. J. J. Winckelmann, *Réflexions sur l'imitation des oeuvres grecques en peinture et en sculpture*, (1755), French trans. Léon Mis, Paris, Aubier, 1954, p. 92.

58. Plato, *Laws*, V, 747b–e.

59. Iamblichus, *Mysteries of Egypt*, I, 2, 6.

60. Hecataeus, F. 119, Strabo, VII, 7, 1.

61. Herodotus, VIII, 44: the Athenians were first called Cranai, when they were Pelasgians; then Cecropidai, under Cecrops; then, when Erechtheus became king, Athenians; and finally, when Ion became their commander, Ionians. But how could any of these names change their Athenian "substance", either for the better or for the worse?

62. Herodotus, II, 91–2.

63. Herodotus, I, 58.

64. Thucydides, I, 2–12.

65. See below, Ch. 3, pp. 79–106.

66. N. Loraux, *The Invention of Athens: The Funeral Oration in the Classical City*, trans. Alan Sheridan, Cambridge MA and London, Harvard University Press, 1986, p. 132.

67. Plato, *Menexenus*, 245d; Loraux, *op. cit* (above. n. 66), pp. 311–27.

68. Isocrates, *Helen*, 68.

69. Isocrates, *Busiris*, 22, 28.

70. Aristotle, *Metaphysics*, I, 1, 981b.

71. A.-J. Festugière, *La révélation d'Hermès Trismégiste*, vol. II, Paris, J. Gabalda, 1949, pp. 168–75; p. 169 for the Aristotle quotation.

72. Diodorus, I, 96.

73. Porphyry, *Life of Pythagoras*, 7–8. Porphyry is here citing a certain Antiphon, the author of a treatise *On the lives of those who excelled in virtue*.

74. O. Murray, "Hecateus of Abdera and Pharaonic kingship", *Journal of Egyptian Archaeology*, 1970, pp. 141–71; S. M. Burstein, "Hecateus of Abdera's History of Egypt", in *Life in a Multicultural Society: Egypt from Cambyses to Constantine and Beyond*, ed. J. H. Johnson, Chicago, University of Chicago Press, 1992, pp. 45–9.

75. See below, p. 102.

76. Diodorus, I, 10–12, 20.

77. Diodorus, I, 28, 4.

78. Such is the thesis of Paul Foucart on the mysteries of Eleusis as borrowings from the religion of Isis, *Les mystères d'Eleusis*, Paris, Picard, 1914. So he, like Victor Bérard on Arcadia, is a "latter-day" supporter of the "old model".

79. Diodorus, I, 28, 7. On Cecrops, N. Loraux, *The Children of Athena*, trans. Caroline Levine, Princeton, Princeton University Press, 1993, pp. 25, 39, 40.

80. Philiochorus, *F.Gr.Hist.* (Jacoby), 328 F. 94. Philochorus, who came from a family of prominent Athenians, was assassinated at the instigation of Antigonus Gonatas. Apart from his *Atthis*, he was the author of books on divination, sacrifices, religious festivals, and a number of other collections. He is a typical representative of the antiquarian and philological erudition of the third century, which combined scholarly history with civic patriotism.

81. Diodorus, I, 29, 5–6.

82. Murray, *op. cit.* (above, n. 74), pp. 144–50, carefully identifies the presence of Hecataeus in Diodorus' text.

83. Manethon, the first "native" to write in Greek (he was a priest of Heliopolis), does not seem to have strayed much from the general framework fixed by Hecataeus. He was writing in the reign of Ptolemy II and, like Hecataeus, opposed Herodotus and contributed to the defence of the native culture, which also chimed with the policies of the early Lagids. See D. Mendels, "Polemical character of Manetho's *Aegyptiaca*", *Purposes of History*, eds H. Verdin and G. Schepens, Louvain, Studia Hellenistica, 30, 1990, pp. 93–4, 106.

84. *F.Gr.Hist.* (Jacoby), 762 F. 3.

85. See below, pp. 103–6.

86. J.-M. André and M.-F. Baslez, *Voyager dans l'antiquité*, Paris, Fayard, 1993.

87. A. and E. Bernand, *Les inscriptions grecques du colosse de Memnon*, Cairo, IFAO, 1970; J. Baillet, *Inscriptions grecques et latines des tombeaux des rois et syringes à Thèbes*, Cairo, Imprimerie de l'Institut, 1920–6.

88. Heliodorus was of Syrian origin. *Ethiopian Story*, trans. Sir Walter Lamb, London, Dent, 1961.

89. Strabo, XVII, 1, 5.

90. Strabo, XVII, 1, 29.

91. Philostratus, *Life of Apollonius*, III, 32.

92. Philostratus, *Life of Apollonius*, VI, 11, 19, VIII, 7: it was the brahmins of India who taught the gymnosophists of Egypt to abstain from eating meat, a principle that Pythagoras then took over from them.

93. G. Fowden, *The Egyptian Hermes*, Cambridge, Cambridge University Press, 1986, p. 196.

94. Porphyry, *On abstinence*, II, 26, 4, citing the book *On piety* by Theophrastus. See J. Bouffartigue, *Porphyry*, preface to book II, Paris, Les Belles Lettres, 1979, pp. 3–71.

95. Detienne and Vernant, *op. cit.* (above, n. 32); J.-L. Durand, *Sacrifice et labour en Grèce ancienne*, Paris, La Découverte/École française de Rome, 1986, p. 195: "The story of Sopatros [an account of the first sacrifice in Athens] provides a perfect explanation of the basis upon which a civic society was founded: gathering together to eat the sacrificed animal, commensality around the shared-out portions of meat", with the slaughtering of the animal being "denied".

96. On the importance of this movement, see below, p. 99f.

97. Plutarch, *On the malice of Herodotus*, 856–7.

98. Plutarch, *On Isis and Osiris*, 364 A.

99. Plutarch, *On Isis and Osiris*, 354 E.

100. Plutarch, *On Isis and Osiris*, 351 F, 375 D: Isis is linked with "knowing", Typhon with "blinding", and Osiris is a compound of *hosios* (holy) and *hieros* (sacred).

101. Plutarch, *On Isis and Osiris*, 375 E–F.

102. Plutarch, *On Isis and Osiris*, 377 C–D.

103. Porphyry, who was born in Tyre, first studied under Longinus, in Athens, then moved to Rome to follow the teaching of Plotinus. After his master's death, in 268, he became the director of the Neo-Platonic School. He edited Plotinus' *Enneads* and was the author of a number of works. He was both a philosopher and, even more, a critic, who demonstrated that the "Book of Zoraster" was a fake and, in his treatise *Against the Christians*, established that the Book of Daniel was written at a late date.

104. See below, p. 99.

105. Porphyry, *On abstinence*, II, 5.

106. Porphyry, *On abstinence*, II, 47.

107. Porphyry, *Lettera ad Anebo*, ed. R. Sodano, 2, 10; Joseph Bidez, *Vie de Porphyre*, Hildesheim, G. Olms, 1964 (Ghent, 1913, pp. 80–7).

108. Iamblichus, *Mysteries*, VII, 5. Des Places, the French translator, cites an extract from the *Corpus hermeticum*, XVI, 2, where the force of the Egyptian is contrasted to the false graces of the Greek: "Therein lies the whole philosophy of the Greeks, the sound of words. As for ourselves, we do not use just words, but sounds that are full of efficacy".

109. Porphyry, *op. cit.* (above, n. 107), IV, 6, 8. An edition of the fragments of Chaeremon exists: Chaeremon, *Egyptian Priest and Stoic Philosopher*, Leiden, 1984.

110. Porphyry, *op. cit.* (above, n. 107), II, 52, 3. On "the friend of god", see P. Brown, *Genèse de l'antiquité tardive*, trans. Aline Roussel, Paris, Gallimard, 1983, pp. 121–2 (= *The Making of Late Antiquity*, Cambridge MA, Harvard University Press, 1993).

111. Lucian, *Philopseudês*, 34, ed. and commentary J. Schwartz, Paris, Les Belles Lettres, 1951, pp. 55–6: we know of a certain Pachratês, a prophet at the temple of Heliopolis, whose learning so impressed Hadrian that he doubled his salary.

112. A. J. Festugière, *Études d'histoire et de philologie*, Paris, Vrin, 1975, pp. 141–50; G. Fowden, *The Egyptian Hermes*, Cambridge, Cambridge University Press, 1986, p. 75.

113. Fowden, *op. cit.* (see above, n. 112), p. 39; Clement of Alexandria, *Stromateis*, V, 7, 1.

114. Bernal (*op. cit.* [above, n. 8], I, p. 145), who is certainly consistent, reckons that, even if the *Corpus* is heterogeneous, "in all probability" it contains passages that go back to the sixth century BC. The presence of far more ancient philosophico-religious ideas is "highly likely", as is its "fundamentally Egyptian" character. A Greek influence is detectable only in the latest of its texts, and is hard to discern given that "Pythagorean and Platonic philosophies were largely dependent upon Egyptian religion and thought".

115. That is the position of Fowden, *op. cit.* (above, n. 112), pp. 73–5, who distinguishes between, among other things, the different types of hermetic writings: the technical texts and the philosophical ones have neither the same impact, the same structure, nor the same references.

116. Festugière, *La révélation d'Hermès Trismégiste, op. cit.* (above, n. 7), vol. I, p. 20.

117. Iamblichus, VIII, 265.

118. F. Yates, *Giordano Bruno and the Hermetic Tradition*, repr. Chicago, University of Chicago Press, 1964, pp. 12–17. Ficino published his translation of Plato in 1483, a Latin translation of Plotinus in 1492, and an edition of Iamblichus in 1497.

119. A. Grafton, *Defenders of the Text*, Cambridge MA, Harvard University Press, 1991, pp. 163, 301 n. 38, for the quotation from Ficino's *Editio princeps* (1471).

120. E. Iversen, *The Myth of Egypt and its Hieroglyphs in European Tradition*, Copenhagen, Gec Gad, 1961, pp. 47–9, 65.

121. Plotinus, *Enneads*, V, 8, 6.

122. Grafton, *op. cit.* (above, n. 119), p. 293 n. 47.

123. I. Casaubon, *De rebus sacris et ecclesiasticis exercitationes XVI*, Geneva, 1654, p. 76, cited from Grafton, *op. cit.* (above, n. 119), p. 292 n. 38.

124. *Corpus herm.*, XVI, 1–2 (trans. Festugière).

125. Grafton, *op. cit.* (above, n. 119), p. 293 n. 47.

126. For Casaubon, the word-play based on Greek etymologies constitutes clear proof, for instance the play on *kosmos*. Poimandres declares that it was with reason that the world was called order (*kosmos*), for it does compose an order (*kosmei*) of the whole collection of beings (*Corpus herm.*, IX, 8). And are *kosmos* and *kosmei* therefore words from ancient Egyptian, asks Casaubon (Grafton, *op. cit.* [above, n. 119], p. 153)?

127. Grafton, *op. cit.* (above, n. 119), p. 161.

128. Iversen, *op. cit.* (above, n. 120), p. 97.

129. A. Kircher, *Prodromus Coptus sive Aegyptiacus*, Rome, 1636, p. 172, cited by Grafton, *op. cit.* (above, n. 119), p. 296 n. 68.

130. Champollion, *Précis du système hiéroglyphique des anciens Egyptiens*, Paris, 1824, an Address to the King.

3   THE INVENTION OF THE BARBARIAN AND AN INVENTORY OF THE WORLD

1. Herodotus, I: the opening passage of the *Histories* (modified translation); W. Nippel, "La costruzione dell'altro", in *I Greci, I: Noi e i Greci*, ed. S. Settis, Turin, Einaudi, 1996, pp. 166–83.

2. Thucydides, I, 3, 3.

3. *Iliad*, II, 867.

4. Strabo, XIV, 2, 28.

5. *Odyssey*, 8, 294: *agriophonos* is used to describe the Sintians of Lemnos; see E. Lévy, "Naissance du concept de Barbare", *Ktèma*, 9, 1984, pp. 7–9. Since J. Jüthner's *Hellenen und Barbaren: Das Erbe der Alten*, Leipzig (no publisher named), 1923, many works have been devoted to the Barbarians: *Grecs et Barbares*, Fondation Hardt, *Entretiens sur l'antiquité classique*, VIII, Vandoeuvres and Geneva, 1962; F. Skoda, "Histoire du mot *Barbaros* jusqu'au début de l'ère chrétienne", *Actes du colloque franco-polonais d'histoire*, Nice, Université de Nice, 1981, pp. 111–26; M. M. Sassi, "I Barbari", in *Il Sapere degli Antichi*, ed. M. Vegetti, Milan, Boringhieri, 1985, pp. 262–78; W. Nippel, *Griechen, Barbaren und "Wilde": Alte Geschichte und Sozialanthropologie*, Frankfurt, Fischer, 1990; *Hellenismos: quelques jalons pour une histoire de l'identité grec*, ed. S. Saïd, Leiden, Brill, 1991, in particular the contributions by E. Lévy, "Apparition des notions de Grèce et de Grecs", pp. 47–69, and M. Trédé, "Quelques définitions de l'hellénisme au IVe siècle avant J.-C. et leurs implications politiques", pp. 71–81.

6. Herodotus, I, 57; C. Darbo-Peschanski, "Les Barbares à l'épreuve du temps", *Metis*, IV. 2, 1989, pp. 238–40.

7. Hecataeus, *F.Gr.Hist.* (Jacoby), 1 F. 119.

8. Herodotus, VIII, 73.

9. Herodotus, I, 58.

10. Thucydides, I, 6, 6.

11. In political and diplomatic intercourse, the Persians were certainly now partners, now opponents, but they did not embody the hereditary enemy; see Y. Thébert, "Réflexions sur l'utilisation du concept d'étranger: évolution et fonction de l'image du Barbare à Athènes à l'époque classique", *Diogène*, 112, 1980, pp. 97–100.

12. See below, p. 163f.

13. Aeschylus, *Persians*, 745–8. The play, staged in 472, marks an important moment in the construction of the stereotype of the Barbarian. On the role of tragedy in the construction of Greek identity, see E. Hall, *Inventing the Barbarian: Greek Self-Definition through Tragedy*, Oxford, Clarendon Press, 1989.

14. Aeschylus, *Persians*, 180.

15. G. W. F. Hegel, *Aesthetics: Lectures on Fine Arts*, 2 vols, Oxford, Oxford University Press, 1975; *Lectures on the Philosophy of World History*, Cambridge and London, Cambridge University Press, 1975.

16. Herodotus, VII, 43. In the political context of the fourth century, Isocrates was to refer to the Trojan War; for example, *Helen*, 67–8.

17. Euripides, *The Trojan Women*, 764, where Andromache, the Barbarian woman, speaks, in connection with the fate of Astyanax, of the Greeks who are the inventors of "barbaric tortures" (*barbara kaka*).

18. Herodotus, I, 4.
19. Herodotus, IX, 120; VII, 33.
20. Herodotus, IX, 116, and, echoing the prologue, Herodotus goes on to say: "Artaÿctes was right, in a certain sense, in saying that Protesilaus made war on the king's country; for the Persians consider that the whole of Asia belongs to them, and to their reigning king".
21. *Iliad*, II, 698–702. See D. Boedeker, "Protesilaos and the end of Herodotus' *Histories*", *Classical Antiquity*, 7, 1988, pp. 30–48; A. Severyns, *Recherches sur la Chrestomathie de Proclus*, II, part 4, Paris, 1963, p. 83.
22. See below, Ch. 4, p. 157.
23. J. S. Mill, *Discussions and Dissertations*, 11, 1859, p. 283 (in a review of Grote's *History of Greece*).
24. Herodotus, II, 147.
25. Herodotus, I, 96.
26. See the innovative works of Pascal Payen, *Les îles nomades: conquérir et résister dans l'Enquête d'Hérodote*, Paris, Éditions de l'École des Hautes Études en Sciences Sociales, 1997.
27. F. Hartog, *The Mirror of Herodotus: The Representation of the Other in the Writing of History*, trans. Janet Lloyd, Berkeley, Los Angeles and London, 1988, pp. 322–39.
28. Herodotus, V, 78.
29. J.-P. Vernant, *Myth and Thought among the Greeks*, London, Routledge & Kegan Paul, 1983, pp. 212–34.
30. Herodotus, VII, 34.
31. Herodotus, VIII, 109.
32. Herodotus, I, 8.
33. Herodotus, V, 92 (he kills his wife, then has sexual relations with her).
34. Herodotus, VI, 75.
35. Aristotle, *Politics*, I, 1253a2–7.
36. Herodotus, VIII, 144, cf. II, 49, where it is stated that the cult of Dionysus is, precisely, not *homotropon* with Greek customs.
37. J. Goody, *The Domestication of the Savage Mind*, Cambridge, Cambridge University Press, 1977; M. Detienne, ed., *Les savoirs de l'écriture*, Lille, Presses universitaires de Lille, 1988; F. Hartog, "La storiografia tra passato e presente", in *I Greci. II, 2*, ed. S. Settis, Turin, Einaudi, 1997, pp. 959–81; "Ecriture, généalogies, archives: histoire en Grèce ancienne", in *Mélanges Pierre Lévêque*, Besançon, Presses Universitaires de Lille, 1991, vol. V, pp. 177–88.
38. The verb *graphein* can also mean to write, draw or paint: see C. Jacob, *L'empire des cartes*, Paris, Albin Michel, 1992, p. 39.
39. A. Peretti, "I peripli arcaici e Scilace di Carianda", in *Geografia e geografi nel mondo antico*, ed. F. Prontera, Bari, Universal Laterza, 1983, pp. 71–113.

The most famous of these voyages are those of Skylax of Caryanda, who was, it is said, sent by Darius to India, and that of the Phoenician Hanno (the chronology here is far from certain) to the Atlantic coast of Africa. These truly were voyages of discovery, and so were exceptional *periploi*.

40. Strabo, I, 3, 21; J. S. Romm, *The Edges of the Earth in Ancient Thought: Geography, Exploration and Fiction*, Princeton, Princeton University Press, 1992, pp. 28–31.

41. Diogenes Laertius, *Lives*, II, 1–2. See C. Jacob, *Géographie et ethnographie en Grèce ancienne*, Paris, A. Colin, 1991, pp. 36–7. On geography, apart from Prontera's collection mentioned above (n. 39), see, among others, C. Van Paassen, *The Classical Tradition of Geography*, Gröningen, J. B. Wolters, 1957; William Arthur Heidel, *The Frame of the Ancient Greek Maps*, New York, American Geographical Society, and Baltimore, Lord Baltimore Press, 1937, repr. 1976; P. Janni, *La mappa e il periplo: cartografia antica e spazio odologico*, Università di Macerta, Publ. della Fac. di Lett. e Filos., XIX, Rome, 1984; Federica Cordano, *La geografia degli Antichi*, Rome, Laterza, 1992.

42. Herodotus, V, 49.

43. Herodotus, IV, 36.

44. Herodotus, II, 143.

45. Herodotus, III, 122. See P. Vidal-Naquet, *The Black Hunter*, trans. Andrew Szegedy-Maszak, Baltimore and London, Johns Hopkins University Press, 1986, pp. 45–6.

46. Herodotus, I, 1–5; Hartog, *Le miroir d'Hérodote*, Paris, Gallimard, 1991, p. xx.

47. Herodotus, III, 139. A *theoros* was a man sent to consult an oracle or take part in a religious festival. On the philosophical voyage, see M. M. Sassi, "Il viaggio e la Festa: note sulla rappresentazione dell'ideale filosofico della vita", in *Idea e realtà del viaggio*, eds Giorgio Camassa and Silvana Fasce, Genoa, 1991, pp. 21–2.

48. Diogenes Laertius, VIII, 8.

49. Herodotus, I, 30. Croesus' exact words are: *philopheôn gên pollên theôriês heineken epelêluthas*, "philosophizing, you have travelled over much of the earth in order to see". This is the first time that *philosophein* appears.

50. Herodotus, IV, 76; see below, pp. 116–33.

51. J. Redfield, "Herodotus the tourist", *Classical Philology*, 80, 1985, p. 106.

52. Herodotus, II, 33; G. E. R. Lloyd, *Polarity and Analogy*, Cambridge, Cambridge University Press, 1966, pp. 342–5.

53. Hartog, *op. cit.* (see above, n. 27), pp. 14–19, 212–59.

54. Herodotus, IV, 100–2.

55. Herodotus, III, 106, 116.

56. Herodotus, IX, 122; J. Jouanna, "Causes de la défaite barbare chez Eschyle, Hérodote, Hippocrate", *Ktèma*, 6, 1981, pp. 3–15.

57. Hippocrates, *Airs, Waters, Places*, XII.

58. C. Calame, "Nature humaine et environnement: le racisme bien tempéré d'Hippocrate", *Science et racisme*, Lausanne, Éditions Payot, 1986, pp. 75–99.

59. Hippocrates, *Airs*, XIV, XVI.

60. Hippocrates, XIV.

61. Herodotus, IV, 142.

62. Hippocrates, *Airs*, XII.

63. Plutarch, *The Fortune of Alexander*, I, 332 A; see below, Ch. 5, pp. 154–6. For a linguistic approach to the concept, M. Casevitz, "Sur la notion de mélange en grec ancien (Mixobarbare ou Mixhellène)", *Mélanges Étienne Bernand*, Annales littéraires de l'université de Besançon, 454, Paris, 1991, pp. 121–39.

64. Herodotus, I, 135; II, 91; IV, 76.

65. Herodotus, IV, 106.

66. Herodotus, IV, 76–7; Hartog, *op. cit.* (see above, n. 27), pp. 61–83.

67. Herodotus, III, 38.

68. Herodotus, VII, 104.

69. Thucydides, I, 6, 6.

70. Thucydides, III, 82–3.

71. M. I. Finley, "La constitution des ancêtres", in *Mythe, mémoire, histoire*, Paris Flammarion, 1981, pp. 209–51 (= "The ancestral constitution", in *The Use and Abuse of History*, London, Penguin, 1990). Such eponymous lists were first published in about 350 at Thasos, 335 at Miletus, even earlier in Athens.

72. Isocrates, *Panegyricus*, 50.

73. Pierre Carlier, *La royauté en Grèce avant Alexandre*, Strasbourg, 1984, pp. 512–13, together with the references to the texts of the *Laws* and the *Politics*. C. Préaux, *Le monde hellénistique*, Paris, PUF, 1978, vol. I, p. 181f.

74. Isocrates, *Busiris*; see above, pp. 62–3.

75. Diogenes Laertius, VI, 73, 103; see M.-O. Goulet-Cazé, *L'ascèse cynique*, Paris, Vrin, 1986.

76. M. Detienne, *Dionysus Slain*, trans. M. and L. Muellner, Baltimore, Johns Hopkins University Press, 1979, pp. 153–68.

77. Ephorus, *F.Gr.Hist.* (Jacoby), 70 F. 42.

78. Diodorus, I, 9, 5.

79. Porphyry, *On abstinence*, II, 5, 1; R. Sorabji, *Animal Minds and Human Morals: The Origins of the Western Debate*, London, Duckworth, 1993, pp. 175–8.

80. *Dictionnaire des philosophes antiques*, ed. R. Goulet, Paris, Éditions du CNRS, 1994, pp. 760–4.

81. Dicearchus, F. 49 (Wehrli); Porphyry, *On abstinence*, IV, 2, 2–8.

82. Photius, *Library*, 250, 49 (VII, 451b11–16). Although the diversity in ways of life is great and the cultural distance between those who are civilized and those

who are not seems immense, at the same time Agatharchides feels that the Hellenistic world has somehow shrunk. Twenty-five days sufficed to move from the north (Lake Maeotis) to the south, with its great heat (Ethiopia), following the "meridian" discovered by early cartography (*ibid.*, 455a3–5).

83. Strabo, IV, 4, 2. It is also possible to trace a certain affinity between the Celts and the Homeric heroes and, more generally, a return to a vision of origins painted in the colours of the Golden Age. See A. J. Voillat Sauer, "Entre exotisme et héroisme; les Celtes de Posidonios", *Études de Lettres: Revue de la faculté des lettres, Université de Lausanne*, April–June 1992, pp. 114–20.

84. Diodorus Siculus, II, 59–60; M. Sartori, "Storia, utopia e mito nei primi libri della Biblioteca historica di Diodoro Siculo", *Athenaeum*, 62, 1984, pp. 492–536.

85. A. J. Festugière, *Contemplation et vie contemplative selon Platon*, Paris, Vrin, 1936.

86. Plato, *Epinomis*, 987a, 987d.

87. Aristotle, *Politics*, VII, 7, 1327b20f.

88. Strabo, I, 4, 9. It is worth noting that excellence and urbanity (*asteioi*) go hand in hand; see below, Ch. 4, pp. 123–4.

89. P. M. Fraser, *Ptolemaic Alexandria*, Oxford, Clarendon Press, 1972, vol. II, pp. 448–79; *Alexandrie IIIe siècle avant J. C.*, eds C. Jacob and F. de Polignac, Paris, Autrement, Mémoires series, 1992.

90. C. Jacob, "Lire pour écrire: navigations alexandrines", in *Le pouvoir des bibliothèques*, eds M. Baratin and C. Jacob, Paris, Albin Michel, 1996, pp. 47–83.

91. Strabo, II, I, 2; see C. Jacob, "Fonctions des cartes géographiques", in Detienne, *Les savoirs de l'écriture*, *op. cit.* (see above, n. 37), pp. 289–96.

92. C. Préaux, "L'élargissement de l'espace et du temps dans la pensée grecque", *Bulletin de l'Académie royale de Belgique (Lettres)*, 54, 1968, pp. 208–66.

93. Jacob, "Fonctions des cartes", in *Le pouvoir des bibliothèques*, *op. cit.* (see above, n. 90), p. 295. Claudius Ptolemy, in the second century AD, was to note the ultimate achievement of this kind of scientific geography, which was understood to be an exact cartographic representation of the earth.

94. See below, Ch. 5, p. 189.

95. Strabo, II, 5, 11.

4 GREEK VOYAGES

1. Isocrates, *Philip*, 132.

2. G. Daverio Rocchi, *Frontiera e confini nella Grecia antica*, "L'Erma" di Bretschneider, Rome, 1988; M. Casevitz, "Les mots de la frontière en grec", *La frontière*, Travaux de la Maison de l'Orient, 21, 1993, pp. 17–24; "Sur *eschatia*: histoire du mot", in *Frontières célestes dans l'antiquité*, ed. Aline Rousselle, Perpignan, Presses universitaires de Perpignan, 1995, pp. 19–30; D. Rousset,

"Les frontières des cités grecs: premières réflexions à partir des documents épigraphiques", *Cahiers du Centre Glotz*, V, 1994, pp. 97–126.

3. Herodotus, IV, 76.

4. J.-J. Barthélemy, *Voyage*, vol. II, p. 2.

5. Herodotus, IV, 76–7.

6. F. Hartog, *The Mirror of Herodotus: The Representation of the Other in the Writing of History*, trans. Janet Lloyd, Berkeley, Los Angeles and London, 1988, pp. 61–84.

7. Plato, *Republic*, X, 600a.

8. Strabo, VII, 3, 9; Diogenes Laertius, I, 41.

9. Ephorus, *F. Gr. Hist.* (Jacoby), 70 F. 42, 182; Jan Fredrik Kinsdstrand, *Anacharsis, the legend and the Apophthegmata*, Stockholm, Almquist och Wiksell, 1981, pp. 81–102.

10. Diogenes, I, 41.

11. Plutarch, *Life of Solon*, V, 1–2; Diogenes, I, 101–2.

12. *Real Encyclopädie* (Pauly Wissowa), s. v. Hermippos; A. Momigliano, *Alien Wisdom: The Limits of Hellenization*, Cambridge, Cambridge University Press, 1975.

13. F. H. Reuters, *Die Briefe des Anacharsis*, Berlin, Akademie Verlag, 1963; Antisthenes, the founder of Cynicism, was believed to have included him in a meeting of the Seven Sages: *The Cynic Epistles: A Study Edition*, ed. A. J. Malherbe, Missoula MT, 1977.

14. Maximus of Tyre, *Dissertatio*, 25. Abbé Barthélemy may have got from this the idea of a tour of Greece by Anacharsis the Younger.

15. Lucian, *Anacharsis or on the Gymnasia*, 38.

16. Montesquieu, *Apologie des Lettres persanes*, in *Oeuvres completes*, Bibliothèque de la Pléiade, Paris, Gallimard, 1949, I, p. 374.

17. Plutarch, *Life of Solon*, V.

18. Plutarch, *Banquet of the Seven Wise Men*, 156 A.

19. Strabo, VII, 3, 11; Hartog, *op. cit.* (above, n. 6), pp. 166–71.

20. Plutarch, *Banquet of the Seven Wise Men*, 150 D.

21. Lucian, *Anacharsis*, 18.

22. Lucian, *Anacharsis*, 30, 39.

23. Lucian, *Toxaris*, 4.

24. Lucian, *Toxaris*, 5.

25. Lucian, *Toxaris*, 8. Pausanias, himself an initiate of Eleusis, considers that, of all the admirable things of Greece, the Mysteries and the Olympic Games are what the gods care about most (V, 10, 1).

26. Lucian, *Toxaris*, 9. The town was probably Beroia: see C. P. Jones, *Culture and Society in Lucian*, Cambridge MA, Harvard University Press, 1986, p. 11.

27. Plutarch, *Banquet of the Seven Wise Men*, 155 B.

28. Plutarch, *Banquet of the Seven Wise Men*, 163 E.

29. Diogenes, I, 105.

30. Diogenes, I, 101. The rest of this text records several anecdotes that indicate, rather, that the Persian is closer to the Cynics than Solon's pupil is.

31. Grimm, *Correspondance littéraire*, 14, p. 355, cited by P. Vidal-Naquet, *Politics Ancient and Modern*, trans. Janet Lloyd, Oxford, Polity, 1995, p. 15.

32. M. Rebérioux, "Anacharsis Cloots, l'autre citoyen du monde", in *Thomas Paine, citoyen du monde*, ed. G. Kantin, Paris, Éditions Creaphis, 1990, pp. 34, 38.

33. M. Detienne and J.-P. Vernant, *Cunning Intelligence in Greek Culture and Society*, trans. Janet Lloyd, Hassocks, Harvester Press, 1978.

34. Forgetting what his brother has said, he accepts this "gift" from all the gods, Pandora (Hesiod, *Works*, 85–9). The same goes for his role as distributor in the myth of Protagoras (Plato, *Protagoras*, 321c).

35. *Odyssey*, IX, 273, 370.

36. *Odyssey*, IX, 442.

37. The fox and the octopus are particularly prominent among the animals endowed with *mêtis* (Detienne and Vernant, *op. cit.* (see above, n. 33), pp. 27–55).

38. See above, Ch. 1, pp. 22–3.

39. A. Schnapp-Gourbeillon, *Lions, héros, masques*, Paris, Maspéro, 1981, pp. 195–7, 205, where the author uses the expressions "*animalité-prétexte*", "*animalité-réflet*".

40. Homer, *Iliad*, X, 485–8.

41. See below, p. 137.

42. U. Dierauer, *Tier und Mensch im Denken der Antike: Studien zur antiken philosophie*, Amsterdam, B. R. Grüner, 1977.

43. Plato, *Protagoras*, 322a; Aristotle, *Parts of Animals*, 656a, 5–10.

44. Isocrates, *Nicocles*, 6.

45. Aristotle, *Politics*, I, 1252b8, 1253a24.

46. Diodorus Siculus, I, 8; J. de Romilly, "Thucydide et l'idée de progrès", *Annali della Scuola normale superiore di Pisa*, XXXV, 1966, pp. 146–7.

47. Plato, *Protagoras*, 322c. *Aidôs* designates the ability to recognize the "other" as an *alter ego*.

48. Aristotle, *Politics*, I, 1253a26–9. This calls to mind the famous *hupsipolis–apolis* opposition in Sophocles (*Antigone*, 370), which suggests the ever-present danger of a reversal: if a man chooses the way of the laws and the justice of the gods, he is *hupsipolis*, quintessentially of the *polis*, but the minute he gives way to crime, he becomes *apolis*: he no longer has a *polis*, is quite literally no longer anybody, even loses the status of a human being.

49. P. Chantraine, *Études sur le vocabulaire grec*, Paris, Klincksieck, 1956, pp. 34–5; P. Bourgeaud, "The Countryman", in *The Greeks*, trans. G. Lambert and T. Lavender, Chicago and London, University of Chicago Press, 1995.

50. Pollux, IX, 12: *agroikos ho skaios*, gauche, clumsy, stupid; Suda: *aphrôn, dusko-los, sklêros, apaideutos.*

51. Aristophanes, *Clouds*, 239.

52. Thucydides, II, 14–16; Y. Garlan, *Recherches de poliorcétique grecque*, Athens, BEFAR, 1974, pp. 44–65.

53. Aristophanes, *Clouds*, 43–52.

54. Aristophanes, *Clouds*, 398; J. Taillardat, *Les images d'Aristophane*, Paris, Les Belles Lettres, 1965, p. 262.

55. Aristophanes, *Clouds*, 492, 628, 1398.

56. This is the title of a number of lost comedies credited to Antiphanes, Anaxilas, Philemon and Menander, whose *Dyskolos* is, precisely, a country bumpkin.

57. Menander, *Fragment*, 97 (Kock III, 30).

58. Theophrastus, *Characters*, 4.

59. Aristotle, *Nicomachean Ethics*, 2, 1104a26; 2, 7, 1108a26; *Eudemus*, 2, 1230b19; 3, 7, 1234a5.

60. The index of L. Branwood (Leeds, W. S. Mancy and Sons, 1976) notes thirty or so occurrences of *agroikos* and its derivatives. Plato and stupidity is a whole subject in itself. L. Jerphagnon has given an account of the fools set on stage in the Dialogues (*Revue du métaphysique et de morale*, 76, 1971, pp. 24–31). It is possible, as C. Gaudin ("*Euêtheia*: la tradition platonicienne de l'innocence", *Revue philosophique de la France et de l'étranger*, 1981, pp. 145–68) has suggested, to show that what is elaborated is a theory of innocence. To call some-one *euêthês* is to say quite clearly that he is a fool. But Plato, in one of his customary reversals, rehabilitates "naive simplicity", primarily by setting it in opposition to what he calls *kakoêtheia*, an ugly character.

61. Plato, *Republic*, VIII, 560d5; X, 607b4; *Symposium*, 194c2; *Theatetus*, 174d8; *Laws*, IX 880a4. But this does not prevent Socrates, on a number of occasions, from defending one form of rusticity: in particular, faced with sophists and pre-tentious rhetoric, he says, "I rusticize" (*agroizomai*; *Phaedrus*, 269b1; *Theatetus*, 146a6). But of course Socrates is a torpedo-fish, and a torpedo-fish is an animal endowed with *mêtis*.

62. C. Mossé, "Le statut des paysans en Attique au IVe siècle", in *Problèmes de la terre en Grèce ancienne*, ed. M. I. Finley, Paris and The Hague, Mouton, 1973, pp. 179–86. Following a decree of Antipatros (322), which struck thousands off the list of citizens, we know that 10,000 people left Attica for Thrace. They included many poor peasants.

63. See above, p. 95.

64. It is worth noting that, as a result of a false etymology of *agroikos*, modern Greek formed the word *groikos*, meaning intelligent.

65. Plato, *Laws*, V, 745d.

66. Xenophon, *Oeconomicus*, IV, V.

67. Borgeaud, *op. cit.* (see above, n. 49), pp. 233–4.

68. F. Frontisi, "Artémis bucolique", *Revue de l'histoire des religions*, 1, 1981, pp. 54–5.

69. Theocritus, *Idylls*, I, 1–3.

70. Theocritus, *Idylls*, VII, 25.

71. Aristophanes, *Acharnians*, 738; J. Taillardat, *Les images d'Aristophane*, Paris, Les Belles Lettres, 1965, p. 257.

72. Barthélemy, *Voyage*, vol. IV, p. 75.

73. Polybius, XX, 4.

74. Aristophanes, *Acharnians*, 872; *kollikophagos*, an eater of coarse barley bread.

75. Aristophanes, *Acharnians*, 904–5.

76. Plutarch, *On the eating of flesh*, I, 995e. Clearly Polybius has given this theme a historicizing and rationalizing treatment.

77. Pindar, *Olympians*, VI, 88.

78. Strabo, who gives the name of this people, suggests the comparison.

79. *Corpus paroemiographorum graecorum*, eds E. Leutsch and F. Schneidewin, Hildesheim, Olms, 1965, I, p. 151.

80. Plutarch, *Political precepts*, 803 D.

81. *Corpus paroemiographorum*, I, p. 223, 357; II, p. 333.

82. Philostratus, *Life of Apollonius*, VII, 7.

83. Hippocrates, *Airs*, XXIV.

84. J. Michelet, *Leçons inédites de l'École normale*, ed. F. Berriot, Paris, Éditions du Cerf, 1978, p. 91.

85. Thucydides, II, 48.

86. Menander, *The Woman of Samos*, 458.

87. In Plutarch, for example (*Life of Theseus*, 24), the common folk, the poor (*idiô-tai* and *penêtes*) are contrasted to the *dunatoi* or *prôtoi* (the influential class). To underline the (apparent) disqualification of a character, Lucian was to present him as an *agroikos* and an *idiôtês*, which was a way of saying that he was of no account (*Hermotimos*, 81).

88. Suda, s. v. *idiôtai: anti tou politai*.

89. M. de Certeau, *La fable mystique*, Paris, Gallimard, 1982, pp. 49–58.

90. M. de Certeau, "L'illettré éclairé dans l'histoire de la lettre de Surin sur le Jeune Homme du Coche (1630)", *Revue d'ascétique et de mystique*, 44, 1968, pp. 404–9.

91. Diogenes Laertius, VI, 38; M.-O. Goulet-Cazé, *L'ascèse cynique*, Paris, Vrin, 1986, p. 60.

92. Plutarch, *On the eating of flesh*, I, 6, 995 D; M. Detienne, *Dionysus Slain*, trans. M. and L. Muellner, Baltimore, Johns Hopkins University Press, 1979, pp. 64–5.

93. Aelian, *Varia historia*, X, 11.

94. For Diogenes, a true education is "a moral education, founded upon training for a simple and frugal life"; see Goulet, *op. cit.* (see above, n. 91), p. 153.

95. Diogenes Laertius, VI, 54.

96. Dio Chrysostom, IX, 9.

97. Plutarch, *Bruta animalia ratione uti*. On the position of Aristotle and its consequences, R. Sorabji, *Animal Minds and Human Morals: The Origins of the Western Debate*, London, Duckworth, 1993, in particular pp. 12–16.

98. Herodotus, IV, 94; I, 180.

99. Juvenal, *Satire*, X, 50.

100. Cicero, *Letters*, CCXVI (Att. VII, 7), where "in the fashion of the Abderites" (in Greek) means a stupid or crazy way to behave; *On the nature of the gods*, I, 120.

101. Demosthenes, *Speeches*, XVII, 23.

102. Lucian, *How to write history*, I: this is an English rendering of the translation-adaptation of P. Bayle, which is to be found in his *Dictionnaire historique*, "Abdera" article, pp. 33–41. Lucian tells this story as a preface to his reflections on how to write history. The people of Abdera, declaiming in the streets as though they are tragic actors, put him in mind of all the men who were currently setting about writing the history of the wars against the Parthians, all of them thinking that they were some kind of Thucydides.

103. E. Kant, *Le conflit des facultés en trois sections*, Fr. trans. J. Gibelin, Paris, 1935, pp. 95–7 (= *The Conflict of the Faculties*, trans. Mary J. Gregor, New York, Abaris Books, 1979).

104. Barthélemy, *Voyage*, vol. V, p. 209.

105. J.-C. Berchet, "Et in Arcadia ego", *Romantisme*, 512, 1986, pp. 90–1.

106. P. Borgeaud, *The Cult of Pan in Ancient Greece*, trans. K. Atlass and J. Redfield, Chicago and London, University of Chicago Press, 1988.

107. Herodotus, VIII, 73.

108. Thucydides, I, 2, 3; see above, pp. 59–60.

109. Thucydides, I, 2, 6.

110. Pausanias, VIII, 1, 4.

111. Herodotus, I, 66; Apollonius Rhodius, IV, 263–265; Alcaeus, F. 245.

112. See above, p. 108; M. Detienne and J.-P. Vernant, *La cuisine du sacrifice en pays grec*, Paris, Gallimard, 1979, pp. 58–63 (= *The Cuisine of Sacrifice among the Greeks*, trans. Paula Wissing, Chicago and London, University of Chicago Press, 1989).

113. See above, p. 100.

114. Pausanias, VIII, 4, 1.

115. Pausanias, VIII, 2, 3–7; M. Jost, *Sanctuaires et cultes d'Arcadie*, École française d'Athènes, Paris, Vrin, 1985, pp. 258–9; Bourgeaud, *op. cit.* (see above, n. 49), pp. 62–5.

116. These stories are recorded by Pliny the Elder in his *Natural History*, VIII, 81, 82; Jost, *op. cit.* (see above, n. 115), pp. 259–60.

117. Philostratus, *Life of Apollonius*, VIII, 7. Pausanias passes rapidly over Mount Lycaeum: "On this altar they sacrifice in secret to Lycaean Zeus. I was reluctant to pry into the details of the sacrifice. Let them be as they are and were from the beginning" (VIII, 38).

118. Pausanias, VIII, 3, 6–7.

119. Pausanias, VIII, 22, 4; Scholium on Apollonius Rhodius, II, 1054.

120. Jost, *op. cit.* (see above, n. 115), p. 558.

121. Pausanias, VIII, 14, 1–3.

122. Pausanias, VIII, 17, 6.

123. Pausanias, VIII, 19, 3.

124. Pausanias, VIII, 22, 3. See F. Frontisi-Ducroux, "Artémis bucolique", *Revue de l'histoire des religions*, 1, 1981, pp. 54–6; P. Ellinger, "La légende nationale phocidienne: Artémis, les situations extrêmes et les récits des guerres d'anéantissement", *Bulletin de correspondance hellénique*, suppl. XXIII, Athens, École française d'Athènes, 1993, p. 335: "Artemis controls not only the frontiers between cultivated and wild space, but also, in a far more general fashion, at all levels of human activity, the frontiers between Nature and Culture, Civilization and Savagery".

125. Pausanias, VIII, 42, 6–7; Jost, *op. cit.* (see above, n. 115), pp. 312–17.

126. Polybius, IV, 20–1.

127. This is the name of the Spartan education system; see A. Brelich, *Paides e Parthenoi*, Rome, Edizione dell'Ateneo, 1969, pp. 209–13.

128. The etymology of their name is not without interest: *Kunaitheis (kuôn, aithôn)*, designating both their colour and their behaviour.

129. Polybius, IV, 21, 5–8. Pausanias says nothing about this appalling reputation of the Cynaethians, but does mention a statue of Hadrian in their agora.

130. Strabo, VIII, 8, 1.

131. C. Habicht, *Pausanias' Guide to Ancient Greece*, Berkeley, University of California Press, 1985, pp. 9–18.

132. F. Hartog, "Premières figures de l'historien en Grèce: historicité et histoire", in *Figures de l'intellectuel en Grèce ancienne*, eds N. Loraux and C. Miralles, Paris, Belin, 1998.

133. Pausanias, I, 26, 4 (*panta homoiôs epexionta ta Hellênika*).

134. The expression is frequently used to open a passage or to conclude it, for example, Pausanias, II, 13, 3, 14, 4, 29, 1; VI, 17, 1; VIII, 54, 7; see Habicht, *op. cit.* (see above, n. 131), pp. 20–3.

135. Pausanias, I, 39, 3; III, 11, 1.

136. Pausanias, V, 10, 1.

137. For example, this linking formula: "My story next requires me to describe whatever is notable at Pallantion" (Pausanias, VIII, 43, 1).

138. Pausanias, VIII, 8, 3.

139. P. Veyne, *Did the Greeks Believe in their Myths?*, trans. Paula Wissing, Chicago and London, University of Chicago Press, 1988.

140. Pausanias, VIII, 2, 4–7.

141. Pausanias, VIII, 33.

142. Chateaubriand, in an article in the *Mercure de France*, July 1807, cited by Berchet, *op. cit.* (see above, n. 105), pp. 101–2.

143. On the theme of ruins, see J. Elsner, "From the pyramids to Pausanias and Piglet: monuments, travel and writing", in *Art and Text in Ancient Greek Culture*, eds S. Goldhill and R. Osborne, Cambridge, Cambridge University Press, 1994, pp. 248–51.

144. Pausanias, VIII, 53, 5.

145. Pausanias, V, 1, 1; VIII, 54, 7, for example.

146. Pausanias, IX, 15, 6; J. Elsner, "Pausanias: a Greek pilgrim in the Roman world", *Past and Present*, 135, 1992, pp. 18–19.

147. Pausanias, VIII, 42, 11–13.

148. Pausanias, II, 35, 8; Habicht, *op. cit.* (see above, n. 131), p. 156.

149. Pausanias, VIII, 5, 5.

150. Pausanias, I, 38, 7.

151. Elsner, "Pausanias: a Greek Pilgrim", *op. cit.* (see above, n. 146), pp. 20–5.

152. Victor Bérard, *De l'origine des cultes arcadiens*, Paris, Thorin, 1894, p. 6.

153. Bérard, *op. cit.* (see above, n. 152), pp. 7, 8.

154. Bérard, *op. cit.* (see above, n. 152), pp. 27, 323.

155. M. Bernal, *Black Athena: The Afroasiatic Roots of Classical Civilization*, London, Free Association Books, 1987–91, vol. I, pp. 380–1. Bernal reckons that Bérard, who was not constrained within the limits of a particular discipline, probably went further than was necessary (with his idea of a Phoenician Mediterranean), which is why it is so easy to discredit his hypotheses. In a recent book on the cults of Arcadia, by M. Jost (see above, n. 115), Bérard is mentioned only in a note relating to Zeus Lykaios, whose origins he believed to be Phoenician.

156. Bérard, *op. cit.* (see above, n. 152), p. 6.

157. Bérard, *op. cit.* (see above, n. 152), p. 364.

158. Pausanias, VIII, 44, 4; 14, 5. On the road to Orchomenus there is a mound reputed to be the tomb of Penelope. After being expelled by Odysseus, on account of her infidelity, she was said to have died in Mantinea (VIII, 12, 6).

159. Dionysius of Halicarnassus, *Roman Antiquities*, I. 31–2.

160. Pausanias, VIII, 26, 7; Jost, *op. cit.* (see above, n. 115), p. 537.

161. Ovid, *Fasti*, II, 267–302. The arrival of Evander, who was an exile, is reported by Ovid in Book I, 461f.

162. B. Snell, *The Discovery of the Mind*, trans. T. Rosenmeyer, New York, Harper and Rowe, 1960, pp. 281–309 (paperback, Oxford, Blackwell, 1953).

163. Livy, *Preface*, 5.

164. Virgil, *Eclogues*, X, 31–6, 42–3.

165. E. Panofsky, "*Et in Arcadia ego*: on the conception of transcience in Poussin and Watteau", in *Philosophy and History: Essays Presented to E. Cassirer*, eds R. Klibansky and H. J. Patton, Oxford, Clarendon Press, 1936, p. 230. The theme is again treated in E. Panofsky, *L'oeuvre d'art et ses significations: essais sur les "arts plastiques"*, Fr. trans. by Bernard and Marthe Teyssèdre, Paris, Gallimard, 1969, pp. 278–302.

166. Panofsky, "*Et in Arcadia ego*", *op. cit.* (see above, n. 165), pp. 232–40.

167. J. W. Goethe, *Roman Elegies*: "Certainly you are a world, O Rome, but without Love, / The world would not be a world, / Nor would Rome be Rome".

168. This story could be pursued further. In a text on Greece, dated 1922, Hofmannstahl wrote that Goethe was now "regarded as a Roman". Between him and us stands "the huge head of the Ludovisi Juno". We are thus reminded that he had never seen original fifth-century sculpture and that the famous serenity that Winckelmann and he made so much of was simply an expression of "a moment in the German soul, nothing more" (*Erzählungen und Aufsätzen* II, Frankfurt, Fischer, 1957, p. 672).

169. J. G. Droysen, *Histoire d'Alexandre le Grand*, Fr. trans. J. Benoist-Méchin, Paris, Grasset, 1935 (repr. Brussels, Éditions Complexe, 1981), which in 1877 became the first volume of a *History of Hellenism*, 1887, that was never completed. See the fundamental study by Benedetto Bravo, *Philologie, histoire, philosophie de l'histoire: étude sur J. G. Droysen historien de l'antiquité*, Hildesheim, Georg Olms Verlag, 1988; C. Wagner, *Die Entwicklung Johann Gustav Droysen als Althistoriker*, Bonn, Rudolf Habelt, 1991; W. Tarn, "Alexander the Great and the unity of mankind", *Proceedings of the British Academy*, 19, 1933, pp. 123–66; repr. in *Alexander the Great*, Cambridge, Cambridge University Press, 1948; see the critical remarks by E. Badian, "Alexander the Great and the unity of mankind", *Historia*, 7, 1958, pp. 425–44.

170. P. Goukowsky, *Essai sur les origines du mythe d'Alexandre*, vol. I, Nancy, Presses universitaires de Nancy, 1978, pp. 111–14.

171. See above, pp. 84–5.

172. Polybius, I, 2, 3; see above, Ch. 5, p. 163.

173. The bibliography is immemse; see P. Ceausescu, "La double image d'Alexandre le Grand à Rome", *Studi Classici*, XVI, 1974, pp. 153–68, and the pages devoted to the Roman Alexander by P. Vidal-Naquet in "Flavius Arrien entre deux mondes", postface to Arrian, *Histoire d'Alexandre*, Paris, Éditions de Minuit, 1984, pp. 330–43.

174. Ceausescu, *op. cit.* (see above, n. 173), pp. 158, 159.

175. Livy, IX, 17–19.

176. Plutarch, *On the Fortune of the Romans*, 326 B. Some commentators have suggested dating this account of Plutarch's visit to Rome to the late seventies. But that is not necessarily correct. Others, on the contrary, regard it as a late work. See the introduction in the edition produced by F. Frazier and C. Froidefond, Paris, Les Belles Lettres, 1990, pp. 15–19.

177. Pseudo-Callisthenes, *The Alexander Romance*, I, 29, Fr. trans. G. Bounoure, Paris, Les Belles Lettres, 1992, a story put together in Alexandria in about the third century AD.

178. On *On the Fortune of Alexander* I and II, see the articles in the Belles Lettres edition cited in n. 176, pp. 89–109. These speeches have often embarrassed commentators on Plutarch. What are we to make of this rhetorical Alexander? Set him aside, by questioning the authenticity of the treatises? Pay him scant attention, by attributing the treatises to a youthful Plutarch bent on showing off his rhetorical skills, and by stressing that the mature Plutarch of the *Lives* was yet to appear? Or ascribe the differences to the difference in genres: on the one hand biography, with all its particular demands and its moral message (*The Life of Alexander*), on the other rhetoric, with its own rules, objectives and its own kind of verisimilitude (the treatise *On the Fortune of Alexander*)? The former work was intended for private use (self-improvement), the latter was basically a public speech (concerned, in this case, with collective identity).

179. Plutarch, *On the Fortune of Alexander*, 328 B–329.

180. Arrian, *Anabasis*, VII, 11, 8–9.

181. Plutarch, *On the Fortune of Alexander*, 329 C.

182. Plutarch, *On the Fortune of Alexander*, 329 E–F.

183. Marcus Aurelius, *Meditations*, VIII, 3.

184. In his speech *On royalty*; M.-H. Quet, "Rhétorique, culture et politique", *Diologues d'histoire ancienne*, 4, 1978, pp. 59–62; Glen Warren Bowersock, *Greek Sophists in the Roman Empire*, Oxford, Clarendon Press, 1969, pp. 110–12. But even if Dio does introduce Alexander several times, in particular with Diogenes, he does not present him as the embodiment of the ideal sovereign.

185. Guillaume de Sainte-Croix, *Examen critique des anciens historiens d'Alexandre le Grand*, Paris, Delauce et Lesueur, 1804, pp. 86–7.

186. Vidal-Naquet, "Flavius Arrien entre deux mondes", *op. cit.* (n. 173), pp. 311–43; P. A. Stadter, *Arrian of Nicomedia*, Chapel Hill, University of North Carolina, 1980.

187. See above, p. 83.

188. Arrian, I, 11, 5–7.

189. Herodotus, VII, 54; Arrian, I, 11, 6.

190. Arrian, VII, 43; I, 11, 7–8.

191. Arrian, I, 12, 1, 4.

192. B. G. Niebuhr, cited by Bravo, *op. cit.* (see above, n. 169), p. 278.

193. C. Préaux, "Réflexions sur l'entité hellénistique", *Chronique d'Egypte*, 40, 1965, pp. 129–139; Bravo, *op. cit.* (see above, n. 169); L. Canfora, *Ellenismo*, Bari, Laterza, 1987, pp. 49–69.

194. Droysen, *Alexandre le Grand, op. cit.* (see above, n. 169), 1981 repr., p. 44. The second edition of Droysen's *Geschichte Alexanders des Grossen*, 1877, begins as follows: "The name of Alexander designates the end of one world epoch (*Weltepoche*) and the beginning of a new one".

195. Droysen, *Geschichte, op. cit.* (see above, n. 194), 1833, letter to G. Friedlaender.

196. Droysen, *Geschichte, op. cit.* (see above, n. 194) 1833, p. 469, and for the theme of union, in particular, pp. 428, 463.

197. Bravo, *op. cit.* (see above, n. 169), p. 242.

198. J. G. Droysen, *De Lagidorum regno: Kleine Schriften*, II, Leipzig, 1843, p. 351.

199. Droysen, *Kleine Schriften*, II, *op. cit.* (see above, n. 198), pp. 419–20; Bravo, *op. cit.* (see above, n. 169), p. 219.

200. J. G. Droysen, *Vorwort zur Geschichte des Hellenismus II*, 1843, in *Geschichte des Hellenismus*, vol. 3, Munich, D. T. V., 1980, p. xxii.

201. Droysen, *Kleine Schriften*, II, *op. cit.* (see above, n. 198), p. 384.

202. Bravo, *op. cit.* (see above, n. 169), pp. 240–1.

5 ROMAN VOYAGES

1. Dionysius of Halicarnassus, *Roman Antiquities*, I, 72, 2. One manuscript has *after* Odysseus, not *with* Odysseus.

2. C. Ampolo, "Enea ed Ulisse nel Lazio da Hellanico a Festo", *Parola del passato*, 47, 1992, pp. 321–41; F. Solmsen, "Aeneas founded Rome with Odysseus", *Harvard Studies in Classical Philology*, 90, 1986, pp. 93–110. On Aeneas as a figure of reconciliation between the Greeks and the Trojans, hence also for the Romans, A. Momigliano, "How to reconcile Greeks and Trojans", *Settimo contributo alla storia degli studi classici e del mondo antico*, Storia e Letteratura, Rome, 1984, pp. 437–61.

3. E. Bickerman, "Origines gentium", *Classical Philology*, 47, 1952, pp. 65–81.

4. Montaigne, *Essays*, Ch. XXXI; E. M. Duval, "Lessons of the New World: design and meaning in Montaigne's 'Des Cannibales' and 'Des Coches'", *Yale French Studies*, 64, 1983, pp. 95–112.

5. Plutarch, *Pyrrhus*, 16, 6–7; *Flamininus*, 5, 6 (the Greeks, learning of the army and behaviour of Titus Quinctius Flamininus, now on Greek soil, had the same thought as Pyrrhus, who, for his part, was in Italy).

6. Pausanias, I, 12, 1.

7. F. W. Walbank, *Polybius*, Berkeley, University of California Press, Walbank et al., 1972; *Polybe: entretiens sur l'antiquité classique*, XX, Fondation Hardt, Geneva, 1974.

8. Pausanias, VIII, 8–9: *epi gên kai thalassan pasan planêtheiê*.

9. Polybius, XII, 27.

10. A. Momigliano, "Atene nel III secolo A. C. e la scoperta di Roma nelle Storie di Timeo di Tauromenio", in *Terzo contributo alla storia degli studi classici e del mondo antico*, Storia e Letteratura, Rome, 1966, p. 61.

11. Polybius, XII, 27, 10–28, 5, in particular.

12. Momigliano, "Polybius' reappearance in Western Europe", in Walbank et al., *Polybe, op. cit.* (see above, n. 7), pp. 347–72.

13. F. Hartog, *Le XIXe siècle et l'histoire: le cas Fustel de Coulanges*, Paris, PUF, 1988, p. 30.

14. Cicero, *On the republic*, II, 27: "Polybium nostrum, quo nemo fuit in exquirendis temporibus diligentior".

15. M. Dubuisson, *Le latin de Polybe: les implications historiques d'un cas de bilinguisme*, Paris, Klincksieck, 1985.

16. Polybius, I, 3, 3–4.

17. On Flavius Josephus, see P. Vidal-Naquet, "Flavius Josèphe ou du bon usage de la trahison", preface to *La guerre des Juifs*, Paris, Éditions de Minuit, 1977.

18. Polybius, I, 4, 1.

19. Polybius, XXXVII, 22, 2; *Iliad*, VI, 448–9.

20. Polybius, VI, 2, 9.

21. Walbank, *Polybius, op. cit.* (see above, n. 7), pp. 155–6.

22. C. Nicolet, *Le métier de citoyen dans la Rome républicaine*, Paris, Gallimard, 1976 (= *The World of the Citizen in Republican Rome*, trans. P. S. Falla, London, Batsford, 1980), pp. 25–6.

23. C. Nicolet, "Polybe et les institutions romaines", in Walbank et al., *Polybe, op. cit.* (see above, n. 7), pp. 230, 243, 254, 255. Nicolet also thinks that Polybius' remarks, which are at odds with the traditional view of Roman public law, find a parallel (if not their origin) in the speeches and actions of Cato (*ibid.*, p. 251).

24. P. Gauthier, review of Nicolet's *Métier de citoyen*, *Commentaire*, 2, 1979, p. 320.

25. P. Gauthier, "Grandes et petites cités: hégémonie et autarcie", *OPUS*, VI–VIII, 1987–9, pp. 187–97.

26. Isocrates, *Areopagiticus*, 14. This was also the period when the Athenians were seeking or invoking the "ancestral constitution".

27. Aristotle, *Politics*, III, 1276b29.

28. Polybius, VI, 2, 8.

29. Polybius, VI, 3, 7: "It is evident that we must regard as the best constitution a combination of all these three varieties, since we have had proof of this not only theoretically but by actual experience, Lycurgus having been the first to draw up a constitution – that of Sparta – on this principle".

30. Polybius, VI, 10, 8–9; E. Lévy, "La Sparte de Polybe", *Ktèma*, 12, 1987, pp. 63–79.

31. Cicero, *On the republic*, II, 1, 2; Nicolet, "Polybe et les institutions romaines", *op. cit.* (see above, n. 23), pp. 243–55.

32. Polybius, VI, 50, 3–4.

33. Strabo, I, 2, 15–16.

34. Dionysius of Halicarnassus, *Roman Antiquities*, I, 6, 5. On Dionysius and the period as a whole, see E. Gabba, *Dionysius and the History of Archaic Rome*, Berkeley, University of California Press, 1991.

35. Isocrates, *Panegyric*, 50.

36. Dionysius, *Orators*, I, 1, 7.

37. Dionysius, *Orators*, I, 3, 1.

38. Dionysius, *Orators*, I, 4, 1; A. Hurst, "Un critique dans la Rome d'Auguste", *Aufstieg und Niedergang der römischen Welt*, II, 30. 1, 1982, pp. 839–65.

39. Dionysius, *Antiquities*, I, 4, 2; I, 8, 4.

40. Dionysius, *Antiquities*, I, 8, 1.

41. Dionysius, *Antiquities*, I, 8, 3; I, 90, 1.

42. Polybius, IX, 2–7.

43. Dionysius, *Letter to Cnaeus Pompey*, 6.

44. Dionysius, *Antiquities*, I, 8, 3; 11, 1.

45. Dionysius, *Antiquities*, I, 7, 3.

46. D. Musti, "Tendenze nella storiografia romana arcaica: studi su Livio e Dionigi d'Alicarnasso", *Quaderni urbinati di cultura classica*, 10, 1970, pp. 5–158; D. Briquel, "L'autochtonie des Etrusques chez Denys d'Halicarnasse", *Revue des études latines*, LXI, 1983, pp. 65–86.

47. See C. Ampolo, *Plutarco: le vite di Teseo e Romolo*, Fondazione Lorenzo Valla, Anraldo Mondadori Editore, 1988, in particular pp. 262–78.

48. J.-L. Ferrary, *Philhéllenisme et impérialisme*, Rome, BEFAR, 1988, in particular pp. 537–9.

49. Dionysius, I, 10–13.

50. Even if the Roman historians were following a Greek *muthos* (I, 11, 1), the important point is that it was they who were recounting it.

51. Even if they are not themselves autochthonous, the Romans are descended from people who were, namely the Arcadians. However, Dionysius does not make anything of this point.

52. See, for example, how (I, 45f.) Dionysius treats the *aporia* of Aeneas' voyage, in an attempt to establish "credibility".

53. Dionysius, VII, 70–1.

54. J.-P. Thuillier, "Denys d'Halicarnasse et les jeux romains", in *Mélanges de l'école française de Rome (Antiquity)*, 87, 1976, pp. 563–81.

55. This points up the theme of Rome's greater authenticity. Dionysius cites as an example (VII, 72) the total nudity of the fighters: it was not customary in Homer's day, nor is it currently, in Rome. It was the Spartans who introduced this in Greece.

56. Strabo, I, 2, 9: "And, too, it was on the basis of Homer's actual knowledge that the Cimmerians lived about the Cimmerian Bosphorus, a gloomy country in the north, that he transferred them, quite appropriately, to a certain gloomy region in the neighbourhood of Hades – a region that suited the purpose of his mythology in telling of the wanderings of Odysseus". See J. S. Romm, *The Edges of the Earth in Ancient Thought: Geography, Exploration and Fiction*, Princeton, Princeton University Press, 1992, pp. 183–96.

57. More generally, Dionysius' demonstration belongs amid all the Greeks' reflections on the origins of peoples (a genre in itself) (see E. Bickerman, *op. cit.* [see above, n. 3]). It is also linked to the phenomenon (increasingly manifest from the Hellenistic period on) registered by epigraphy and to which L. Robert frequently drew attention: the use of the idea of kinship (*sungeneia*). The decrees and language of the chancellery gave way to claims of this kind. Thus the little city of Heraclea (Latmos) claimed kinship with the Aetolians (L. Robert, *Documents d'Asie Mineure*, Paris and Athens, École française d'Athènes–de Boccard, 1987, pp. 177–85). See also D. Musti, "Sull'idea di *sungeneia* in iscrizioni greche", *Annali della Scuola normale superiore di Pisa*, 32, 1963, pp. 225–39.

58. The earliest French translation of Dionysius is dated 1723. See now Dionysius of Halicarnassus, *Roman Antiquities*, a translation of Books I and II by V. Fromentin and J. Schnäbele, Paris, Les Belles Letttres, 1990.

59. P. C. F. Daunou, professor at the Collège de France from 1819 to 1830. The twenty volumes of his *Cours d'études historiques* were published posthumously in 1842. His verdict on Dionysius is to be found in vol. XIII, p. 96.

60. *Les antiquitéz Romaines de Denys d'Halicarnasse*, by Father F. Le Jay. The 1723 translation, initially anonymous, was by Bellanger. See C. Grell, "Les origines de Rome: mythe et critique. Essai sur l'histoire au XVIIe et au XVIII siècles", *Histoire, Economie, Societé*, 2, 1983, pp. 255–80.

61. Pouilly opened the debate with his "Dissertation sur l'incertitude de l'histoire des quatre premiers siècles de Rome" (15 December 1722), *Mémoire de l'Académie*, vol. VI. Sallier counterattacked (devoting no fewer than four articles to the affair); then Fréret became involved (17 March 1724) with his "Sur l'étude des anciens historiens et sur le degré de certitude de leurs preuves".

62. Beaufort published the first edition in 1738 in Utrecht, the second in 1750, reprinted in Paris in 1866. On Beaufort, see Moussa Raskolnikoff, *Histoire romaine et critique historique dans l'Europe des Lumières: la naissance de l'hypercritique dans l'historiographie de la Rome antique*, Rome, École française de Rome, 1992.

63. Beaufort, *L'incertitude, op. cit.* (see above, n. 62), p. 138 (1899 edition).

64. Beaufort, *L'incertitude, op. cit.* (see above, n. 62), p. 129.

65. Beaufort, *L'incertitude*, *op. cit.* (see above, n. 62), p. 135.

66. E. Schwarz, *Real Encyclopädie*, V, 1905, s. v. Dionysios, coll. 934–61.

67. Max Egger, *Denys d'Halicarnsse: essai sur la critique littéraire et la rhétorique chez les grecs au siècle d'Auguste*, Paris, A. Picard,1902, p. 232.

68. Egger, *op. cit.* (see above, n. 67), p. 294.

69. Apart from the classic work by G. W. Bowersock, *Augustus and the Greek World*, Oxford, Oxford University Press, 1965, and that by Gabba, *Dionysius and the History of Archaic Rome*, *op. cit.* (see above, n. 34), see the many articles by Gabba devoted to Dionysius, in particular "La *Storia di Roma arcaica* di Dionigio d'Alicarnasso", *Aufstieg und Niedergang der römischen Welt*, II, 30, 1, 1982, pp. 799–816. Once the *Antiquities* are treated not as history, but rather as a historiography of origins, Gabba sees two reasons to take an interest in Dionysius: he provides evidence of the way of thinking of a Greek in the Augustan period; and, thanks to his fidelity to his sources, he makes it possible to understand something of the methods and aims of the Roman annalists of the second and first centuries BC. Gabba reckons that the "constitution of Romulus" of Book II echoes a political pamphlet written at the time of Sulla. See also C. Schultze, "Dionysius of Halicarnassus and his audience", in *Past Perspectives*, ed. I. Moxon, Cambridge, Cambridge University Press, 1986, pp. 121–41.

70. Dionysius, I, 89, 3.

71. Dionysius, I, 5, 3.

72. For example, the Aborigines against the Barbarians (Sicels) (Dionysius, I, 16, 1), and the Aborigines together with the Pelasgians, also against the Sicels (*ibid.*, I, 20, 1).

73. Dionysius, I, 89, 4.

74. Cato, *Origins*, I, 19: "It is not in fact proved that Romulus and his people did not know Greek, that is to say Aeolian, at this time. That is what Cato declares in his Roman archaeology as does the very scholarly Varro in the preface to his writings on Pompey: Evander and the other Arcadians had in the past come to Italy and had spread the Aeolian language among the Barbarians". See E. Gabba, "Il Latino come dialetto greco", in *Mélanges A. Rostagni*, Turin, Bottega d'Erasmo, 1963, pp. 188–94.

75. Dionysius, I, 90, 1.

76. Dionysius, I, 60.

77. Dionysius, II, 2, 2.

78. Dionysius, I, 85, 4.

79. M. Casevitz, *Le vocabulaire de la colonisation en grec ancien*, Paris, Klincksieck, 1985, pp. 128–30, 202–5.

80. Dionysius, I, 85, 6.

81. Hesiod, *Works and Days*, 11–16.

82. Dionysius, I, 87, 1–2.

83. On the other hand, once Rome had overcome this crisis in which it had almost foundered even before being born, it was described by Dionysius as a *polis koinotatê* (Dionysius, I, 89, 1).

84. Dionysius, I, 87, 3: *apo te tou adelphou kai politikês allêloktonias.*

85. In Dionysius' view, "the most credible" account is the one in which Remus dies even before the real foundation got under way. But other writers do not share this view.

86. Plutarch, *Life of Romulus*, 9, 2: "The residents of Alba would not consent to give the fugitives the privilege of intermarriage with them, nor even receive them as fellow-citizens". Plutarch produces two proofs in support of this: the abduction of the Sabine women, which was not simply a stroke of aggression, but a necessity imposed by the lack of women for them to marry; and the creation of a sanctuary to the god Asylum, when the town was as yet barely founded, in which they welcomed all comers.

87. Isocrates, *Helen*, 36; *Panathenaicus*, 129.

88. Dionysius, II, 7–14.

89. Dionysius, II, 12, 4.

90. Dionysius, II, 9–10.

91. Dionysius, II, 11, 2.

92. Dionysius, II, 16–17. The openness of the city, resulting in mixture, is in this context presented as an indubitable mark of the superiority of Rome. See P. Gauthier, "*Générosité* romaine et *avarice* grecque: sur l'octroi du droit de cité", in *Mélanges d'histoire ancienne offerts à William Seston*, Paris, de Boccard, 1974, pp. 207–15; "La citoyenneté en Grèce et à Rome: participation et intégration", *Ktèma*, 6, 1981, pp. 167–79. Dionysius reckons that it was sheer numbers, rather than the favour of Fortune, that enabled Rome to surmount its most serious crises, as for example following the disaster of Cannae. On the other hand, he is much more reserved about the freeing of slaves, which, he claimed, was in his day giving rise to unjustifiable abuses.

93. Dionysius, I, 89, 1.

94. Claude Nicolet, *L'inventaire du monde*, Paris, Fayard, 1988, p. 18; C. Jacob, *Géographie et ethnographie en Grèce ancienne*, Paris, A. Colin, 1991, pp. 147–66; Christiaan Van Paassen, *The Classical Tradition of Geography*, Gröningen, J. B. Wolters, 1957, pp. 3–32; *Strabone: Contributi allo studio della personalità e dell'opera*, vol. I, ed. F. Prontera, and II, ed. G. Maddoli, Perugia, Università degli Studi, 1984, 1986.

95. Strabo, II, 5, 18, 25.

96. Strabo, I, 1, 2.

97. Strabo, I, 2, 3.

98. Strabo, I, 2, 7.

99. Strabo, I, 2, 29.

100. Strabo, I, 1, 16.

101. Strabo, I, 2, 4; see above, p. 177.

102. Strabo, I, 1, 23.

103. See above, p. 102.

104. Strabo, II, 5, 26; author's italics.

105. Aristotle, *Politics*, I, 1252b8.

106. Aristotle, *Politics*, III, 3, 1276a24–30, together with the remarks by Gauthier, "*Générosité* romaine et *avarice* grecque, *op. cit.* (see above, n. 92), pp. 176–7.

107. *L'Europa nel mondo antico*, ed. M. Sordi, Milan, Vita e Pensiero,1986.

108. J.-L. Ferrary, "L'empire romain, l'oikoumène et l'Europe", in *L'idée de l'Europe au fil de deux millénaires*, Paris, Beauchesne, 1992, pp. 39–54; F. Hartog, "Fondements grecs de l'idée d'Europe", *Quaderni di Storia*, 43, 1996, pp. 5–17.

109. Nicolet, *L'inventaire du monde*, *op. cit.* (see above. n. 94), pp. 46, 48; Ferrary, "L'empire romain, l'oikoumène et l'Europe", *op. cit.* (see above, n. 108), pp. 39–54.

110. Ferrary, "L'empire romain, l'oikoumène et l'Europe", *op. cit.* (see above, n. 108), p. 43.

111. Ovid, *Fasti*, II, 684; Nicolet, *L'inventaire du monde*, *op. cit.*, (see above, n. 94), pp. 126–7.

112. J. H. Oliver ("The ruling power", *Transactions of the American Philosophical Association*, vol. 43, 4, 1953, pp. 873–1003) dates the speech to 143, when Herodes Atticus, his former teacher, was *consul ordinarius*, on the occasion of the celebration of the anniversary of Rome (21 April). C. A. Behr believes it should be dated to 155, when Aelius Aristides made a second (?) voyage to Rome. On eulogistic literature, see L. Pernot, *La rhétorique de l'éloge dans le monde gréco-romain*, Paris, Institut d'études augustiniennes, 1993.

113. G. W. Bowersock, *Greek Sophists in the Roman Empire*, Oxford, Clarendon Press, 1969, pp. 43–59; E. L. Bowie, "Greeks and their past in the Second Sophistic", in *Studies in Ancient Society*, ed. M. I. Finley, London, Routledge and Kegan Paul, 1974, pp. 166–209.

114. Aelius Aristides, *To Rome*, 60–1.

115. Aelius Aristides, *To Rome*, 24–6.

116. Aelius Aristides, *To Rome*, 106, and *Iliad*, XX, 307–308; Aelius Aristides, *To Rome*, 101 and *Iliad*, XV, 193.

117. P. Veyne, *Les grecs ont-ils cru à leurs mythes?*, Paris, Éditions du Seuil, 1983.

118. Not exactly the crowning achievement of history, perhaps, since for Aristides there was, strictly speaking, no history for Rome: it existed in a timeless present.

119. Virgil, *Aeneid*, VI, 851–3: "Remember thou, O Roman, to rule the nations with thy sway – these shall be thine arts – to crown Peace with Law, to spare the

humbled, and to tame in war the proud!"; see Pernot, *op. cit.* (see above, n. 112), vol. 2, pp. 759–60.

120. Aelius Aristides, *To Rome*, 70.

121. Aelius Aristides, *To Rome*, 102.

122. Aelius Aristides, *To Rome*, 63; Nicolet, *Le métier de citoyen, op. cit.* (see above, n. 22), pp. 32–7.

123. One further side to Plutarch's attitude is given expression in his *Precepts of Statecraft*, in which he explains to a young man how the Greek cities must continue to manage their own affairs, at the same time retaining the friendship of the powerful Romans; J. Boulogne, *Plutarque: un aristocrate grec sous l'occupation romaine*, Lille, Presses universitaires de Lille, 1994. Paul Veyne calls Plutarch "a nationalist who favoured the Roman hegemony" (*Annuaire du Collège de France*, 1992–3, p. 766). In the same text Veyne shows that Dio of Prusa was critical of the Roman order. In his speech addressed to the Rhodians, he opposes the reuse of old statues on which the names of the original men to whom they were dedicated were rubbed away so that the powerful of the present day could be honoured. Veyne reads this as "a Greek nationalist manifesto" (*ibid.*, p. 763). It does indeed, like Pausanias' work, reflect the idea of *to Hellênikon* as a historical patrimony: one to be maintained and passed on and which also provided rules for action in the present day.

124. Montaigne, *Journal de voyage*, ed. F. Rigolot, Paris, PUF, 1992, p. 111.

125. Montaigne, *op. cit.* (see above, n. 124), p. 100.

126. Montaigne, *op. cit.* (see above, n. 124), p. 127.

127. J. J. Winckelmann, *Kleine Schriften Vorreden-Entwürfe*, ed. W. Rehm, Berlin, De Gruyter, 1968, p. 8; E. Pommier, "Winckelmann: l'art entre la norme et l'histoire", *Revue germanique internationale*, 2, 1994, pp. 17, 21.

128. J. J. Winckelmann, *Briefe* (13 September 1760); J.-R. Mantion, "L'histoire de l'art a-t-elle (un) lieu? Winckelmann depuis Rome", in *Winckelmann: la naissance de l'histoire de l'art à l'époque des Lumières*, ed. E. Pommier, Paris, La Documentation française, 1991, pp. 199–200.

129. J. W. Goethe, *Italienische Reise: Goethes Werke*, XI, Munich, Beck, 1978, p. 147.

130. W. von Humboldt, *Werke*, V, Darmstadt, Wissenschaftliche Buchgesellschaft, 1981, p. 216.

131. F. Hartog, "Faire le voyage d'Athènes: J. J. Winckelmann et sa réception française", "Winckelmann et le retour à l'antique", in *Entretiens de La Garenne Lemot*, Nantes, Repro-Dactyl Service Nantes, 1995, pp. 127–45.

132. J. J. Winckelmann, *Histoire de l'art*, Fr. trans. 1789, vol. 3, p. 263.

133. von Humboldt, *op. cit.* (see above, n. 130), p. 216.

134. Where he was asssassinated on 8 June 1768. J. Pigeaud, "Torniamo a Roma: vers quelle antiquité?", *Entretiens, op. cit.* (see above, n. 131), p. 49.

CONCLUSION

1. G. Flaubert, *La tentation de saint Antoine: oeuvres complètes*, Paris, Gallimard, 1951, vol. I, pp. 92, 95.
2. See above, p. 90.
3. *Life of Apollonius*, I, 34.
4. *Life of Apollonius*, VIII, 30.
5. C. Cavafy, *The Complete Poems*, London, 91.
6. *Life*, I, 14.
7. This list could be expanded to include the *Library* of the pseudo-Apollodorus, which is dated to the late second–early third century AD. Its three books provide a recapitulation, in the form of a genealogy, of the whole collection of Greek mythical traditions from the reign of Ouranos down to the Trojan War.
8. Lucian, *Alexander* (which cites Apollonius as a member of that brotherhood of charlatans).
9. *Real Encyclopädie*, s. v. Apollonios; E. Meyer, "Apollonios von Tyana und die Biographie des Philostratos", *Kleine Schriften*, Halle, M. Niemeyer, 1924, vol. II, pp. 133–91. In this important study Meyer concludes that Philostratus turns the life of Apollonius into a novel and that he is a "product and representative not of the first century but well and truly of the first decade of the third". E. L. Bowie, "Apollonius of Tyana, tradition and reality", *Aufstieg und Niedergang der römischen Welt*, Berlin and New York, W. de Gruyter, 1978, II, XVI, 2, pp. 1652–99, continues in this same vein, adding details and corrections to Meyer's thesis. D. Del Corno provides an interesting introduction to his *Vita di Apollonio di Tiana*, Milan, Adelphi, 1988. Finally, see G. Anderson, *Philostratus. Biography and Les Belles Lettres in the Third Century AD*, London, C. Helm, 1986. In Chs VII to XII (which are devoted to Apollonius), Anderson, in opposition to Meyer, undertakes a systematic re-evaluation of the historical Apollonius and the veracity of Philostratus, but is not always convincing. An overall assessment can be found in the *Dictionnaire des philosophes antiques*, ed. R. Goulet, Paris, Editions du CNRS, 1989, no. 284. Little is known about Philostratus. Tradition records four men of this name, all belonging to the same family, which originated in Lemnos. The author of the *Life* is the second of these (*c.*165–245 AD). See A. Billault, "Le personnage de Philostrate dans *La Vie d'Apollonios de Tyane*: autoportrait de l'auteur en biographe", in *L'invention de l'autobiographie d'Hésiode à saint Augustin*, Paris, Presses de l'École normale supérieure, 1993, pp. 271–8.
10. J. Sirinelli, *Les enfants d'Alexandre*, Paris, Fayard, 1993, notes (in the same vein as Meyer), p. 368: "All in all, the *Life of Apollonius* is one of the key works of the period that begins with the Severan dynasty. Philosophy, with its new promises, the principles of the new political pact, the new demands of religious

sensibilities – all are tackled in a composition that essentially borrows from the most traditional but also the most convenient of forms".

11. *Life*, I, 34.

12. *Life*, IV, 16; Apollonius is, in particular, very concerned to rehabilitate Palamedes.

13. Dionysius the Periegete, *La description de la terre habitée*, Fr. trans. C. Jacob, Paris, Albin Michel, 1990.

14. Philostratus, *Heroicus*, Leipzig, Teubner, 1977.

15. P. Goukowsky, *Essai sur les origines du mythe d'Alexandre*, Nancy, Annales de l'Est, 1981, vol. II, p. 83.

16. *Life*, II, 12, 43; III, 52–8 (the return journey by sea is modelled on Alexander's). The account is also close to the Pseudo-Callisthenes' *Romance of Alexander*.

17. *Life*, III, 16.

18. *Life*, V, 4; it also contains a bronze statue of Themistocles.

19. *Life*, VI, 1; *Odyssey*, I, 22–5.

20. *Life*, II, 31, III, 16.

21. *Life*, III, 43.

22. *Life*, I, 7.

23. *Life*, III, 13, 14.

24. *Life*, I, 20.

25. *Life*, VIII, 19.

26. *Life*, IV, 1–20; VIII, 7; in particular J.-P. Vernant, *L'individu, la mort, l'amour: soi-même et l'autre en Grèce ancienne*, Paris, Gallimard, 1989, p. 231, which refers the reader to the works of P. Brown.

27. *Life*, I, 17.

28. *Life*, II, 27.

29. *Life*, V, 28.

30. *Life*, I, 21.

31. Isidore Lévy, *Recherches sur les sources de la légende de Pythagore*, Paris, Leroux, 1926, pp. 130–6, which compares the two "Lives".

32. *Life*, I, 32.

33. *Life*, VI, 11.

34. *Life*, VIII, 19.

35. *Life*, VIII, 11–12. In the *Odyssey*, the nymphs' cave, with its two entrances (XIII, 102f), is situated on Ithaca, not on Calypso's island.

36. F. Buffière, *Les mythes d'Homère et la pensée grecque*, Paris, Les Belles Lettres, 1956, p. 461.

37. *Life*, VIII, 7; above, p. 68.

38. *Life*, V, 24.

39. *Life*, VI, 11.

40. The bibliography for the "Pythagorean question" is, suitably enough, bottomless. The best presentation of it seems to be that by W. Burkert, *Weisheit und*

Wissenschaft Studien zu Pythagoras, Philolaus und Platon, Nuremberg, H. Carl, 1962.

41. J.-P. Vernant, "Le Dionysos masqué des *Bacchantes* d'Euripide", *L'homme*, 93, 1985, p. 51.

42. *Life*, I, 2.

43. G. Flaubert, *La tentation de saint Antoine: oeuvres complètes*, Paris, Gallimard, 1951, vol. I, p. 104.

Index